THE CHILD'S INTERESTS IN CONFLICT

European Family Law Series

Published by the Organising Committee of the
Commission on European Family Law

THE CHILD'S INTERESTS IN CONFLICT

The Intersections between Society, Family, Faith and Culture

Edited by
Maarit Jänterä-Jareborg

intersentia
Cambridge – Antwerp – Portland

Intersentia Ltd
Sheraton House | Castle Park
Cambridge | CB3 0AX | United Kingdom
Tel.: +44 1223 370 170 | Fax: +44 1223 370 169
Email: mail@intersentia.co.uk
www.intersentia.com | www.intersentia.co.uk

Distribution for the UK and Ireland:
NBN International
Airport Business Centre, 10 Thornbury Road
Plymouth, PL6 7 PP
United Kingdom
Tel.: +44 1752 202 301 | Fax: +44 1752 202 331
Email: orders@nbninternational.com

Distribution for the USA and Canada:
International Specialized Book Services
920 NE 58th Ave. Suite 300
Portland, OR 97213
USA
Tel.: +1 800 944 6190 (toll free) |
Fax: +1 503 280 8832
Email: info@isbs.com

Distribution for Germany and Switzerland:
Stämpfli Verlag AG
Wölflistrasse 1
Postfach 5662
3001 Bern
Switserland
Tel.: +41 31 300 66 77
Email: verlag@staempfli.com

Distribution for Europe and all other countries:
Intersentia Publishing nv
Groenstraat 31
2640 Mortsel
Belgium
Tel.: +32 3 680 15 50 | Fax: +32 3 658 71 21
Email: mail@intersentia.be

The Child's Interests in Conflict. The Intersections between Society, Family, Faith and Culture

ISBN 978-1-78068-346-1
D/2016/7849/12
NUR 822

British Library Cataloguing in Publication Data. A catalogue record for this book is available from the British Library.

PREFACE

This collection consists of nine contributions on situations where the interests of society, family, faith and culture concerning the child's welfare are in conflict. The focus is thus on one of the burning issues of any pluralistic, multicultural society encountering a diversity of norms, whether legal, cultural or faith-based. The English summary of the Swedish Law Commission's report *Strengthened Protection against Forced Marriages and Child Marriages*, which formed the basis of Sweden's 2014 law reform in the field, is included in order to demonstrate societal responses to encountered problems.

My thanks go to all the speakers, chairpersons, and participants at the "Families, Faith and Functions, The Child in the Intersections between Family, Society, Faith and Culture" symposium, held at Uppsala University in May 2013 on the occasion of the fifth anniversary of the university's multidisciplinary research programme "The Impact of Religion: Challenges for Society, Law and Democracy". One of the most vital themes of this research programme, funded as a Linnaeus Centre of Excellence (2008–2018) by the Swedish Research Council, is "Family and Society". I wish to thank, in particular, my dear colleague and co-convener of the symposium Professor Anna Singer, as well as the Wenner-Gren Foundation and FORTE Research Council. Thanks are due also to Karolina Markgren LLM who assisted me with the drafting of the index and the final editing of this volume. All the presentations have been updated and rewritten for the purpose of this publication.

Uppsala, November 2015 Maarit Jänterä-Jareborg

CONTENTS

LIST OF AUTHORS

Marie-Claire Foblets
Director at the Max Planck Institute for Social Anthropology (Law and Anthropology Department), Halle, Germany; Professor of Law and Anthropology, Faculty of Law, Catholic University of Leuven, Belgium

Sanne Hofman
Legal Advisor in Child Rights, Save the Children, Norway; Chair of the Norwegian Forum for the UN Convention on the Rights of the Child

Staffan Janson
Senior Professor of Public Health at Karlstad University; guest Professor of Pediatrics, Uppsala University

Maarit Jänterä-Jareborg
Professor of Private International Law and International Civil Procedure, Faculty of Law, Uppsala University; Former Deputy Director of the Research Program 'The Impact of Religion: Challenges for Society, Law and Democracy' (Centre of Excellence 2008–2018), Uppsala University, Sweden

Sanna Koulu
LL.D., Lecturer in Child and Family Law, University of Rovaniemi, Finland

Göran Lambertz
Justice of the Supreme Court of Sweden; Chair of the Law Commission on strengthened protection from forced marriages and child marriages; former Chancellor of Justice

Jane Mair
Professor of Private Law, School of Law, University of Glasgow, Scotland

Sanna Mustasaari
Doctoral candidate, Faculty of Law, University of Helsinki, Finland

Esin Örücü
Professor Emerita of Comparative Law, University of Glasgow, Scotland, and Erasmus Universiteit Rotterdam, the Netherlands

Kirsten Sandberg
Professor of Law, Department of Public and International Law, University of Oslo, Norway

Louise Ellen Teitz
Professor of Law, Roger Williams University School of Law, Rhode Island, USA; Former First Secretary of The Hague Conference on Private International Law

THE CHILD IN THE INTERSECTIONS BETWEEN SOCIETY, FAMILY, FAITH AND CULTURE

Maarit JÄNTERÄ-JAREBORG

1. INTRODUCTION

The various contributions in this book address situations of conflict between society and the child's family regarding what lies in the child's best interests. In these cases, from society's point of view, the child is exposed to a significant harm or risk of harm. Society's actions are based on state law. According to the parents' understanding, on the contrary, the child is harmed or risks being harmed if the parents' outlook on the issue is not respected, be it the manner in which the child is to be brought up, the shaping of the child's cultural or religious identity, the child's education, underage marriage, or circumcision of a boy child. The parents' outlook is often based on a cultural or faith-based understanding of the issue, indicating that a normative system other than state law is relevant. In some cases, and in particular in cross-cultural marriages, only one of the parents has this frame of reference. The focus of the contributions is, consequently, on children with links to different cultures and faiths, in a European and particularly a Nordic (Scandinavian) context. The problems identified are, nevertheless, in no way unique to Europe and are addressed in a manner which can be expected to be of interest even outside this geographic context.

A core issue is how the legal system should respond to the increasing and no longer negligible normative diversity in society, in situations where majority values concerning children's welfare differ from minority values, and where the family's claim to decisional autonomy collides with state law. Cultural encounters take place today as never before, and the individuals concerned seek justice from a broader normative perspective than before.[1] Expressed in more trendy language, the challenge is how the legal system should "navigate" between the competing claims and conflicting interests, having regard to the fact that the threatened values have gradually developed in society, alongside increased welfare and increased emphasis on the rights of women and children.[2] What in this context can qualify as inviolable rights and liberties with no exceptions?[3] The reported tensions are often linked to the presence of recently established migrant communities within a country. In these situations an allegedly secular and equal society encounters religiously or culturally motivated practices. The tensions are also due to a *revaluation* of previously tolerated practices, usually among minority groups, brought about by a new awareness of the risks involved. In this respect, the impact of the United Nations Convention on the Rights of the Child (CRC), which strives to place the child in the centre as an autonomous individual with rights of his or her own, is evident. As the child's ultimate guardian, society is expected to intervene whenever there is a suspicion of malpractice or abuse of children within its jurisdiction.

---

1 In the current system of *law*, differences of treatment are usually only permitted when a legally relevant connecting factor to another state calls for that state's jurisdiction or the application of a foreign state's law. These are cases regulated by *private international law*, in each state. In the kinds of situations we are dealing with now, however, a person's "identity" and "belonging" are not marked by nationality, domicile or habitual residence as in private international law, thus falling (at least primarily) beyond the scope of the rules of this discipline. It is not the states' legal systems that clash, but the norm and value systems followed by distinct minority groups in relation to values promoted by the majority society, as embodied in state law.

2 Another increasingly important element in many Western countries (including all the Nordic states) is legal protection and recognition of sexual minorities. This important development falls, however, outside the scope of this book.

3 This is a particular challenge for Western liberalism. According to Mavies Maclean and John Eekelaar this is "because of the tension between the liberal values of respecting difference and the autonomy-enhancing features of individuals identifying with particular cultures, and the autonomy-restricting aspects of cultural membership, including the apparently illiberal practices of some cultural groups, for example, with respect to gender equality in family law. Furthermore, in human rights discourse, the rights of the individual to respect for his or her cultural and religious beliefs and practices may conflict with the rights to equality of treatment, personal safety and autonomy." M. Maclean and J. Eekelaar (eds.), *Managing Family Justice in Diverse Societies*, Hart Publishing 2013, p. 1.

In all of the situations to be discussed, a disturbing intersectionality is present on different levels.[4] In these cases, the person at the centre of the conflict is not only a child by definition and as such a vulnerable person to be protected, but also a child "belonging" to a "minority group" or to parents of "mixed origin". How do children fare in situations where majority and minority values are in conflict with each other in substance, within fields strongly influenced by religion, culture and tradition? Adding to the complexity is the fact that there is no unanimity on what these factors or elements consist of and how they relate to each other.[5] Is it possible to address a child's identity, preferences and convictions separately from the parents', or should society accept that in certain cases the identity and interests of the child "merge" with those of the parents?[6]

All decision-making in public bodies and courts of law should be anchored in the relevant legal sources. Even if variations exist among legal systems regarding the hierarchy of these sources, they essentially consist of legislation (with the country's constitution at its head), treaty law, statements made in the official *travaux préparatoires* to adopted legislation, court precedents and, to a varying degree, analyses and interpretations given in the legal literature. The decision-maker encounters two major challenges in this respect. The first has to do with the extent to which normative sources other than law can be taken into account, if at all.[7] The second challenge is the increasingly multi-layered nature of law, consisting of a mix of national and international regulations on children as well as other human rights instruments. How universally should international instruments be interpreted and applied, and how do they relate to the other normative systems established in the form of cultural or faith-based practices?

---

4 The concept of intersectionality was originally developed within the field of gender studies in order to highlight the connections between gender and racism. See e.g. Kimberle Crenshaw, "Mapping the Margins: Intersectionality, Identity Politics, and Violence Against Women of Color" (1990–91) 43 *Stanford Law Review* 1241–1299. Intersectionality as a concept has later on been extended to other fields as well, in order to better understand the interconnectedness of various factors (variables) such as gender, class, age, nationality, sexual orientation, etc.

5 Practices which are a part of a religion may qualify for protection under a constitutionally protected freedom of religion and conscience, as well as under the ECHR, contrary to practices motivated by culture or traditions. For this reason alone, drawing a line between "religion" and "culture" or "tradition" may be relevant. Concerns about other protected rights or other people's rights can nevertheless impose restrictions on the exercise of freedom of religion as well.

6 See Jane Mair in this volume, sections 3.1 and 3.3.1–3.3.2.

7 Constructions such as the *action's societal adequacy* have been developed in the legal literature and in the case law of courts, in order to grant societal acceptance to actions which otherwise would be punishable according to state law but find support in other norm systems accepted by society. In this chapter (section 8), examples of this are found in the Swedish and Finnish courts' reasoning to drop the charges which were based on legislation concerning physical assault, against parents who had had their son circumcised.

2. FOCUS ON EUROPE AND THE NORDIC STATES – BUT WITH GLOBAL IMPLICATIONS

As the majority of the authors in this volume are active in the Nordic states (in particular Sweden, but also Finland and Norway) the focus is inevitably on the current situation in these states. A comprehensive and general European view is, nevertheless, present in the contributions of Marie-Claire Foblets and Jane Mair in particular. The case law of the European Court of Human Rights (ECtHR) analysed by Sanna Mustasaari and Sanna Koulu is equally of general European interest. Louise Ellen Teitz also draws our attention to international attempts to bring the Muslim countries into a framework of global legal cooperation in respect of children's welfare, initiated by The Hague Conference on Private International Law through the so-called Malta Process. Esin Örücü's concerns for adult interests systematically overriding those of the child are *per se* universal in nature.

The special attention given to the situation in the Nordic countries, but in a more general European context, is also motivated by other concerns.

First, after the Second World War, the Nordic states have become important destinations of refuge from politically unsettled parts of the world. The most striking example is probably Sweden (with a population of approximately 10 million inhabitants), which is expected to receive in 2015 alone 190,000 asylum seekers, primarily from Syria and Iraq. It is through the new public presence of Islam[8] that religion has re-emerged in Scandinavia, challenging the majority society's notion of religion as a private concern[9] *and* what qualifies as secular or confession-free.[10] To give an example, in spite of the Nordic states' reputation of

8 Other important Muslim groups consist of refugees from the ethnically Muslim parts of the former Yugoslavia, who arrived in the course of the 1990s, and Turks (in particular Kurd minorities) since the 1960s. Jewish minorities, on the other hand, have lived in the Nordic countries for several centuries; Jews qualify as a national minority group in the Nordic States under the Council of Europe Framework Convention for the Protection of National Minorities (1994). The Chileans, who arrived after the brutal defeat of Salvador Allende's experiments on socialism, did not actively bring their religion (Roman Catholicism in their case, if any) into the public eye. This also appears to apply to the Greeks (Greek Orthodox Church) who in periods of political turbulence in Greece have sought refuge in Scandinavia and in particular Sweden.

9 The "privatisation of religion" can be dated to start towards the end of the 19th century, when the state took over many of the traditional activities of the church, such as education and care of needy persons. Parallel to this development, legislation was secularised, for example by removing the clergy's enrolment in various kinds of matters of the family. In a Nordic setting secularisation of law, by keeping it separate from religion, has been regarded as necessary for promoting the values of a modern, equal welfare society. Exceptions exist, such as faith communities' right, upon state authorisation, to officiate marriages with full legal effects in all the Nordic states. See, e.g., Maarit Jänterä-Jareborg, "The Legal Scope for Religious Identity in Family Matters – The Paradoxes of the Swedish Approach", in J. Mair and E. Örücü (eds.), *The Place of Religion in Family Law: A Comparative Search*, Intersentia 2011.

10 More generally on the issue see Anders Bäckström (coordinator), *Welfare and Values in Europe, Transitions related to Religion, Minorities and Gender, Volume 1: Northern Europe: Sweden, Norway, Finland and England*, Uppsala University 2011.

being among the most secular countries in the world, each of them has a national (Evangelical Lutheran) Folk's Church of which the majority of the population are members. Even if the large majority of the members of the national church take no part in its activities, there is a general acceptance of originally faith-based elements in the obligatory school system, such as the tradition of celebrating the ending of the two annual school terms in the local church or – less obviously – music lessons including traditional songs with a Christian message. It is increasingly being debated whether these elements are in conflict with, in particular, Muslim and Jewish children's identity and, as a result, how a line should be drawn between traditions, based on the country's cultural heritage and Christian (Evangelical Lutheran) confessional elements.[11] The answer is important; for example, according to Swedish law, no confessional elements are permitted in the school curriculum.[12]

Second, legislation is widely used as a tool for *social engineering* in order to abolish various forms of discrimination and inequality of treatment in both private and public spheres of life. A multicultural society offers not only new challenges but also new prospects for using legislation to set the standards and limits for societal acceptance.[13] In addition to legislation, the Nordic states' public school system with a fixed nationwide curriculum constitutes society's main channel for shaping children and young people into citizens who share the values of the state. The many applications for exemptions from certain kinds of education elements in the school curriculum, seen by the parents as an infringement of the family's culture or faith, illustrate the tensions.[14]

Third, the Nordic societies have since the 1930s been organised as social welfare states, with an extensive public sector in charge of general welfare (education, health care, care of the needy through distribution of social welfare benefits, etc.). The population in general has a high degree of trust in the state and public bodies,

---

11 Martin Scheinin's comment on the issue captures the problem: "The majority religion, often in a secularized or symbolic form, may be present in the law and in public institutions to the extent that individuals not belonging to the Lutheran Church may experience as a lack of respect for their own freedom of thought, conscience and religion." Martin Scheinin, "Secular Human Rights Perspectives, As a Challenge to Nordic Law & Religious Solutions", in L. Christoffersen et al. (eds.), *Law & Religion in the 21st Century – Nordic Perspectives*, Djof Publishing 2010, p. 548. See also Pamela Slotte, "A Little Church, a Little State, and a Little Commonwealth at Once, Towards a Nordic Model of Religious Instruction in Public Schools", in *Law & Religion in the 21st Century – Nordic Perspectives*, ibid., pp. 239–268.

12 According to the interpretation by Swedish National School Agency (*Skolverket*), gatherings related to the school year may take place in church facilities *but only on condition that all elements of faith are absent*. See Anna Ekström and Claes-Göran Aggebo, "Gud får inte vara med när skolan samlas i kyrkan", *Dagens Nyheter*, 25 November 2012 ("God may not attend when the school assembles in church"). This interpretation was much debated during the Uppsala symposium in May 2013 (Preface), after the presentation given by the Agency's Director General Anna Ekström. It can be questioned on the basis that in any active church milieu religion is inevitably present.

13 See for example Göran Lambertz on how legislation forbidding child marriages can be expected to change people's behaviour and protect children from being married off; Göran Lambertz in this volume, sections 3.5 and 6.

14 See Sanna Mustasaari and Sanna Koulu in this volume, sections 3–4.

and far-reaching expectations of the quality of various kinds of social services. With the state being the ultimate guarantor of each citizen's welfare, in particular children's, its intrusions in the private sphere of the family are generally not questioned.[15] Newcomers from politically and economically unstable countries, on the other hand, seldom have any positive previous experience of state involvement and tend to regard the family as the only reliable source of material welfare. Religion, culture and traditions may, in addition, offer the spiritual meaning of life and the setting for how family life is to be conducted. Public intrusion is not welcomed in what the family regards as its sphere of autonomy. These different positions create an additional potential for tensions.

Fourth, the Nordic societies' approach to the new challenges of diversity is a curious mix of both attempts to accommodate, in a manner which often compares favourably with that of most other European jurisdictions, and sending strong signals of disapproval through legislation regarding practices not to be tolerated. These developments are largely independent of developments in other European countries and have received little international attention. In many cases, the Nordic experiences can be expected to be of general relevance.

In a multicultural context, the Nordic states are increasingly engaged in protecting any child under the age of 18 years from entering into a marriage.[16] The concern here is that an early marriage deprives the child of the right to develop his or her full potential, for example through lost educational and labour market opportunities.[17] Society is responsible for ensuring that all children receive equal chances in life, and should counteract restrictive traditional views, such as the notion of the woman's proper place being in the home, or that sex and pregnancy outside of marriage are shameful. Other current concerns relate to children's physical integrity, in particular how to protect girls from genital mutilation[18] and how to control religiously or culturally motivated circumcisions of boys. The requirement for all children under the age of 16 to participate in an education system following an obligatory curriculum established by the state has resulted in numerous legal disputes on the scope for exceptions with reference to (in essence) the family's convictions. Since attending school is a duty and not only a right of the child, the parents are responsible for making sure that the child attends. If they fail to do so, the state has access to economic sanctions in the form of injunctions

15 See Olav Helge Angell, in Bäckström, *supra* note 10, p. 122.

16 Denmark, however, has introduced a 24 year age limit, among many other conditions within the law of migration, for any person (without citizenship within the EES) to be able to receive residence permit in Denmark on the basis of marriage to a Danish national or person legally resident in Denmark. The original concern of this legislation was to counteract forced and arranged marriages involving family members in Denmark and family members outside the EES area. A similar government bill has been presented in Norway.

17 See Göran Lambertz in this volume, section 2.1.

18 See, for example, the Swedish Act (1982:316) on prohibition of genital mutilation of women. The victim's consent to such an act is irrelevant, and the perpetrator is to be sentenced to prison for, usually, a maximum of four years but, in case of grave circumstances, up to ten years.

(fines), to be ordered by court. In practice, this sanction can be effective only if the family has an income or assets. If a child is taken into public care because his or her parents are unable to care for him or her according to prevailing societal standards, the child's new placement should be decided with due regard to the child's ethnic, religious, cultural and linguistic background.

All these issues are, from different perspectives, touched upon in the various contributions to this book. While it is easy to claim that law protects or should protect children and their identity, it is much more difficult to define what this means in practice and what benefits it might bring, as Jane Mair points out.[19] Sanna Mustasaari and Sanna Koulu find the parents' convictions to be the key, whereas Marie-Claire Foblets fears that these convictions risk being increasingly overrun. Kirsten Sandberg's and Sanne Hofman's studies in Norway regarding placements of children into care outside of their home demonstrate that society often tolerates much more neglect, in particular emotional neglect, from parents with another cultural background or with a traumatic refugee background, perhaps out of fear of generalising cultural-specific aspects of child-raising to the whole group or culture. Göran Lambertz draws attention to the lawmaker's difficulty regarding how to deal with situations where the disputed practices only are exercised within minority groups or among newcomers.[20] Since it is in society's interest not to stigmatise its minorities, a fair balance must be struck between the concurring demands in order not to hamper inclusion and a sense of belonging.

Marie-Claire Foblets reminds us about the growing uneasiness of Jewish and Muslim minority groups with what they perceive as a selective policy of intrusion in their traditions and practices. Under the cover of the protection of human rights and fundamental freedoms, society seeks to restrict certain of their rights, while ignoring the fact that these had historically been granted precisely in the name of religious freedom.[21] Circumcision of boys for religious or cultural reasons, for example, has become a growing European concern. Staffan Janson's

---

19 See Jane Mair in this volume, sections 1 and 2.2. Not all identities are regarded as worthy of protection by society, such as honour-based identities imposed by the family on its members at the expense of the individual's own needs and rights. This is the position taken in a Swedish appellate court judgment of July 2015. Swedish social authorities had placed a young woman, aged 19 years, into forced care because she risked her health and possibly even her life in her family environment (to be taken by force abroad and forced into marriage). Her wish to be reunited with her family, because of her strong feelings of guilt for dishonouring her family by the separation, was disregarded. In the court's opinion, her home environment differed from fundamental societal norms. She needed to be protected against her own actions, in this case returning to her parental home. Two members of the court were of a dissenting opinion and did not qualify the young woman's own behaviour as socially self-destructive, justifying a forced care order. Kammarrätten i Stockholm, judgment 17 July 2015 case No. 1414–15. The circumstances were similar in the case decided by the Swedish Supreme Administrative Court, HDF 2015 ref. 7. In that case, however, the young woman's attempts to have contact with her "honour-oriented" family did not, in the Court's opinion, qualify as "socially destructive" and justify a continued forced care order (applicable in Sweden to young persons under the age of 21).

20 See Göran Lambertz in this volume, section 3.

21 See Marie-Claire Foblets in this volume, section 1.3.1.

description of the medical profession's growing opposition towards this practice, out of respect for the child's physical integrity and autonomy, illustrates this clash between rights.[22] The so-called Malta Process, initiated by The Hague Conference on Private International Law and described in this volume by Louise Ellen Teitz, demonstrates a search for a common understanding between Western and Muslim states about the best interests of the child, when the child is situated in the middle of a cross-border, cross-cultural dispute on parental responsibilities. Importantly, the Malta Process strives to build upon mutual trust and confidence, instead of provoking confrontation, for example by striving to highlight differences in the essence and manner of exercise of parental rights and duties.

3. HOW HUMAN RIGHTS INSTRUMENTS TACKLE THE CHILD'S CONFLICTING INTERESTS

In all countries, it is a relatively new development to view children as holders of rights of their own. Children's interests were previously, both privately and publicly, largely subsumed under those of their parents, children being in essence treated as their parents' assets.[23] The successive recognition of childhood as a period of utmost importance for the child's further development has changed the underlying premises of legislation on children. Importantly, this development paved the way for the adoption of the United Nations Convention on the Rights of the Child (CRC) in 1989, which in turn has significantly contributed to the strengthening of children's rights, nationally and internationally. In Sweden, a major shift took place in 1979 through the explicit prohibition of all forms of corporal punishment and demeaning treatment of the child. Sweden was the first country in the world to introduce such a prohibition; to date, 37 other countries have successively followed.[24] The Swedish legislation's definition of parental responsibilities reflects this position in an accurate manner, by stating that "children are entitled to care, security and a good upbringing. They shall be treated with respect for their person and their distinctive character and may not be subjected to corporal punishment or any other humiliating treatment".[25] The holders of parental responsibilities must not only provide the child with a

22 See Staffan Janson in this volume.

23 On this, see in particular Jane Mair in this volume, section 1.

24 In 2014, Brazil joined "the camp" as the 38th state in the world. Annika Rydman, "Hipp Hipp Hurra! I år fyller Barnkonventionen 25 år", *Barn Nr 2/2014*, p. 45.

25 Children and Parents Code Ch. 6 §1 (Sweden). See further, Swedish Report on Question 8, K. Boele-Woelki, B. Braat and I. Curry-Sumner (eds.), *European Family Law in Action, Volume III: Parental Responsibilities*, Intersentia 2005, pp. 178 f. See also Marjorie Smith and Ann Phoenix, "Variation and Change in Normative Parental Discipline: Persuasion or Legislation?", in M. Maclean and J. Eekelaar (eds.), *Managing Family Justice in Diverse Societies*, Hart Publishing 2013, pp. 295–310.

good and secure home environment, but they must also be attentive to the child's individuality and growing needs of personal integrity.

But even if parental responsibilities are to be exercised in the child's best interests, secondary to any parental interests, practice and reality are often different and society falls short of providing adequate protection. The case study carried out by Kirsten Sandberg and Sanne Hofman concerning children with a different cultural ethnicity (than "majority Norwegian") and taken into public care in Norway makes this point brutally explicit. Refugee children, for example, needed to experience neglect to a far greater extent than other children, apparently out of regard for the parents' difficult situation.[26] The cases demonstrated on the other hand that physical violence was not accepted by Norwegian child care authorities but regarded as "universal" proof of the parents' lack of caring ability.

On another level, we encounter the parents' expectations that they will be able to shape their children's identity in accordance with their own, a problem addressed by both Jane Mair and Sanna Mustasaari and Sanna Koulu.[27] In spite of all the child-centred language in national and international law, the view that parents know what is best for their children is deeply rooted and respected.[28] This view appears to find support in the CRC, due to its recognition of parental guidance in the child's exercise of the conventional rights.[29] Parental rights, however, risk restricting the child's autonomy. Tensions are inevitable when the state, in particular through its obligatory school system, claims to be in charge of the child's education and socialisation. From society's point of view, public school attendance offers the necessary opportunity for the child to come into contact with others, both adults and children, outside of the family and the parental circles.

Measured on the basis of the number of ratifications, the CRC is the most successful human rights convention ever adopted.[30] Primarily under the guidance of the Convention's supervisory body, that is, the UN Committee on the Rights of the Child, four principles enshrined within the CRC have emerged as fundamental and are expected to govern all measures taken in respect of children, namely (i)

---

26 See Kirsten Sandberg and Sanne Hofman in this volume, section 4.

27 See Jane Mair in this volume, section 3.3.1. See also Sanna Mustasaari and Sanna Koulu in this volume, section 2.

28 See, for example, Jane Mair in this volume, section 2.

29 The same applies to the ECHR, see Sanna Mustasaari and Sanna Koulu in this volume, sections 1–2.

30 Of all current UN Member States (2015), only the United States has abstained from acceding to the CRC. On the other hand, numerous states – including the majority of Muslim states – have entered general (such as to the extent it is in compliance with Islam) or specific reservations (certain articles) against the Convention. Reservations by Muslim states address, in particular, two specific aspects of the CRC, namely the freedom of thought, conscience and religion (Article 14), and adoption (Article 21). See Lena-Maria Möller, "Improving Women's Rights through Children's Rights? The Reform of Custody Laws in Contemporary Muslim Jurisdictions", in Maarit Jänterä-Jareborg and Hélène Tigroudja, *Women's Human Rights and the Elimination of Discrimination*, The Hague Academy of International Law, Martinus Nijhoff Publishers 2016 (forthcoming).

equal treatment of all children within a state's jurisdiction; (ii) regard for the child's best interests as a primary consideration; (iii) the child's right to life and development; and (iv) the child's right to be heard. It should, however, not be forgotten that the CRC is aimed to operate in very different kinds of states and legal systems.[31] For this reason alone it must be questioned whether any uniform interpretation of the CRC is ever possible, or even desirable.

On the contrary, when adopting the Convention, the world community must have understood and accepted that each contracting state will be inclined to interpret and apply the CRC in a manner that the said state considers reasonable but with respect for the rights granted by the Convention. The universal notion of human rights, applicable in the case of the CRC to every child, should not be confused with a requirement for a uniform application in all contracting states. On a national level, however, within the state's jurisdiction, each state is under the duty to treat all children equally (Article 2). In cases of tensions, such as those addressed in this volume, the Convention provides us with very few clear-cut answers. Since it also acknowledges the child's right to identity on national, cultural, religious and family-based grounds,[32] any uniformity of treatment could be claimed to be debatable.[33] Whereas the CRC aims to promote both the "universal" child's and the "individual" child's interests, in each concrete case the interests of the individual child should, according to the Committee on the Rights of the Child, take priority.

The Nordic states are currently much engaged in discussions on human rights, in particular how to best promote children's rights. Norway has implemented the CRC as legislation of a higher rank, to be given precedence in the case of conflict with ordinary legislation.[34] The Convention's signal effect is said to have increased as a result of this "upgrading", strengthening the rights of children in Norwegian society. In Finland, the CRC has been implemented as ordinary legislation. In its inaugural declaration in October 2014, Sweden's new government (led by the Social Democratic Party) promised to implement the CRC as directly applicable legislation in Sweden. A law commission is to deliver its proposal to this effect by March 2016, including how potential conflicts between the provisions of the CRC and Swedish domestic law are to be tackled in order to give the CRC the intended

---

31 As phrased by Jane Mair, international conventions on human rights are an abstraction of general principles but they become real through national and local implementation. See Jane Mair in this volume, section 3. The many reservations to the CRC find an important explanation in states' uncertainty regarding whether their legal system fulfils the standards established in the Convention. By making a reservation, the state strives to safeguard that it will not be alleged breaking against its conventional duties. Germany, for example, initially had several reservations against the Convention which it later on withdrew. Another motive is uncertainty regarding the CRC's compatibility with the ratifying state's fundamental principles.

32 On the markers of identity acknowledged by the CRC, see Jane Mair in this volume.

33 On the basis of the nationality test alone, the European Union Court (ECJ) found in the case of *Garcia Avello*, C-148/02, that Belgium was guilty of discrimination by treating Spanish-Belgian children's right to a surname according to the same rules as applied to children of only Belgian nationality. The children in question were habitually resident in Belgium with their parents.

34 See Kirsten Sandberg and Sanne Hofman in this volume, section 2.

effect. The basic vision is, at the same time, that the CRC sets the "minimum rights standard" and that domestic legislation is to be continuously revisited in order to strengthen children's rights.[35] The promised implementation of the CRC marks a reconsideration of the previous understanding according to which Swedish law is in full conformity with the CRC.[36] The European Convention on Human Rights and Fundamental Freedoms (ECHR) has been implemented in the form of directly applicable legislation in all the Nordic countries. In the light of case law, the ECHR's impact is continuously increasing.

Due to the lack of a precise content of human rights and, not least, children's rights under the CRC, taking these rights seriously may result in increased conflicts.[37] Whereas we can readily agree that human rights are universal, in the sense that they apply or should apply to every human being, we do not agree on any uniform interpretation of these universal rights, worldwide or in a regional context. Voices differ even within the same jurisdiction. The debates on circumcision of boys on the grounds of religion or tradition illustrate this point well. A contracting state's CRC obligations are, furthermore, restricted to children within its jurisdiction (Article 2),[38] although each state has the right to protest against other states' violations of the Convention.

As Jane Mair points out, although the standard at the outset appears to be objective, what in the end is regarded to be in the individual child's interests "is open to broad and varied interpretation" and "lies at the heart of many disputes".[39]

---

35 Norway's reported positive experiences of the incorporation of the CRC is an important motivation regarding Sweden's corresponding plans. The Commission's (*Barnrättighetsutredningen*) directives are issued in Dir. 2013:08, supplemented by Dir. 2015:17, Ministry of Social Affairs. Maarit Jänterä-Jareborg acts as an expert member in this law commission.

36 See e.g. Memorandum by the Ministry of Social Affairs (*Socialdepartmentet*) *Hur svensk lagstiftning och praxis överensstämmer med rättigheterna i barnkonventionen – en kartläggning*, Ds 2011:37, Regeringskansliet 2011.

37 For example, arguments based on other normative systems than law may need to be taken increasingly into account in all decision-making.

38 For any scholar of private international law, the term *jurisdiction* refers to national jurisdiction to take measures of, e.g., protection. The right to exercise jurisdiction is largely determined by international conventions between states. Instruments such as the European Union's Brussels II *bis* Regulation of 2003 on parental responsibilities and the 1996 Hague Child Protection Convention all set clear limits to a participating state's right to exercise jurisdiction. If the child's habitual residence is not in that state but in another participating state, the instruments prevent the state (where, e.g., the child is present) from taking any other than *provisional protective measures*. Romanian Roma children begging on the streets of Sweden and sleeping in huts and deserted cars with their parents thus fall outside Sweden's jurisdiction except where urgent protective measures are necessary. The jurisdiction to take the necessary protective measures rests with Romania (an EU Member State) alone, as the state of habitual residence of the children. Begging in public places is not forbidden under Swedish law.

39 See Jane Mair in this volume, section 2.1. See also Sanna Mustasaari and Sanna Koulu in this volume, section 2. Göran Lambertz provides a useful example of a pregnant girl's interest in receiving a dispensation to marry before the age of 18 years; otherwise the girl risks being dishonoured and abandoned by her very traditional family. In his opinion, the signal effect of a strict law, which leaves no scope for any exceptions, weighs heavier than meeting the

From the legal system's perspective, access to different understandings can provide a useful tool for flexibility, of value in particular in multicultural settings. This flexibility can, however, endanger the basic principle of any *Rechtsstaat* in respect of legal certainty and predictability, requiring that it should be clear at the outset what is legitimate or not. Evidently, the CRC cannot stand on its own, but needs to be supplemented by other international instruments, national legislation and court precedents. The potential impact of the general comments by the CRC Committee on the interpretation of any provision of the CRC is reduced by the fact that in most states (or all states?) these comments are not acknowledged as binding or established legal sources, thus preventing their direct application. The impact of the Third Optional Protocol to the CRC (2011), which establishes an individual complaints procedure for violations of children's rights, still remains to be seen. A similar complaints procedure under an optional protocol to the UN Convention on the Rights of Women and the Elimination of Discrimination appears to have been without any significant effect.

Accession to the CRC nevertheless obliges the states parties to respect and promote the rights established in the Convention. This implies, for example, that the states abstain from any measures that restrict or infringe upon these rights, that the states protect the child from any such restrictions or infringements by other actors, and safeguard for each child the exercise of the conventional rights. Society – meaning primarily the state and its administration – has become the child's agent, imposing duties on public and private actors in relation to the child, also within traditionally private domains. From the point of view of the family, society's engagement can amount to intrusion, questioning or restricting the family's traditional autonomy and the culture the family is part of. But even if society formally places the child on a pedestal in terms of rights, the child risks falling into the shadow of others and their interpretations of what best serves the child.

Many of the authors in this volume fear that decision-making takes place "over the child's head", that is, without the child and his or her best interests being truly in the centre. Whereas Mustasaari and Koulu raise concerns that the child risks being "a pawn in the conflict of parents and the state",[40] Örücü compares the child with a sacrificial lamb.[41] In Mair's analysis, children turn out to be simultaneously both "the most precious and the most insignificant".[42] In her opinion, we need to be clear whether the child's identity to be protected is the identity into which the child is born, that is, that of his or her parents, or an identity to be shaped in the course of the years of growing up, in which case it is an open identity. Importantly, children and their interests cannot be seen in isolation from the society where

girl's immediate situation. This is an example where children's collective interests overrun the interests of an individual child. See Göran Lambertz in this volume, sections 4.2–4.4.

40 See Sanna Mustasaari and Sanna Koulu in this volume, section 2.

41 See Esin Örücü in this volume.

42 Jane Mair in this volume, section 3.

they grow up and go to school. Parents, on the other hand, may wish to continue to adhere to the values of their state of origin or their special faith or culture and to promote a certain lifestyle that differs from that of majority society. Mustasaari and Koulu emphasise that children suffer the social consequences of parental decisions, for example, in relation to their peers. It is, furthermore, the child's future that risks being jeopardised when a child is deprived of equal educational opportunities.[43] Lambertz argues that the child's fundamental right to maximum development of his or her personal capacities must supersede any other interests.[44] In his opinion, this concern should exclude any recognition of marriages where one party is under the age of 18 years.

Sandberg and Hofman refer to the care needs of the child, in relation to which regard for the child's cultural background remains subsidiary, though relevant.[45] Foblets' approach is that of sustainable accommodation and the balancing of interests, in a spirit of striving to understand the essence of what is at stake for the concerned persons.[46]

As a professor of paediatrics, Janson, on the contrary, is not willing to support any interventions on the child's physical integrity for other than strictly medical reasons.[47] For the medical profession in Scandinavia, the boy child's right to be heard and to make decisions of his own has become a crucial criterion in the context of religiously or culturally motivated circumcisions of boys. Teitz's point of entry, focusing primarily on international child abduction across cultural and confessional borders, is basically that of neutrality, in order for states to be able to establish any successful framework for legal cooperation across national borders.[48] Whichever state exercises jurisdiction on the agreed basis should be free, according to this model, to interpret the child's best interests in accordance with the values of its own legal and cultural system. In cross-border cases, there can be reason to interpret the principle of the child's best interests more broadly and take into account other factors than what might apply in a purely domestic case, but without sacrificing the child's welfare.[49]

---

43 See Sanna Mustasaari and Sanna Koulu in this volume, section 2.

44 See Göran Lambertz in this volume.

45 See Kirsten Sandberg and Sanne Hofman in this volume, section 8. Roma children's forced care placements into families not belonging to the Roma community are debated in Sweden, as a violation of the children's identity rights. See Henrik Sundström, "Utred misstankarna om massomhändertagande" (Investigate the suspicions on large-scale forced care orders), *Dagens Nyheter*, 10 August 2015, p. 6. In Sweden, the Roma are a national minority group to be protected in accordance with the Council of Europe (1994) Framework Convention for the Protection of National Minorities.

46 See Marie-Claire Foblets in this volume, section 1.2.

47 See Staffan Janson in this volume, sections 3.1 and 4.2.

48 See Louise-Ellen Teitz in this volume.

49 See e.g. the reasons provided by Baroness Hale of Richmond in the child abduction case of *Re J* [2005] UKHL 40; [2006] 1 AC 80, para. 25: "In all non-Convention cases the courts have consistently held that they must act in accordance with the welfare of the individual child. If

4. THE CHILD'S RIGHT TO RELIGIOUS IDENTITY

Children's right to a religious identity is central in the majority of the contributions, either as a matter of principle (Mair), or in a specific context, such as the right to be exempted from certain elements of the residence state's otherwise obligatory school curriculum (Mustasaari and Koulu) or through circumcision of boys as a part of a Jewish and Muslim religious rite marking belonging (Foblets, to be compared with Janson). Concerns of identity-making are often present, directly or indirectly, in custody disputes and other disputes on parental responsibilities between parents of different religions or beliefs (Mair, and Teitz). It also comes into play when deciding with whom to place a child, removed from parental care (Sandberg and Hofman). Nor is it possible to fully grasp the essence of informal religious marriages involving a child (Lambertz) without including the child's religious identity as an element of relevance.

Numerous provisions of the CRC are of immediate relevance when assessing the child's right to a religious identity,[50] in particular Article 14. But several other international instruments also have a say, in Europe in particular the European Convention on Human Rights and Fundamental Freedoms (ECHR) and its First Protocol.[51] The Member States of the European Union also need to take EU law into account. The core issue is how to approach the child's right to identity independently and separately from that of the parents' and whether the identity to be protected is that into which the child is born or an identity which the child can acquire by choice. If the latter, the child's future autonomy must be safeguarded until he or she is able to take a sufficiently informed and independent decision on the issue.

In a European context, Article 2 of the First Protocol to the ECHR explicitly confirms the parents' right to ensure that their children are educated in conformity with the *parents'* own religious and philosophical convictions. Consequently, in the European Court's case law analysed by Mustasaari and Koulu, the convictions of the parents have been decisive when a child applies for exemption from certain kinds of school classes, such as music lessons, dancing, swimming lessons or sex education. The CRC is more diffuse in this respect, and it can be criticised for expressing double standards. On the one hand, its preamble and numerous specific articles link the child's identity and harmonious development to that of the child's parents and family, and the child's ethnic, cultural and religious background. On the other hand, the Convention's fundamental principles signal the child's uniqueness and independence from the interests of others. Affording children the

they decide to return the child, that is because it is in the best interests to do so not because the welfare principle has been superseded by some other consideration."

50 Besides Article 14, Articles 15, 20(3), 28–30, and the preamble of the CRC are of relevance. On their contents, see Jane Mair in this volume.

51 On this Protocol and its Article 2 (right to education), see Sanna Mustasaari and Sanna Koulu in this volume.

religious identity of their parents could be seen as "a state benefit to the parents in recognition of the role they play in child raising", Mair argues.[52] By doing so, we contribute towards labelling children. Religious behaviour and practices are not necessarily passed directly from one generation to another and can be understood differently by the different generations, in particular in a secular surrounding.[53] On the other hand, it remains uncertain to what extent children are able to have or acquire a separate identity of their own. Case law indicates that the child's own position is seldom clear.[54] In the opinion of Mustasaari and Koulu, children have an interest in an "effortless belonging", by acquiring an identity which is not grounded in choice.[55] In the case of conflicts, a consequence analysis test should be carried out, from the point of view of the individual child, with regard to the pros and cons of granting or denying the exemption.[56]

The authors in this volume emphasise that children's religiousness should not be viewed from a parental perspective. So when is a child mature enough to take a religious stance? Mair suggests making an analogy with the provisions on consent to medical treatment.[57] This also appears to be Janson's position, in the context of circumcision of boys. Marriage requires an even stricter standard, at least from the perspective of Swedish law. The child's religious sentiment requesting marriage is not sufficient to legitimise a marriage, which under Swedish law can be validly concluded only after the child's 18th birthday.[58]

5. NAVIGATING BETWEEN PARENTS' CONVICTIONS AND THE STATE'S INTEREST IN EQUAL EDUCATION FOR ALL

In their contribution, Sanna Mustasaari and Sanna Koulu discuss the possibility of children being exempted from certain lessons and school activities on the grounds of freedom of religion, with special regard to the European Court's case law. Usually, there is a conflict between a curriculum fixed by the state and binding on all schools on a nationwide basis, and the convictions of the parents. The

52 Jane Mair in this volume, section 3.1.2.

53 Jane Mair in this volume, section 3.2.2. See also Esin Örücü in this volume. This concern has, repeatedly and more bluntly, been voiced by Richard Dawkins. "I want everybody to flinch whenever we hear a phrase such as 'Catholic child' or 'Muslim child'. Speak of a 'child of Catholic parents' if you like; but if you hear anybody speak of a 'Catholic child', stop them and politely point out that children are too young to know where they stand on such issues, just as they are too young to know where they stand on economics or politics." Richard Dawkins, *The God Delusion*, Black Swan, 2007, p. 25.

54 Sanna Mustasaari and Sanna Koulu in this volume.

55 Sanna Mustasaari and Sanna Koulu in this volume, section 5.

56 Sanna Mustasaari and Sanna Koulu in this volume, section 5.

57 Jane Mair in this volume, section 3.3.2.

58 Göran Lambertz in this volume, section 4.1.

authors draw attention in particular to the case of *Kjeldsen et al. v. Denmark* (1976), concerning exemption from sex education classes. In its judgment, the Court established a prohibition on the state to pursue aims of indoctrination which do not respect the parents' religious and philosophical convictions. Mustasaari and Koulu are critical of the Court's reasoning in general, which in their opinion takes far too little account of the wellbeing and interests of the concerned children.

Mustasaari and Koulu draw additional attention to developments in Sweden,[59] in the light of recent Swedish case law and a law reform carried out in 2011, which aimed at restricting the scope of any exceptions from the otherwise mandatory school education. The Swedish Supreme Administrative Court's judgment *HFD 2013 ref. 49*, denying an Orthodox Jewish family habitually resident in Gothenburg, Sweden, the continued right to keep their four daughters out of Sweden's general school system, demonstrates society's overriding demands to be in charge of all children's education (and socialisation), even if it requires special and far-reaching arrangements.[60] In this case, the dictates of family's religion governed every hour of the day, making home schooling (supported by online school education) the only option from the family's (and their faith's) perspective.[61] In the Court's opinion, the reasons provided by the parents did not qualify as extraordinary enough (as required by the revised law) to justify home schooling.[62]

Parents' preference for home schooling is usually motivated by their desire to educate the children in the family's religious, philosophical or cultural setting, but it can also be an expression of their lack of trust in the state.[63] Society, in turn, is reluctant to accept home schooling not only for concerns of quality and the lack of full control over its exercise but also due to the important role of the public school system in socialisation of children. It is in the state's interests to promote societal integration and to contribute, through the educational system, to an increased understanding of different cultures and faiths,[64] in addition to the dissemination of other knowledge. The Swedish approach could be claimed to fall within the state's margin of appreciation under the ECHR and to be in line with Article 29 of the CRC.[65]

---

59 Regarding the developments in the other Nordic countries, see Pamela Slotte, "A Little Church, a Little State, and a Little Commonwealth at Once, Towards a Nordic Model of Religious Instruction in Public Schools", in L. Christoffersen et al. (eds.), *Law & Religion in the 21st Century – Nordic Perspectives*, Djof Publishing 2010, pp. 239–273.

60 In Sweden, for example, the schools must provide children with a warm lunch, etc. every school day. The menu must respect pupils' dietary restrictions, for example for religious reasons.

61 The girls were 7–14 years of age. The parents had lived in Sweden since 1991.

62 The Swedish School Act, Ch. 24 §23.

63 See Jordi Ribot, "How much Family Conduct do we need to Regulate through Family Law?", in M. Maclean and J. Eekelaar (eds.), *Managing Family Justice in Diverse Societies*, Hart Publishing 2013, p. 288.

64 See Johanna Schiratzki, *Barnets bästa i ett mångkulturellt Sverige, En rättsvetenskaplig undersökning*, Iustus Förlag 2005, p. 158. See also the case of *Konrad v. Germany*, decided by the ECtHR on 11 September 2006.

65 According to Pamela Slotte, in the Nordic legal culture "religious freedom in school education is about realizing tolerance, rather than viewing religious freedom as meaning that public

What steps can society take if the child does not attend school? In Sweden, the state has access to injunctions, as a mechanism to force the parents to abide the law. This sanction is ineffective if the parents lack an income or assets. There are cases where parents belonging to the Maranatha sect[66] have defied the law and kept their children at home. This neglect of children's education has not been considered sufficient for society to remove the children from the care of their parents.[67] Swedish Roma children's high drop-out rates from the country's school system, reportedly due to insensibility towards Roma culture and harassment in the school environment, remain a considerable problem.[68]

It should be added that under Swedish law, faith communities have the right to found and operate schools, on the condition that the education is capable of giving the pupils knowledge and capacities essentially equivalent to those provided by the public schools and that the education corresponds with the general goals and values of the state curriculum.[69] The school needs state authorisation, but is then entitled to full public funding under the same conditions as the ordinary schools in Sweden. Its diplomas are furthermore recognised by the state. This is an example of accommodating the education of religious heritages and spiritual values, as a *supplement* to the state's obligatory curriculum. The system is, however, highly contested, primarily on the grounds that the required state supervision and control remain insufficient and that faith-based schools lack qualifications (or the ambition) to integrate their pupils into Swedish society and to properly disseminate the values which society expects to be shared by all its members.

---

school education should be conceptualized in religious terminology. Religious instruction is not equalled with religious 'teaching'. Tolerance forms part of what is understood by 'neutrality'. The task of the state is to counteract negative estimation of difference. However, abolishment of difference, of plurality as such is not the goal." Pamela Slotte, "A Little Church, a Little State, and a Little Commonwealth at Once, Towards a Nordic Model of Religious Instruction in Public Schools", in L. Christoffersen et al. (eds.), *Law & Religion in the 21st Century – Nordic Perspectives*, Djof Publishing 2010, p. 267.

66 The Maranatha is classified as a Christian Pentecostal movement.

67 See Hanna Kjöller, "Extremisterna som håller barnen hemma" (The extremists who keep their children at home) *Dagens Nyheter*, 22 November 2014. Removal of children from parental care against the parents' wishes requires, according to the ECtHR, that the child is exposed to dangerous practices or to physical or psychological harm. See case of *Vojnity v. Hungary*, ECtHR, judgment of 12 February 2013, para. 37. Generally speaking, the parents' convictions, their religious devotion or their irrational worldviews do not qualify as a ground for removing children from parental care, irrespective of how extreme in nature the secular society perceives them to be.

68 The Roma are recognised as a national minority group in Sweden, under the Council of Europe's Framework Convention for the Protection of National Minorities from 1994 (to which Sweden is a state party). The Convention's monitoring body has urged Sweden to take measures to improve Roma children's right to education, in an inclusive environment free from harassments.

69 On state funding of religious education of the youth in Sweden, see further, Maarit Jänterä-Jareborg, "Religion and the Secular State in Sweden", in *Religion and the Secular State: National Reports, Interim Reports issued on the occasion of the XVIIIth International Congress of Comparative Law*, under the direction of J. Martinez-Torrón and W. Cole Durham, Jr., 2010, pp. 683–685 (final edition, 2015).

6. REMOVAL OF CHILDREN FROM PARENTAL CARE

Most states have special solutions and special child-care institutions to provide shelter and care for children who cannot live and be taken care of in their parental home.[70] This protection can be offered in the form of placing the child in a so-called children's home with professional, employed staff. It can also involve a foster family placement (family home placement) where a private home, regulated and supervised by a competent authority, receives children and offers them a home for a longer or shorter period of time. Seen from the parental perspective, this placement may be "voluntary", in the sense that the child's parents have consented to it. If the placement takes place without parental consent, it is an "involuntary" or "forced" placement. The positions of legal systems differ as regards the impact of the care order. In some states, for example Norway and Sweden, the parents remain as the child's legal custodians and guardians but lose the right to daily care of the child and all related decision-making. In other states, the intrusion on their legal parental rights and duties may go further.

In this volume, care placements of children outside their parental home are studied from a primarily Norwegian point of view but with special regard to the CRC and its Article 20(3).[71] This provision requires the state to pay due regard to the desirability of continuity in a child's upbringing and to the child's ethnic, religious, cultural and linguistic background. Under Norwegian law,[72] a child may be taken into public care in the event of serious neglect of the child's physical or mental needs, due to failure to follow up a child's special need for health care or training, because of violence or sexual or psychological abuse of the child, or risk of severe damage to the child's health or development. These grounds indicate a serious parental inability to take sufficient responsibility for the child. Other solutions must have been tried earlier or at least considered but found to be insufficient. Finally, it has to be determined whether it is in the child's best interests to be taken into care.[73]

Kirsten Sandberg's and Sanne Hofman's survey of Norwegian care orders concerned children with a different ethnic and cultural background from that of majority Norwegian society.[74] The results indicated a far-reaching tolerance towards parental behaviour, for example, by "interpreting" it to be in line with "normal parental behaviour" in a given ethnic group or by demonstrating a far-

70 See Katharina Boele-Woelki and Maarit Jänterä-Jareborg, "Protecting Children against Detrimental Family Environments under the 1996 Hague Convention and the Brussels II bis Regulation", in K. Boele-Woelki et al. (eds.), *Convergence and Divergence in Private International Law – Liber Amicorum Kurt Siehr*, Eleven International Publishing 2010, pp. 126 ff.

71 See Kirsten Sandberg and Sanne Hofman in this volume.

72 See Norwegian Child Protection Act, section 4-12.

73 See Kirsten Sandberg and Sanne Hofman in this volume, sections 2 and 7.

74 See further Kirsten Sandberg and Sanne Hofman in this volume, section 1.

reaching "understanding" towards the parents' traumatic background, as an excuse. What a child needs is to a certain extent culturally determined. Equally, the term "caring ability" implies a cultural and normative perspective of care. A particular challenge faced by the competent authorities was to decide to what extent deviations from the Norwegian majority standard could be accepted before taking the child into public care. There was, however, no tolerance of any kind of physical abuse of the child. When this was detected, the child was removed from parental care.

In the placement decisions studied, Norwegian authorities generally strived to take into account the child's cultural background, regarding it as an essential element when assessing the best interests of the child. This was, however, not a decisive criterion and the outcomes varied. In Sandberg's and Hofman's opinion, a forced care order creates far-reaching obligations for the state to strive to place a minority group child in the culture where the child belongs or to ensure that the child has the possibility of retaining his or her cultural identity, having regard to Article 30 of the CRC. It follows that minority group children should preferably be placed in the care of a family home belonging to the same ethnic or cultural group as the child or in a family where at least one of the foster parents speaks the mother tongue of the child. In Sandberg's and Hofman's opinion a foster home that does not share the child's background should be required to be prepared to support the child in practicing his or her culture. An additional way to support this right is by safeguarding the child's contact with the biological family or by appointing a support person or an extra home of the same cultural background where the child may, for example, spend some weekends.

Sandberg's and Hofman's study does not cover cross-border placements of children. Importantly, two relatively recent child protection instruments explicitly strive to regulate them, namely the 1996 Hague Convention on Cross-Border Child Protection[75] and the European Union's Brussels II *bis* Regulation of 2003.[76] Under both instruments, the decision by a competent authority to place a child into care in another state may only take place if the competent authority of the contemplated state of placement consents to it. These instruments can be expected to pave the way for society to place children abroad more frequently, having regard to the child's best interests, the free movement of persons (within the EU), mutual trust between the cooperating states and, not least, "the desirability of continuity in a child's upbringing and to the child's ethnic, religious, cultural and linguistic

75 Convention of 19 October 1996 on Jurisdiction, Applicable Law, Recognition, Enforcement and Co-operation in Respect of Parental Responsibility and Measures for the Protection of Children, see in particular Article 33. With few exceptions the member states of the EU are parties to this Convention.

76 Council Regulation (EC) No. 2201/2003 of 27 November 2003 Concerning Jurisdiction and the Recognition and Enforcement in Matrimonial Matters and Matters of Parental Responsibilities, Repealing Regulation (EC) No. 1347/2000, OJ (EU) 2003 L 338, see in particular Article 56.

background", as defined by Article 20(3) of the CRC.[77] In particular, placements with close relatives living in another country can turn out to be an option in respect of young children. So far, very few cases appear to have gone to court concerning care placements of children abroad. How the procedure is to take place under the Brussels II *bis* Regulation, in the case of an institutional placement of a child in another European Union Member State, is clarified by the preliminary ruling of the European Union Court in *C-92/12 Health Care Executive, PPU*. This case was unusual in that it concerned a teenager placed in forced care due to her own destructive behaviour and the risk of her committing suicide. No suitable care alternative existed in the child's state of habitual residence (Ireland) whereas adequate care could be provided in an institution in England.

Two recent cases, the one from Norway and the other from Sweden, indicate the potential for global conflict when society places children into care independently of the children's (faith-based) cultural origin. In the Norwegian case, children of Indian origin but habitually resident in Norway were removed from their parents' care due to serious shortcomings in their home environment, and placed in a Norwegian family's home. These measures were extensively and critically reported in Indian media, under headlines such as "Hands off Norway of Hindu Children".[78] The case was in the end settled on a high diplomatic level between the two countries, and the children were placed in the care of close relatives in India. In the Swedish case, the children of a Malaysian diplomat couple were removed from the parents' care and placed in a Swedish family's home because the parents had systematically physically assaulted their children as a disciplinary measure.[79] This case also became a national concern in the children's country of origin, and was widely reported in the media. Criticism was raised in particular against the children's placement with a Swedish family that was neither Muslim nor Malaysian. After the Malaysian Deputy Minister of Foreign Affairs had paid a visit to Sweden, the children were removed to Malaysia to the care of their relatives, the country's Prime Minister himself receiving them. Both cases demonstrate not only different outlooks on which state has "jurisdiction" to take the necessary measures but also the importance to be given to the child's culture

---

77 See Katharina Boele-Woelki and Maarit Jänterä-Jareborg, "Protecting Children against Detrimental Family Environments under the 1996 Hague Convention and the Brussels II bis Regulation", in K. Boele-Woelki et al. (eds.), *Convergence and Divergence in Private International Law – Liber Amicorum Kurt Siehr*, Eleven International Publishing 2010, pp. 126 ff.

78 See, for example, A. Malhotra, "Leave the Kids Alone, Norway", *The Hindu*, 29 January 2012, and A. Malhotra, "Personal Law Is Valid in Norway, Too", *The Tribune*, 30 January 2012. See also Maarit Jänterä-Jareborg, "Religious Personal Laws, Freedom of Religion, Human Rights and Public Policy in Private International Law", in *The 90th Birthday of Boutros Boutros-Ghali, Tribute of the Curatorium to Its President*, The Hague Academy of International Law, 2012, p. 169 f.

79 The parents were also sentenced by a Swedish court for this crime. The case received extensive media coverage in Sweden in the beginning of 2014. See e.g. "Diplomatpar häktat – ska ha slagit sina barn" (A diplomat couple arrested for hitting their children), *Expressen*, 22 January 2014; "Barnmisshandel i Sverige – ministerfråga i Malaysia" (Child assault in Sweden – a concern of the Malaysian government), *Dagens Nyheter*, 24 January 2014.

of origin. In both cases the CRC was officially given credit for enabling the final and amicable settlement between the states concerned.

7. PROTECTING CHILDREN FROM MARRYING

This volume includes as an Annex the English summary of the final report, published in 2012, of a law commission appointed by the Swedish government to investigate and analyse the practice of forced marriages and child marriages in Sweden and to propose counteractive measures. It is not a coincidence that this summary starts by reciting heart-breaking narratives of girls in Sweden who were married off as children, against their own will and often during a visit abroad, as part of a transaction between two families. When the state needs to justify a controversial law reform, in this case a reform which could be feared to stigmatise minorities, narratives on individual cases are far more persuasive than any uncertain figures. The law commission's proposals were on the whole approved by Parliament, and a bill was passed. According to the revised Swedish legislation, applicable since 1 July 2014, no child (defined as person under the age of 18 years) may enter into a legally valid marriage in Sweden. Marriages celebrated abroad are regarded as invalid (null and void) in Sweden if either one of the parties – the child or the other intended spouse – at the time of the marriage had a connection to Sweden in the form of Swedish nationality or habitual residence in Sweden. In this way, the legislation strives to prevent any evasion of Swedish law in situations where the parties, at the time of the marriage, had reason to take the Swedish prohibition into account.[80] Persuading, luring or forcing a child to marry, *formally or informally*, can constitute a crime according to the new law. In Sweden, informal marriages usually take place in a religious or tradition-bound setting, through rites that the involved parties or families regard as binding. It follows that such a marriage needs to be dissolved according to the same normative system; a criterion which the law commission used to define the vague concept of "informal marriage".[81]

In his contribution to this book, the commission's chair Justice Göran Lambertz draws attention to the conflicting interests at stake.[82] He describes child

80 If, however, the marriage – involving a child as a party – was concluded at a time when no such connection existed to Sweden, the marriage may be recognised in Sweden if validly concluded according the law of the state of the habitual residence or nationality of the spouses. In this setting, Sweden's private international law rules promote recognition, unless there is special reason to dissociate from the marriage out of concern for Swedish public policy, which usually is to be interpreted restrictively in cross-border cases. It is not uncommon among asylum seekers that one of the spouses, now applying for asylum in Sweden, was under 18 years at the time of the marriage. In these cases, originally lacking Swedish connection, the approach is in favour of recognition of the marriage.

81 On the definition of informal marriages, see Göran Lambertz in this volume, section 2. See also the annexed Summary.

82 See Göran Lambertz in this volume.

marriages as a largely cultural phenomenon which the majority society regards with strong disapproval. For certain minorities, on the contrary, it is a question of an old tradition which is considered to promote the best interests of the family, the group and, in the end at least, the directly concerned child. How should the legislator respond, if at all, in an increasingly diverse society? When a practice considered harmful for children is only exercised by immigrant and minority groups, three particular complicating concerns arise, according to Lambertz.

(a) The group/culture problem, which raises the question whether it is reasonable for the legislator to take the majority standpoint only, and disregard the reasons behind the minority practices.
(b) The family/privacy problem, raising the question of who can ultimately judge best and thus decide what is in the best interests of a child. Under what conditions and to what extent should the legislation interfere with the conducting of what people see as their private or family life?
(c) The risk of stigmatising minorities and their lifestyles and the connected negative consequences, such as increased xenophobia in society which connects child marriages with forced marriages and honour-related violence among minority groups.

A fair estimation, according to Lambertz, is that 400–500 girls under the age of 18 living in Sweden are either married or about to get married, when informal marriages are included. Previous surveys had, furthermore, indicated that approximately 70,000 young persons (16–25 years of age) living in Sweden experience restrictions from their families regarding their choice of a future spouse.[83] Global figures furthermore indicate that child marriages are widely practiced all over the world. Thus, one out of three girls in developing countries is expected to marry before she reaches 18 years of age.

As one of the expert members of the law commission, I have no reason to go into polemics against the conclusions drawn and proposals made, except in one respect. I remain opposed to criminalisation, in the form of specially drafted rules, of acts relating to the conclusion of a child's "informal marriage". My point is that criminalisation can be successfully used only in the case of clearly definable, usually intentional, actions. In my opinion, the concept of informal marriage remains too vague to qualify for criminalisation. Furthermore, it must be asked whether it is objectively more harmful for a person under 18 years of age to be a party to an "informal marriage" than to unmarried cohabitation. This is a relevant issue to raise in a country like Sweden where the law does not prohibit voluntary sex with a person of at least 15 years of age. Partners cohabiting outside of marriage qualify in Swedish law, under certain conditions, for legal protection in the form of

83 *Ungdomsstyrelsens rapport* (Swedish Youth and Education Board), *Gift mot sin vilja* (Involuntarily married), *Ungdomsstyrelsens skrifter* 2009:5, Stockholm 2009.

mutual rights and duties. These conditions do not include any age limit of 18 years. If the group to which the child belongs requires an "informal marriage" for any sexual relations or cohabitation to be acceptable, why should society react against this label when the child is at least 15 years of age and wishes to live together with the other concerned person under the façade of an "informal marriage"? In my opinion, the difference in relation to unmarried cohabitation, legally accepted by society, is not sufficient to justify criminalisation.

Lambertz's rejoinder is that there is a *difference in essence* between the two, brought about by how the concerned group views the nature of the union, in addition to certain formalities on dissolution. These characteristics render an informal marriage just as harmful for the child's full developmental rights as a marriage does. I would, on the contrary, argue that essentially similar phenomena should not be treated differently on the basis of whether it is a practice of the majority population or a practice of minority groups. If protection of children is taken seriously and on an equal basis, a more convincing approach would be to exclude unmarried cohabitation of a child from any legislative protection.[84]

A final point to be raised in this context is how major international instruments, such as the CRC and ECHR, relate to child marriages. It can be noted that the CRC does not forbid contracting states from permitting the child to attain majority at an earlier age than 18 (see Article 1). Probably the most common ground for a child to reach majority earlier is that of marriage. It can be pointed out that many Western jurisdictions permit a person under 18 years of age to marry at least if the dispensation to marry, where required by the law, has been granted by the competent authority. In these countries, child marriages can, consequently, involve members of the majority society too. In Lambertz's opinion, the compatibility of child marriages with the ECHR could be invoked as an infringement of Article 8 (right to private life and right to family life). The case he has in mind is that of a woman married off as a child bringing legal proceedings against the state that did not protect her from the marriage. Girls in particular risk becoming victims of child marriages, due to culturally stereotyped gender roles.[85]

---

84 This would, e.g., require changing the Swedish Act on Cohabitation of 2003 which is Sweden's primary enactment concerning informal cohabitation. On the position of Swedish law, see Swedish national report by Maarit Jänterä-Jareborg, Margareta Brattström and LisaMarie Eriksson, in Katharina Boele-Woelki et al. (eds.), *European Family Law in Action, Volume V: Informal Relationships*, Intersentia 2015.

85 The European Union, for example, links the practice of forced marriages and child marriages with stereotyped gender roles and other prejudices based on the idea of the inferiority or the superiority of either of the sexes. See Conclusions of the Council of the European Union on the promotion and protection of the rights of the child, Brussels 17 December 2014, 17016/14. This outlook is shared by the Council of Europe, for example in its Convention on preventing and combating violence against women and domestic violence (Istanbul Convention, 2011). According to Article 16.2 of the UN Convention on the Elimination of All Forms of Discrimination Against Women (CEDAW) the betrothal and the marriage of a child shall have no legal effect.

In a multicultural society different and opposite concerns can likewise be raised in comparable cases. What about Swedish authorities' categorical refusal (following Sweden's current legislation) to recognise marriages entered into abroad in those cases where a party to the marriage was under 18 years of age, either one of the parties being a Swedish national or habitually resident in Sweden? This practice is illustrated by the precedent of the Swedish Supreme Administrative Court, *HFD 2012 ref. 17*.[86] In this case, the Court confirmed a decision taken by the Swedish Population Registry not to register a marriage which had been validly concluded in Palestine, because the wife-to-be at the time of the marriage was under 18 years of age and habitually resident in Sweden. Her subsequent pregnancy and the occasion of her 18th birthday just ten days after the marriage ceremony were not regarded as sufficient reasons for an exception to recognise the marriage. The woman in this case could equally have an interest in bringing proceedings against Sweden for an infringement of her right to family life. In testing the Swedish legislation's proportionality one must, however, take into account that Swedish law in no way prevents the parties from entering into a legally valid marriage, in a new marriage ceremony, in Sweden or abroad after the woman's 18th birthday. What the parties cannot achieve is legal recognition of the original "marriage date" and the legal effects of a marriage as of that date.

8. CIRCUMCISION OF BOYS: WHAT IS AT STAKE?

The two contributions on circumcision of infants and young boys bring sharply into focus the differences between two contrasting interpretations of this practice, both having the concerned boys' interests as their point of entry. On the one hand, we find the traditional approach which links these interests to the incorporation of the child into the religion, tradition and group to which his parents (or one of them) belong. This incorporation is also seen as a part of the child's upbringing. This approach is, in essence, advocated by Marie-Claire Foblets. The other approach is based on a more individual conception of the child's best interests, emphasising the boy's right to physical integrity when the intervention is irrevocable and not medically motivated and the boy's right to take decisions of his own, including a position on his religion or belonging, once he has attained the necessary maturity to do so. This is Staffan Janson's line of reasoning, in conformity with how the Scandinavian medical profession in general and children's rights advocates in Scandinavia[87] perceive the conflicting interests.

---

86 This restrictive practice goes back to a reform of Sweden's private international law rules on the recognition of foreign marriages, carried out in 2004. See further, Maarit Jänterä-Jareborg, "The Incidental Question of Private International Law, Formalised Same-Sex Relationships and Muslim Marriages", in *Essays in Honour of Michael Bogdan*, Juristförlaget 2013, pp. 157–159.

87 The joint communication by the Nordic Children's Ombudsmen and Nordic Paediatricians, published in September 2013, reiterates this position. In spite of the sharp language of the

Seen together, these two contributions give a comprehensive exposé of the interests involved and the different ways of approaching them.

In the following, I will limit myself to some additional remarks concerning the legal developments in Sweden and Finland. Both states have interesting case law which has passed largely unnoticed internationally. Furthermore, in 2001, as the first state in Europe, Sweden passed legislation on circumcision of boys.

The Swedish Act (2001:499) on circumcision of boys is based on two primary concerns. *First*, it aims to safeguard that boys are circumcised under medically certain and hygienic conditions under anaesthesia, but only after the parents have been properly informed of the risks of the operation and have consented to it. *Second* (if these conditions are met), it confirms the right to circumcision, on religious, cultural or traditional grounds. Previously, only religiously motivated circumcision enjoyed legal protection in Sweden, as a part of the constitutionally protected exercise of freedom of religion.[88] While the 2001 enactment is basically permissive, not abiding by it can result in fines or a prison sentence.

In an important Swedish Supreme Court judgment preceding the 2001 legislation, *NJA 1997 p. 636*, the Court acquitted a defendant who, without using anaesthesia, had circumcised six Muslim boys, between the ages of one-and-a-half and seven; the operations had taken place in the boys' home. In the Court's opinion, the parents had given, on the boys' behalf, the necessary consent.[89] As the operations were motivated by religion by well-intending parents, and had not caused the boys excessive pain or serious medical risks, they qualified in the Court's opinion as *socially adequate actions*.

The 2001 enactment aimed to canalise circumcisions of boys into the general health care system of Sweden, while at the same time (alternatively) permitting a qualified person of the concerned faith community to perform the operation, under regulated terms. This solution was intended, in particular, to accommodate the Jewish tradition of performing the circumcision ritual in the boy's home.[90]

Swedish follow-up studies indicate that the 2001 enactment has indeed resulted in safer operations.[91] There are, however, indications that many Muslim boys

communication, arguing that circumcision of boys contradicts against, *inter alia*, Articles 3 and 12 of the CRC, the signatories call for a "respectful dialogue" between all concerned parties. See also Staffan Janson in this volume, sections 5–6.

88 See Victoria Enkvist, *Religionsfrihetens rättsliga ramar* (The legal framework of the freedom of religion), Iustus Förlag 2013, pp. 175–177 and 180.

89 In an earlier Swedish court decision (Appellate Court of Skåne and Blekinge) of 1996, a Swedish medical doctor who had circumcised a boy was convicted for physical assault, on the ground that he had not sufficiently informed the parents of the level of pain that the operation could cause the child. This case is described by Victoria Enkvist, *Religionsfrihetens rättsliga ramar*, Iustus Förlag 2013, p. 192.

90 See Government Bill, Proposition 2000/01:81.

91 On the impact of the Swedish legislation in practice, see Victoria Enkvist, *Religionsfrihetens rättsliga ramar*, 2013, pp. 198 f. with further references. It is estimated that 3,000 boys are circumcised in Sweden per year. Lotten Wiklund, "Manlig omskärelse en omtvistad sedvänja" (The disputable custom of male circumcision), *Dagens Nyheter*, 28 April 2011.

continue to be circumcised privately, under conditions which do not meet the legal requirements. In these cases the parents appear to lack sufficient information about Swedish law and the right to have the operation performed within the general health care system. Investigations carried out by the Swedish National Board of Health and Welfare have revealed several cases, after the Act's entry into force and also within the public health care system, where the operation had resulted in serious complications for the boy and, in one reported case, the boy's death.[92] This kind of findings explains in part the medical profession's and children rights advocates' opposition to the continued practice of circumcision.

In Finland, there is a call for a similar kind of legislation as that in Sweden.[93] In Finnish case law, several important judgments from the last ten years concern the permissibility of circumcision of boys for religious or cultural reasons. In most of the cases, the public prosecutor brought forth criminal charges against both the person performing the circumcision and the parents, referring to medical complications suffered by the boys. Of particular relevance is the Finnish Supreme Court judgment *KKO 2008:93*, as the currently most authoritative precedent. In this case, the Court acquitted the defendants of charges relating to bodily assault on the boys, with reference to the underlying religious and personal motives of the circumcision and that no harm had been intended. Decisive relevance was to be given to (a) that the operation had been carried out professionally and adequately, (b) that both custodial parents had consented to it, and (c) that the operation could not objectively be regarded as being contrary to the interests of the child.

The same position was taken in a judgment by the Helsinki Court of Appeal in 2011.[94] In a subsequent judgment, again delivered by the Helsinki Court of Appeal in December 2013 and described by Marie-Claire Foblets,[95] the Helsinki Court of Appeal confirms the continued relevance of the previous precedents.[96] The Convention on Human Rights and Biomedicine, adopted by the Council of Europe and more recently ratified by Finland, did not in the Court's opinion render circumcision illegal, contrary to the public prosecutor's interpretation. In the final assessment of all these cases, religion, seen by the parents as promoting the child's well-being and integration into their faith community, takes precedence over the child's physical integrity, or more precisely, the pain and cosmetic injury suffered by the boy and his right to autonomous decision-making.

An even more recent case, decided by the Helsinki Court of Appeal in 2014,[97] raised the relevance of the *father's culture of origin* – in Nigeria – as a justification for the infant boy's circumcision upon the father's initiative but without the mother's consent. The child's Finnish mother did not belong to any

92 Victoria Enkvist, *Religionsfrihetens rättsliga ramar*, Iustus Förlag 2013.
93 See, for example, the 2013 judgment of the Helsinki Court of Appeal reiterating this position.
94 Helsinki Court of Appeal, judgment No. 940, 30 March 2011.
95 See Marie-Claire Foblets in this volume, section 1.3.3.
96 Helsinki Court of Appeal, judgment No. 3184, 5 December 2013.
97 Helsinki Court of Appeal, judgment No. 12, 10 January 2014.

faith community whereas the father was Roman Catholic and the child had been baptised into the Catholic Church. The Court took into account the fact that circumcision has remained a culturally established practice in sub-Saharan Africa among Christians. In Nigeria, for example, 90% of Christian boys are circumcised, according to the Court. Since the operation had been performed medically adequately (by a medical doctor) without any intention of hurting or harming the child, but with the intention of incorporating the child into the father's culture, the criminal charges based on physical assault on the child against the father and the doctor were not accepted. The Court emphasised that the operation could not objectively be regarded to have taken place against the child's interests since it was intended to strengthen his place in his paternal community and culture. The mother's lack of consent – which should have been acquired before the operation, both parents holding parental responsibilities – lacked relevance from the point of view of criminal law.

However, the chairman of the Court dissented, finding the father guilty of physical assault, but wanted to acquit the doctor on the basis of his probable misconception of the situation and requirements. The chairman paid special attention to the three criteria developed by the Supreme Court in its 2008 precedent, adapted to the circumstances of the case at hand. In addition to taking the mother's lack of consent into account, he was not convinced that the third criterion (conformity with the child's best interests) was fulfilled. In his opinion, it could not be ignored that the operation would irreversibly affect the child's identity and have a guiding effect on his future life, having regard to the fact that the child would grow up in a society where circumcision remains exceptional.[98] "To qualify the moral practices of a parent's country of origin as justifications of an action to the detriment of the other custodial parent's wishes and the living milieu of the child risks making justice vague in a manner which should not be accepted in a *Rechtstaat* valuing legal coherence and predictability", he argued (my translation). This judgment has been appealed to the Supreme Court of Finland.[99]

All in all, these judgments and Sweden's 2001 legislation are best described as accommodating in nature. Rites and traditions[100] which the concerned persons experience as essential will not disappear through prohibitions by law, just because they are not society's first preference or part of its own "culture". The boys concerned are arguably not in a fully comparable situation. Contrary to case law, legislation can be used to regulate the borders of what is admissible, in negotiation with those directly concerned. This willingness to accommodate can be compared

98 The so-called "open future argument", in the context of circumcision of boys, is elaborated by Eldar Sarajlic, "Can Culture Justify Infant Circumcision?", *Res Publica 2014*, pp. 337–341. In Finland it has been estimated that approximately 300–350 boys are circumcised pro year; see Helsinki Court of Appeal, judgment No. 3184, 5 December 2013.

99 A decision on whether a review dispensation will be granted by the Finnish Supreme Court or not is expected by the fall of 2015.

100 The notion of "kitchen surgery" is occasionally used, primarily to express disapproval.

with female genital mutilation which, on the contrary, is strictly forbidden by law.[101]

9. COOPERATION INSTEAD OF CONFRONTATION: THE MALTA PROCESS

At the core of the Malta Process, a non-binding soft law mechanism initiated in the early 2000s by The Hague Conference on Private International Law (HCCH) and described by Louise Ellen Teitz,[102] are two international child protection conventions, adopted by the HCCH, namely the 1980 Child Abduction Convention[103] and the 1996 Child Protection Convention.[104] The Malta Process aims to find solutions to cross-border disputes concerning a child, by encouraging dialogue and cooperation between contracting states to the 1980 and 1996 Conventions *and* states with legal systems that are influenced by or based upon Sharia law and which have not joined these conventions.[105] The basic approach has been to agree on certain common core understandings and shared positions, namely:

(a) equal respect for the different legal traditions and systems;
(b) a willingness to explore and consider new solutions; and
(c) the search for approaches arrived at through a process of consensus.

---

101 In Sweden, see Act (1982:316) on prohibition of female genital mutilation. The previous concept of "circumcision of women" has been replaced to mark society's disapproval and the difference in relation to male circumcision. See also Council of Europe Convention on preventing and combating violence against women and domestic violence (Istanbul Convention, 2011) which explicitly includes female genital mutilation and forced marriage among the addressed forms of violence against women and girls. Marie-Claire Foblets, on the other hand, reminds us of evidence that an exclusively punitive approach that singles out particular practices and imposes serious constraints upon specific minority groups and communities adds to the stigmatisation of those who continue to abide by their practices and traditions; in effect, criminalisation comes down to blaming the victim. In her opinion Marie-Claire Foblets in this volume, section 2.3.3.

102 At the heart of the "Malta Process" are the three Malta Conferences, held in St. Julian, Malta in 2004, 2006, and 2009, that laid the groundwork for a gradually increasing dialogue and engagement of Western and Islamic jurisdictions over issues of child abduction and access.

103 Convention on the Civil Aspects of International Child Abduction, concluded in The Hague on 25 October 1980. More than 90 states (2015) all around the globe have acceded to this Convention.

104 Convention on Jurisdiction, Applicable Law, Recognition, Enforcement and Co-operation in Respect of Parental Responsibility and Measures for the Protection of Children, concluded in The Hague on 19 October 1996. More than 40 states are currently (2015) parties to this Convention.

105 According to Louise Ellen Teitz, the ultimate goal of the Malta process is the Islamic states' accession to the Hague Conventions. Among these, Morocco (2010) and Iraq (2014) have already acceded.

The emphasis, in turn, has been on the shared concern for respect for the best interests of the child.[106] Very much in line with what has been agreed in existing bilateral agreements between states with a strong Islamic influence in family law and Western states, the Malta Process in particular seeks to support the child's right to have continued contact with parents living in different countries.[107] Mediation and amicable resolution are emphasised. An important aim is furthermore to combat international child abduction that may occur following arrangements for one parent to relocate or return home with the child. Child abduction is a violation of Islamic law too, in particular because it denies the parent left behind access to the child. The value-neutral approach of the Hague Conventions, as regulations of private international law, has at the outset excellent prospects of bridging different interpretations of the child's best interests. These prospects deserve much more attention.

In practice, nevertheless, there is ample scope for clashes. An important reason, also explained by Teitz, is the gendered nature of Muslim family law, as compared with the Western notion of formal legal equality between the sexes. Muslim family law is gendered both in relation to the role division between men and women (husbands and wives, fathers and mothers), and in their parental rights and duties towards children, in particular in terms of guardianship (only the father) and custody (depending on the child's sex and age). These differences become concrete upon or after parental separation or divorce. Without the guardian father's consent and willingness to cooperate, a mother who has an order for the sole custody of their children cannot have her abducted children returned back to her to the children's state of habitual residence.[108] In the current situation, states can reach agreement on basic values on an abstract, general level but when applied to concrete cases and situations, a shared understanding is much more difficult to achieve.[109] From the point of view of the Western secular and, at least theoretically, gender-neutral society it is furthermore problematic that, under the Islamic concept, a Muslim man's child is to be a Muslim irrespective of the mother's faith (or lack of faith). Furthermore, as has been pointed out by Lena-Maria Möller, "in a legal environment, in which religious affiliation continues to determine the applicable law and Muslim law reigns supreme through constitutional guarantees, the best interests of a Muslim child may very well be interpreted as the child being raised by the Muslim father and not the mother of another faith".[110]

---

106 See Louise Ellen Teitz in this volume.

107 The impact of these bilateral agreements has remained limited, to my knowledge. This is, at least, the Swedish experience. Sweden has a bilateral agreement of this kind with both Tunisia and Egypt.

108 This was the case, for example, in the Swedish appellate court decision, *Göta hovrätt, B 2140–14*, 8 September 2014. In this case the children were unlawfully retained in Lebanon.

109 Art. 3 of the 1980 Hague Convention protects custodial rights (in a broad sense) as such, and these rights are not superseded by any "superior" rights.

110 Lena-Maria Möller, "Improving Women's Rights through Children's Rights? The Reform of Custody Laws in Contemporary Muslim Jurisdictions", in Maarit Jänterä-Jareborg and Hélène

Article 20 of the 1980 Hague Convention is an obvious pitfall in this context. This provision accepts the right of the state of refuge to refuse the return of an abducted child, if the return would not be permitted by the state's fundamental principles on the protection of human rights and fundamental freedoms. Broad agreement has existed among the contracting states that this provision should not be used.[111] The current increased emphasis on human rights and fundamental freedoms in particular in Europe may lead to a reconsideration of the hitherto restrictive approach,[112] which could be unfortunate. In that case, Muslim states could likewise be tempted to emphasise a religious-based best interests test, preventing the child's return to any non-Muslim parent or contact with that parent. The progress made within the Malta Process cannot be taken for granted.

10. THE CHILD AS THE "SACRIFICIAL LAMB" TO SOCIETY, FAMILY, RELIGION AND CULTURE

The book ends with Esin Örücü's provocative comments on the true content of the best interests of the child. In spite of successive improvements, the child remains a "sacrificial lamb", subject to the values of society and parents. Positive constructions, such as the principle of the best interests of the child, have not changed a brutal reality. It will be up to all readers of the various contributions to this book to decide their own position on the issue.

Tigroudja, *Women's Human Rights and the Elimination of Discrimination*, The Hague Academy of International Law, Martinus Nijhoff Publishers 2016 (forthcoming).

111 See, e.g., Rhona Schuz, "The Relevance of Religious Law and Cultural Considerations in International Child Abduction Disputes" (2010) 12 *Journal of Law and Family Studies* 453–497.

112 A recent Swedish Supreme Court judgment, *NJA 2013 p. 1143*, might indicate a development in this direction. In its ruling the Court referred to Art. 20 of the 1980 Hague Convention, in support of its decision not to return the abducted child to the left-behind parent in Turkey, together with Art. 13(1)(b), Art. 8 of the ECHR (right to family life) and Art. 3 of CRC (regard to the child's best interests). Most likely, by doing so the Court wanted to signal that fundamental human rights rules in the CRC and the ECHR are directly applicable as law in Sweden. Under the circumstances, a return order would be a violation of these rules, from the point of view of the requested state, i.e. Sweden. The Court did not question or touch upon the standard of Turkey's family and justice system or the country's ability to abide by fundamental human rights. The six-year-old child had resided in Sweden for almost four years following the abduction from Turkey and had during this period only marginal contact with the left-behind parent. The original Swedish court order (following the child's abduction to Sweden) to return the child to Turkey had not been enforced, because the mother had hidden the child.

BORN OR BECOMING: CHILDREN, RELIGION AND IDENTITY

Jane Mair

1. THE BADGE OF IDENTITY

In contemporary culture, great emphasis is placed on individual identity and image: self-development, self-analysis, finding oneself and defining oneself are all familiar personal goals. In popular media, through psychotherapy and counselling, in the pages of endless self-help manuals, the value of personal journeys and personal growth is repeatedly stressed. Having a clear sense of self and having one's self-identity respected by others are key indicators in modern measurement of wellbeing and personal fulfilment[1] and they are "widely recognised as intrinsically and instrumentally important aspects of a good form of life."[2] But when we talk of identity in these contexts what do we mean?

Our identity is how we feel about ourselves from the inside but it is also how we are badged by others. In response to the question, "what is your identity?" there are many possible answers. How we label ourselves depends at least partially on our assessment of the reason we are being asked. The particular context will often suggest a number of possible labels from which we might choose and we establish our own identity "by constructing a sense of the place and identity of others"[3] around us. How we see ourselves is to a greater or lesser extent informed by how others see us and is the result of a process of construction and negotiation. Establishment of individual identity is linked to the place of the individual within his or her group. Social construction and assertion of one's identity as an individual and negotiating recognition in association with others in community are processes, which can be "encompassed in the phrase 'identity politics'".[4] In Europe, for example, social and political concerns about identity have arisen in the context of migration and the increasing prevalence in European states of unfamiliar minority groups.[5] The social and political drive to define and establish group identity is linked to greater awareness of diversity and the realisation that "relative power … is partly manifested through the ability to name oneself and others".[6]

Identity, along with concepts such as self-expression and respect, are increasingly familiar in legal discourse too. A legal right to identity might be restricted to the relatively limited and easily understood reality of an identity card, birth certificate or administrative record of origin but, borrowing from social, political and psychological discourse, identity can also have much deeper and less certain meanings. What we mean by identity is open to many possible interpretations: our name, our nationality, our family, our job, our sexuality, our ethnic and cultural origins. Some elements of identity are fixed while others are mutable. Some are termed ascriptive, including those identities that "we acquire at birth, that are closed, and that an individual cannot readily enter or exit".[7] Others

---

1 For discussion of the trend towards increased identification of particular personal roles see D.J. Frank and J.W. Meyer, "The Profusion of Individual Roles and Identities in the Postwar Period" (2002) 20(1) *Sociological Theory* 86.

2 Equality and Human Rights Commission, *Identity, expression and self-respect*, Briefing Paper No 9, 2013, available at www.equalityhumanrights.com.

3 M. Minow, "Identities" (1991) 3 *Yale Journal of Law and Humanities* 97 at 98.

4 D.C. Zock, "Decolonizing Law: Identity Politics, Human Rights and the United Nations" (2006) 19 *Harvard Human Rights Journal* 95 at 97.

5 S. Bonjour and B. de Hart, "A proper wife, a proper marriage: Constructions of 'us' and 'them' in Dutch family migration policy" (2013) 20 *European Journal of Women's Studies* 61.

6 M. Minow, "Identities" (1991) 3 *Yale Journal of Law and Humanities* 97 at 99.

7 D.C. Zock, "Decolonizing Law: Identity Politics, Human Rights and the United Nations" (2006) 19 *Harvard Human Rights Journal* 95 at 105.

are elective: open to selection and consisting "of all potential choices of who we want to be".[8] Although identity rights are reduced to legal terms and lawyers may cite them with confident familiarity, their scope is by no means settled and their meaning far from simple.

One element of identity which has attracted considerable interest in recent years is religion. Particularly in Europe, there has been something of a crisis over the re-emergence of religion as a contested issue of contemporary social, legal and academic debate.[9] The European Court of Human Rights and domestic courts within many European states have been grappling with religious identity and religious expression in the context of competing claims between different religious traditions and between religious and secular views. Religion can be an identifying label, used to classify certain individuals or groups, and religion can also be an influential factor in the development of personal and psychological identity. Here, to the uncertainties of what we mean by identity, are added the complexities of meaning, practice and belief attached to religion.

All of these complexities are further stressed when children are involved. Historically, when the concept of childhood was barely recognised, children's individual rights were of little independent concern and their interests were to a large extent subsumed within those of their parents. With the increasing equalisation of family roles and greater focus on the individual child, however, children have emerged as distinct and valued persons in their own right.[10] Whether because children are the citizens of the future or because their wellbeing and happiness is equally valued or because what happens in childhood impacts on the identity of the adult, development, protection and respect for identity are important for children as well as for adults. Identity is highlighted and protected by various legal rules but, while it is easy to say that law protects or should protect a child's identity, it is much more difficult to define what that means in practice and what benefits it might bring. Given the mutable nature of identity, and what we know of child development, what does protection of identity entail when specifically applied to children? Nature or nurture; genetic or social; born or becoming: theories of childhood and attitudes towards child development and personality are complex, inconclusive and prone to change over time. When law tries to capture a fluid concept such as identity in the fixed model of a right, how well can it reflect these possible and contested understandings?

---

8 Ibid.

9 For an overview of areas of concern and a database of cases, see the work of the RELIGARE project: M.-C. Foblets. K. Alidadi, Z. Yanasmayon and J.S. Nielsen (eds.), *Belief, Law and Politics: What Future for a Secular Europe?*, Ashgate 2014.

10 For detailed discussion of theories of childhood and the emergence of children's rights, see D. Archard, *Children, Rights and Childhood*, Routledge 2004.

2. IDENTITY RIGHTS

What legal rights do children have in terms of identity and, in particular, religious identity? General rights designed to protect religion and identity can be found, for example, in the European Convention on Human Rights (ECHR),[11] the UN Declaration of Human Rights[12] and the UN Convention on Civil and Political Rights.[13] These rights are primarily designed for adults although they may be of relevance to children and young persons too. The main focus in this chapter, however, is on the rights encapsulated in the UN Convention on the Rights of the Child (CRC). Specifically drafted to reflect the particular needs of children and young people, the Convention has attracted an unusually high level of international consensus, having been ratified by most countries.[14] By ratification, states are bound by international law to meet the standards and principles required by the Convention and their compliance is monitored[15] by means of reporting obligations. The system of reporting and monitoring has recently been extended through the possibility of submission of individual complaints to the Committee.[16] Formally, through ratification and the reporting process, the CRC has established international benchmarks against which national law is judged. Beyond the strict legal obligations, growing familiarity with the simple language of the Convention's rights has helped them to pass into accepted thought about children, their rights and their place in families and societies.[17]

---

11 Article 9 is of particular relevance.

12 See e.g. Article 18.

13 Including Article 1(1) which guarantees the right to self-determination and Article 18 which provides for freedom of thought, conscience and religion.

14 A notable exception being the US. For discussion of US arguments against ratification see e.g. B.C. Hafen and J.O. Hafen, "Abandoning Children to their Autonomy: The United Nations Convention on the Rights of the Child" (1996) 37 *Harvard International Law Journal* 449 and for discussion from a particular religious perspective, see J. Witte Jr. and D.S. Browning, "Christianity's Mixed Contributions to Children's Rights: Traditional Teachings, Modern Doubts" (2011) 61 *Emory Law Journal* 991.

15 By the UN Committee on the Rights of the Child: for detailed information about the Committee and its workings see www.ohchr.org/EN/HRBodies/CRC/Pages/CRCIndex.aspx. For detailed discussion of the CRC and its impact in Scotland, from the perspective of international law, see J.P. Grant and E.E. Sutherland, "International Standards and Scots Law" in A. Cleland and E.E. Sutherland, *Children's Rights in Scotland,* 3rd edition, W. Green 2009, pp. 40–61.

16 Optional Protocol to the Convention on the Rights of the Child on a Communications Procedure, adopted by Resolution of the General Assembly in 2011 (A/RES/66/138). For discussion see G. de Beco, "The Optional Protocol to the Convention on the Rights of the Child on a Communications Procedure: Good News?" (2013) 13 *Human Rights Law Review* 367.

17 By definition, the CRC is intended to benefit children and therefore it has frequently been translated into child-friendly language and format. In Scotland, for example, versions have been created by Scotland's Commissioner for Children and Young People: www.sccyp.org.uk/rights/picture, and the Scottish Government: www.sccyp.org.uk/ufiles/Scottish-Government-UNCRC.pdf.

2.1. CLEAR AND SIMPLE LANGUAGE

In the Preamble to the Convention, several recitals resonate with broad notions of the development of a child's identity and personality and key themes emerge. There is a clear message to the effect that the identity of a child is closely linked to family life. The "natural environment for the growth and well-being of ... children"[18] is the family and, ideally, "the child, for the full and harmonious development of his or her personality, should grow up in a family environment, in an atmosphere of happiness, love and understanding."[19] The importance of childhood as training for adulthood is highlighted in the consideration that a child "should be fully prepared to live an individual life in society"[20] and be brought up "in the spirit of peace, dignity, tolerance, freedom, equality and solidarity".[21] Although there is no specific reference to religion, the final recital draws attention to the need to take "due account of the importance of the traditions and cultural values of each people for the protection and harmonious development of children".[22] While there is much to recommend the clear and simple words of these aspirations and values, there are also early signposts of the potential conflicts between different religious views on what is best for the child and between "religious" and "secular" conceptions of what is understood by harmonious development.

Several general principles of the Convention are relevant to the religious identity of children. The principle of non-discrimination is set out in Article 2, binding States Parties to "respect and ensure the rights set forth in the present Convention ... without discrimination of any kind" and specifically including religion. Article 2(1) makes it clear that protection against discrimination extends to grounds relating to both the child and the child's parents or guardians. The most well-known of the general principles enshrined in the Convention is that in all actions concerning children, the child's best interests shall be a primary consideration (Article 3). While this is often cited as if it were an objective formula, it is clear that the detailed assessment of what is best for an individual child is open to broad and varied interpretation and this dilemma lies at the heart of many disputes as to the potential benefit or harm of religion – either religion in general or a specific form of religion – to a child. Article 5 strengthens the role of the family in identifying what is best for an individual child by requiring that states shall respect the "responsibilities, rights and duties" of parents and other appropriate family or community members "to provide, in a manner consistent with the evolving capacities of the child, appropriate direction and guidance".

---

18 Recital 5.
19 Recital 6.
20 Recital 7.
21 Recital 7.
22 Recital 11.

Against the background of these general principles, a number of more specific Articles deal with issues of direct relevance to the religious belief, expression and identity of a child. Article 8 offers protection for the preservation of identity in the following terms:

> "1. States Parties undertake to respect the right of the child to preserve his or her identity, including nationality, name and family relations as recognised by law without unlawful interference."

While religion is not mentioned in the Article, commentary on its background and meaning indicates that possible interpretations "can be divided among four categories – familial, tribal, biological and political"[23] and further elaborates that "tribal identity is intended here to include ethnic, cultural and religious identity."[24] It has been explained that this particular article was introduced to tackle a specific problem in Argentina concerning the abduction of children from their families by military authorities and their subsequent disappearance. There was considerable concern at the time about the lack of effective state action to deal with the problem and Article 8 was proposed "to fill this legal void".[25] Although the motivation sprang from a particular concern, the expectation was that, once adopted, the Article should be allowed to develop naturally to reflect changing times and varied domestic settings.

Article 14 deals expressly with religious rights. It requires States Parties to "respect the right of the child to freedom of thought, conscience and religion".[26] It broadly reflects similar adult protection and a distinction, comparable to that made in the ECHR, is drawn between the absolute right to freedom of thought, conscience and religion and the more restricted "freedom to manifest one's religion or beliefs" which may be limited by law where "necessary to protect public safety, order, health or morals or the fundamental rights and freedoms of others".[27] The interaction between parents and children is expressly recognised in Article 14(2), which requires states to:

> "respect the rights and duties of the parents and, where applicable, legal guardians, to provide direction to the child in the exercise of his or her right in a manner consistent with the evolving capacities of the child."[28]

Article 15 provides for a general right to freedom of association but, read in conjunction with Article 14, could protect the child's freedom to join together

23 G.A. Stewart, "Interpreting the Child's Right to Identity in the UN Convention on the Rights of the Child" (1992) 26(3) *Family Law Quarterly* 221 at 225.

24 Ibid., p. 226.

25 Ibid., p. 222.

26 Article 14(1).

27 Article 14(3).

28 For detailed discussion of Article 14 see S. Langlaude, "Children and Religion under Article 14 UNCRC: A Critical Analysis" (2008) 16 *International Journal of Children's Rights* 475.

with others as part of his or her religious faith or practice or to join a particular religious organisation.

Although the Convention is based on the belief that children are best cared for within their own families, it is recognised that for various reasons this will not always be possible. Where a child needs to be cared for in a different environment, there is provision for recognition and protection of the particular identity of the child. When considering options for temporary or permanent care of a child, Article 20(3) requires that States Parties should pay due regard to "the desirability of continuity in a child's upbringing and to the child's ethnic, religious and cultural and linguistic background."

Articles 28–30 all deal with aspects of education which can overlap in various ways with religion[29] and which may contribute to or reflect a child's religious identity. Education as a fundamental developmental right is set out in Article 28 and further elaboration of the aims of education is set out as follows in Article 29:

> "1. States Parties agree that the education of the child shall be directed to
> (a) the development of the child's personality, talents and mental and physical abilities to their fullest potential;
> (b) the development of respect for human rights and fundamental freedoms, and for the principles enshrined in the Charter of the United Nations;
> (c) the development of respect for the child's parents, his or her own cultural identity, language and values, for the national values of the country in which the child is living, the country from which he or she may originate, and for civilisations different from his or her own;
> (d) the preparation of the child for responsible life in a free society, in the spirit of understanding, peace, tolerance, equality of sexes and friendship among all peoples, ethnic, national and religious groups and persons of indigenous origin; ..."

The religious rights of children in minority communities have specific protection in terms of Article 30. In contrast to the individual focus of many of the other Articles, Article 30 highlights in particular the right of the child "in community with other members of his or her group ... to profess and practise his or her own religion."

2.2. BUT COMPLEX MEANINGS

The idea that children have rights of their own has become widely accepted[30] but "developing a theoretical basis for this increasing recognition of children's rights

29 The right to education and the obligation on states to respect the wishes of parents to have their children taught "in conformity with their own religious and philosophical convictions" are also provided for by Article 2 of ECHR Protocol 1.

30 See e.g. M.D.A. Freeman, *The Rights and Wrongs of Children*, Frances Pinter 1983.

remains a work in progress".[31] Some children's rights are quite clearly child-specific and their substance reflects current understanding of childhood, such as Article 29 dealing with education and Article 31 which includes the right "to engage in play". Others, such as Article 14(1) protecting freedom of thought, conscience and religion, are much more in the "mini-me" mould. While familiarity with the adult version may help to inform the meaning of what is extended to children, rights which are controversial and relatively unsettled when exercised by adults are likely to be even more troubling when applied to children.

Individual and universal rights, by their nature, create potential for conflict. Some rights do make specific provision for interaction with others through the inclusion of principles and mechanisms designed to guide their co-existence but in practice this does not always work smoothly. Article 14, for example, sets up the relationship between the child's autonomy to have his or her own religious thoughts[32] and the provision of parental guidance,[33] but while the words and concepts appear relatively simple and familiar, their practical application can be much more complex. How much freedom should a child have in respect of his or her religious beliefs and choices and how does this fit with parental guidance? Where family relations are harmonious and the beliefs of children and parents match, it seems entirely natural that the balance between autonomy and guidance will simply shift over time as the children grow but where there is discord within families there is little clarity or practical assistance. Sylvie Langlaude, in her detailed analysis of Article 14, has highlighted inconsistency in the approach of the UN Committee on the Rights of the Child to the application of the provision and in particular has criticised over-emphasis of the child's autonomy without sufficient appreciation of the importance of family.[34]

It requires little insight to recognise that the process of making rights real is difficult for many reasons: the loftiness of their aspiration, the accommodation of conflicting rights, limited availability of resources. The words of conventions and declarations are easy to say but their promises difficult to deliver. The substance of some rights, while logistically challenging to provide on a universal basis, is at least relatively simple to understand. In respect of other rights, however, it is much less clear what is intended or required and consensus as to their scope or indeed desirability is lacking. Concepts at the heart of certain rights may be undefined, open to a range of interpretations or in some way controversial, and this has been seen in particular in recent years within the context of rights relating to religion: matters of identity, belief and expression.[35] If religious and identity rights give rise

31 R. Dixon and M.C. Nussbaum, "Children's Rights and a Capabilities' Approach: the Question of Special Priority" (2011–12) 97 *Cornell Law Review* 549 at 551.

32 Article 14(1).

33 Article 14(2).

34 S. Langlaude, "Children and Religion under Article 14 UNCRC: A Critical Analysis" (2008) 16 *International Journal of Children's Rights* 475.

35 See e.g. N. Cox, "The Clash of Unprovable Universalisms – International Human Rights and Islamic Law" (2013) 2 *Oxford Journal of Law and Religion* 1.

to uncertainties, problems and concerns, when they are to be exercised by adults,[36] it is inevitable that the discomfort is even greater when the rights in question are applied to children.[37] As Sylvie Langlaude formulates it:

> "Children and religion is a complex issue. It is complex because it does not simply involve children and the state – parents and religious communities are also concerned. Religion is also an emotive subject which matters greatly to children, parents, religious communities and the state. It is complex because it involves theories of rights and childhood. Finally it is about religion, which forms the subject-matter of one of the most complex of human rights."[38]

Religious rights for children are beset by all of these complexities and when the flexible and undefined concept of identity is also added into the mix the complexity is increased. To some extent, however, these complexities are concealed by the relatively simple and familiar words of conventional human rights and children's rights rhetoric. Where problems are identified, the focus is often on what could be done to make the rights work more effectively and less often on the inherent difficulties and uncertainties of what is promised.[39] While it sounds intrinsically reassuring and good that we protect the rights of a child to his or her own identity, what does it mean and how does that protection operate in practice? When law seeks to protect the identity of a child, is it the identity with which the child was born or the identity into which the child will grow? To what extent is identity the product of self-determination or to what extent is it ascribed? And when that identity is grounded in or formed by religion, do we remain equally comfortable about its protection or would we prefer the identity of a child to be nurtured within a system of liberal secular influence?

3. THE SITUATED CHILD: THE BEST AND THE LEAST

Perhaps even less than adults, children do not live in isolation and, in considering what religious identity rights might mean in respect of children, and how they operate in practice, the child needs to be viewed within the communities in which he or she lives and grows: the state, the religious organisation and the family. Although frameworks of legal rights, religious doctrine and family law and life

---

36 An indication of the range of issues concerning religion and law which have caused concern within the EU in recent years is provided by the work of the RELIGARE project: www.religareproject.eu.

37 As Archard has commented, in respect of a child's right to a particular cultural identity, questions "can only properly be answered when the balance between these different claims has been resolved for adults within society": D. Archard, *Children, Rights and Childhood*, Routledge 2004, p. 200.

38 S. Langlaude, "Children and Religion under Article 14 UNCRC: A Critical Analysis" (2008) 16 *International Journal of Children's Rights* 475.

39 See e.g. D.C. Zook, "Decolonizing Law: Identity Politics, Human Rights and the United Nations" (2006) 19 *Harvard Human Rights Journal* 95.

each stress the special nature and value of children, it is often easy in practice for children to be overlooked.[40] They may appear to be at the centre of our child-focused perspective but their views are not always heard and, even when they are heard, not necessarily understood. In many ways, children are simultaneously the most precious and the most insignificant: the best and the least. To some extent this is reflected in their identities within the contexts of state, religion and family.

International conventions on human rights are an abstraction of general principles but they become real through national and local implementation. Scotland is one example of a country which seeks to give effect to the CRC through its family law framework and through its child policy. When child law was substantially reviewed and reformed in the Children (Scotland) Act 1995, the UN Convention was a significant influence.[41] More recently, the Children and Young People (Scotland) Act 2014 has taken further steps to embed the principles of the Convention in Scots child law and practice.[42] Despite being part of the United Kingdom, Scotland has its own legal system, distinct from England and Wales. Since 1999 the Scottish Government has exercised substantial devolved authority, including in respect of family law, and in September 2014 there was a national referendum to decide on the question of independence for Scotland. While the outcome of the referendum was a majority vote in favour of remaining within the UK, the pre-referendum period created a significant opportunity for the Scottish government to signal its vision of Scotland as a society[43] and this included a strong message of commitment to human rights and equality. It is therefore a good time to reflect on the position of children in Scotland: their place within the state, religion and family and the ways in which their place might impact on their religious identity.

3.1. CHILDREN AS CITIZENS: THE IDENTITY OF THE CHILD WITHIN THE STATE

In a classical liberal construction, children are situated and cared for within their families and their relationship with the state is mediated through their parents. As summarised by Archard:

> "The 'family' and the 'state' have most commonly been represented as mutually excluding spheres of action; so much so that an endorsement of the family's social role

[40] For discussion of children in theology see B. Miller-McLemore, "Whither the Children? Childhood in Religious Education" (2006) 86(4) *The Journal of Religion* 635.

[41] For an overview, see J.P. Grant and E.E. Sutherland, "International Standards and Scots Law", in A. Cleland and E.E. Sutherland, *Children's Rights in Scotland,* 3rd edition, W. Green 2009, pp. 40–61.

[42] Sections 1 and 2 place specific duties on ministers and local authorities in respect of the rights of the Convention.

[43] Scottish Government, *Scotland's Future: Your Guide to an Independent Future*, 2013, Edinburgh, available at www.scotland.gov.uk/Publications/2013/11/9348.

in bringing up children may be taken as already setting certain limits to the proper role of the state."[44]

So long as children remain within the care of their families, the state has little direct role to play. To a large extent, this is the model endorsed by the CRC which accords individual rights to children but expects that these rights will normally be fulfilled within the context of the family or moderated through the guidance and direction of parents. In domestic law, the state will accept certain welfare responsibilities towards children in respect of care and protection but usually only as a last resort; stepping in to protect children when they cannot be adequately cared for within their own families. According to this model, the state has an interest in children, not as citizens themselves, but "as *current* human beings to be cared for".[45]

3.1.1. Children in Need

Specific provision is made for this eventuality in the CRC, in those Articles concerning the care of children who have been separated from their families. Here the state is acting *in loco parentis* in caring for a child within public institutional accommodation or arranging for care in a substitute family environment by means of fostering or adoption. Article 20 of the Convention provides that account should be taken of the child's religious background, in arranging for his or her temporary or long-term care. In Scotland, local authorities have a range of responsibilities towards children broadly defined as being "children in need".[46] Decisions about these children should be guided, as in the private context of families, by their welfare[47] and it is specifically stated that, in providing services to promote a child's welfare, the local authority should "have regard so far as practicable to each child's religious persuasion".[48] Similar provision is made in respect of adoption and, in making any decision about the adoption of a child, the court or adoption agency must have regard, as far as reasonably practicable, to the religious persuasion of the child.[49] In both cases, the requirement refers to the religious persuasion of the child himself or herself although, in respect of adoption, section 14 also requires the adoption agency to have regard to the views of the parents, guardians or other relatives.[50]

Although these provisions indicate that the law "in books" in Scotland, respects the religious rights of children, what do we know of the law "in practice"? The religious rights of children and their religious persuasion or identity have attracted

44 D. Archard, *Children, Rights and Childhood*, Routledge 2004, p. 153.
45 Ibid., p. 155.
46 Children (Scotland) Act 1995, s22.
47 Ibid., s16(1).
48 Ibid., s22(2).
49 Adoption and Children (Scotland) Act 2007, s14(4)(b).
50 Ibid, s14(5).

relatively little interest in Scotland and it has been commented on a number of occasions that "we know little about the issues of faith and children who become looked after".[51] It has been noted that local authorities do "not consistently record information about the ethnic and cultural origins of families with whom they work"[52] and until 2011 statistics relating to children in the care of local authorities did not record the child's religious background. In the most recent statistics, which relate to 2012–2013,[53] religious background was included for children who are on the child protection register in Scotland, but for 80% of them the religion was recorded as "not known". Of those where details of religion were included, the entry was "no religion" in 20%. Even where religious identity is taken into account when considering care plans for children, there must be a question over whose religious identity it will be. A significant and increasing proportion of children who are "looked after" by local authorities in Scotland are very young when they enter into care. Of the total number of looked after children in Scotland, those who entered into local authority care under the age of five accounted for 25% in 2003 with this rising to 39% in 2013. At that age it is likely that any protection of the child's religious identity will reflect the religious identity of the birth parents rather than of the child himself.[54]

3.1.2. *Child Citizens*

Another way in which the state establishes a relationship with children is by seeing them "as *future* citizens who must now be trained for their eventual roles in society"[55] and even, in some cases, "not as citizens of the future but citizens now."[56] Signs of such a shift in attitude to children can be seen in recent developments in Scotland, where a new statutory framework seeks to develop a more direct relationship between children and the state. The recently enacted Children and Young People (Scotland) Act 2014 builds on a policy developed to guide local authority dealings with children, known by the acronym of GIRFEC: Getting It Right For Every Child.[57] This new statutory framework is intended primarily

---

51 *Extraordinary Lives: Creating a positive future for looked after children and young people in* Scotland, 2006, Social Work Inspection Agency, para. 27, available at www.scotland.gov.uk/Resource/Doc/140731/0034643.pdf.

52 J. McRae, *Children looked after by local authorities: the legal framework*, Social Work Inspection Agency, available at www.scotland.gov.uk/Resource/Doc/128956/0030715.pdf.

53 *Children's Social Work Statistics Scotland 2012–13*, available at www.scotland.gov.uk/Publications/2014/03/8922.

54 For a very insightful discussion of issues of identity in the context of transracial adoptions see B.B. Woodhouse, "Are You My Mother? Conceptualizing Children's Identity Rights in Transracial Adoptions" (1995) 2 *Duke Journal of Gender Law and Policy* 107.

55 D. Archard, *Children, Rights and Childhood*, Routledge 2004, p. 155.

56 S. Jessop, "Children's Participation: An Arendtian Criticism" (2011) 43(9) *Educational Philosophy and Theory* 979 at 980.

57 For discussion of the policy and consultation as to detailed implementation of it under the new legislation, see Scottish Government, *Getting it right for Children and Families*, 2014, available at www.scotland.gov.uk/Resource/0044/00448228.pdf.

to affect children who are identified as being in need of some form of care and it involves partnership between local authorities and health boards. In keeping with the underlying philosophy of equal commitment to all children, however, some of the new provisions will apply equally to children who are living and thriving within their own family environment. One key innovation of the Act is that every child will be allocated a "named person"[58] whose responsibilities will include "advising, informing or supporting the child or young person".[59] The extent to which this named person will be called upon will obviously depend on the extent to which the child's needs are already being met within his or her family or close community and for many children it will make no significant difference to their daily lives. It is nonetheless a novel appointment, which creates a direct link between individual children and the state.

It is notable that religion is not mentioned specifically in the context of this new legislation, although in the guidance and policy, which will be developed in order to implement the statutory framework, there are a number of ways in which it might be relevant. In appointing the named person for a particular child, will the child's religion be taken into account? How will the advice and support of the named person interact with that of parents and other relatives or mentors? Religion is not mentioned in the Act and nor is the concept of identity but central to the framework for public intervention in the lives of children in need of care is the concept of "wellbeing". Getting it right for every child depends on early and targeted intervention,[60] which will be triggered by identification of the fact that a child has a "wellbeing" need.[61] Wellbeing will be assessed by means of a set of criteria summed up in another acronym, SHANARRI: Safe, Healthy, Achieving, Nurtured, Active, Respected, Responsible and Included.[62] Religion and religious background could most obviously be of relevance in terms of assessing the extent to which a child is "respected" and "included", although there is scope for it to feature in a number of the other assessment criteria. The potential for further complexity and difference in construction of wellbeing in each of these labels is clear.

How children are viewed within the state – as dependants of adult citizens, as "dependent yet evolving citizens"[63] of the future or as child citizens[64] now – is likely to affect how their identities are protected or produced. To afford them the religious identity of their parents is perhaps a state benefit to their parents

58 Children and Young People (Scotland) Act 2014, Part 4.

59 Ibid., s19(5)(1)(a).

60 Ibid., s34.

61 Ibid., Pt 5.

62 Ibid., s96.

63 B.B. Woodhouse, "'Out of Children's Needs, Children's Rights': The Child's Voice in Defining the Family" (1993–1994) 8 *Brigham Young University Journal of Public Law* 321 at 322.

64 For discussion of child citizenship see J. Wall, "Children and Political Representation: The Challenge of the Gift" (2010) 1(5) *Journal of Childhood and Religion* 1.

in recognition of the role they play in child raising. Where the emphasis shifts towards recognition of children as current citizens, their own identity comes to the fore but, in this emerging framework, similar disagreements about what is or is not best for the child's welfare and "wellbeing" are likely to arise.[65] There is a danger that in seeking to protect the individual child we continue to label them and perhaps also to imagine that adults – and governments – have more influence and control over identities and outcomes than is justified by experience.

3.2. CHILDREN AS BELIEVERS: THE PLACE OF CHILDREN WITHIN RELIGION

Religious rights protect deeply personal beliefs and affiliation and seek to respect individual identity. With children, however, there can be uncertainty over the extent to which they have or are capable of forming their own personal beliefs and acquiring their own separate identity. Children are central to religion and religious belief; they are very obviously essential to the survival of religious communities and organisations and they are valued in religious doctrine for the special significance of their birth. But in different religious traditions the position of children can be complex. Original sin and childhood innocence; birth, rebirth and conversion: ideas of children born into a particular religion or growing towards mature belief highlight a range of constructions of children within religious doctrines and communities. Apparent inconsistencies and dualisms are evident in many religions and there are contradictions between the inescapability of predetermined nature and the potential for personal growth and change, which in turn further complicate the meaning of identity.

Within the context of religion and religious organisations, children are primarily thought of as the future. Their status within the faith community is secured by the fact that they are the offspring of current believers or adherents. The particular place of children within different religious traditions will depend on that religion's own internal rules and rituals although it is common for children to be initially introduced and accepted on the basis that they are the children of existing adult members or adherents and then at some later stage to make a further independent commitment. The Church of Scotland, for example, explains the usual progression to membership as being that "infant children of Church members are received into the Church through Baptism. In time it is hoped that the child will come to make his or her own public profession of faith".[66]

---

65 For discussion of some challenges and contradictions see D Stasiulis, "The Active Child Citizen: Lessons from Canadian Policy and the Children's Movement" (2002) 6(4) *Citizenship Studies* 507.

66 The Church of Scotland, *Joining the church*, 2015, available at www.churchofscotland.org.uk/about_us/our_faith/joining_the_church.

3.2.1. Religious Education

While religions commonly ritualise the acceptance of infants of existing members into the religious community, this will be only an initial step leading to the longer-term process of teaching and religious guidance. Despite individual differences in doctrine and ritual, what all religions have in common is the desire to teach the next generation in conformity with their beliefs. Children represent the future and promise survival in a very real sense and parents commonly have religious obligations to bring them up in accordance with the rules of the faith community. These religious obligations have tended to be regarded as private matters for individual religious adherents and their spiritual authorities but, in recent years, they have increasingly emerged across Europe as matters of public concern and seemingly intractable legal dispute within the context of public education. At the heart of these disputes is the conflict between the obligation of the state to provide education for all, the rights of children to access education and the rights of individuals (particularly parents) to bring their children up according to their religious (or other) beliefs and values.[67]

In Scotland, there are longstanding links between religion and education and there is no state commitment to completely secular education.[68] Local authorities have an obligation to secure adequate provision of school education.[69] School pupils are to be educated in accordance with their parents' wishes insofar as compatible with the provision of suitable instruction and training and avoiding unreasonable public expenditure.[70] While the vast majority of schools in Scotland are non-denominational, local authorities may provide denominational schools in response to demand.[71] Currently there are 370 state-funded denominational schools in Scotland: 366 Catholic, one Jewish and three Episcopalian.[72] Religion and religious instruction form part of the curriculum in Scottish schools and accommodation of the wishes and concerns of individual parents is achieved by means of an opt-out "from any instruction in religious subjects and from any religious observance."[73] In keeping with the idea that the state provision of religious education is a benefit for religious parents rather than an independent

---

67 See e.g. the detailed discussion in J. Temperman, "State Neutrality in Public School Education: An Analysis of the Interplay Between the Neutrality Principle, the Right to Adequate Education, Children's Rights to Freedom of Religion or Belief, Parental Liberties and the Position of Teachers" (2010) 32 *Human Rights Quarterly* 865.

68 For discussion see F. McCarthy, "Prayers in the Playground: Religion and Education in the United Kingdom and Beyond", in J. Mair and E. Örücü (eds), *The Place of Religion in Family Law: A Comparative Search*, Intersentia 2011, pp. 235–263.

69 Education (Scotland) Act 1980, s1.

70 Ibid., s28.

71 Ibid., s17.

72 Scottish Government, *Frequently Asked Questions*, 2013, available at www.gov.scot/Topics/Education/Schools/FAQs.

73 Education (Scotland) Act 1980, s9.

right for children,[74] it is the parents who have the right to remove their child from religious education in school. The view of the Scottish Government is that "there is an intrinsic value in learning about religion as well as learning from religion" and that religious and moral education should not be simply about the delivery of information but should also allow for "the idea of 'personal search'" and the "development of a child or young person's own beliefs and values".[75] Far from adopting a stance in favour of neutral education, if such a thing is possible, the Scottish Government's view is that teaching children about religion and belief is the best way to encourage tolerance and strengthen a nation which values diversity.[76]

3.2.2. Child Believers

Children in religion are most often thought of as the children of believers but they might also be constructed as "child believers". Until recently, limited attention has been given to the child as an autonomous religious being.[77] This is evident in the Unicef Handbook for the Convention on the Rights of the Child where it is noted that few states have reflected on the individual religious rights of children in domestic legislation but instead "it is parents who determine the child's religion."[78] Where there has been focus on the child and on children's own religious convictions, it is often to highlight concerns about the lack of capacity of children to "assert, or to choose not to assert, a personal religious identity".[79] Recently, however, there has been increasing interest in research into children, youth and religion,[80] which aims to achieve a better understanding of the active involvement of children. This research stresses further the complexity of how children and young people construct their religious identities. In many secular countries, the sight of young people wearing religious dress raises concerns about indoctrination

---

74 For further discussion, see e.g. S. Grover, "Children's right to be educated for tolerance: minority rights and inclusion" (2007) 19(1) *Education and the Law* 59.

75 Scottish Government, *Curriculum for excellence: religious and moral education principles and practice*, 2012, available at www.curriculumforexcellencescotland.gov.uk. In Scotland there is provision for both religious education and religious observance, with the latter involving practising religion or participating in some other form of "reflection".

76 Scottish Government, *Scotland's Future*, 2013, available at www.scotland.gov.uk/Publications/2013/11/9348.

77 See e.g. B. Miller-McLemore, "Whither the Children? Childhood in Religious Education" (2006) 86(4) *The Journal of Religion* 635.

78 UNICEF, *Implementation Handbook for the Convention on the Rights of the Child,* Pt 1, 3rd edition, 2007, p. 185.

79 J. Shulman, "Who Owns the Soul of the Child?: An Essay on Religious Parenting Rights and the Enfranchisement of the Child" (2012) 6 *Charleston Law Review* 101 at 120. See too S. Langlaude, "Indoctrination, Secularism, Religious Liberty and the ECHR" (2006) 55 *International and Comparative Law Quarterly* 929.

80 P.J. Hemming and N. Madge, "Researching children, youth and religion: Identity, complexity and agency" (2012) 19(1) *Childhood* 38.

or undue family pressure, because it is perceived as "counter-cultural".[81] Empirical research into how teenagers in Scotland engage with Christianity highlights, however, the extent to which "being a very faithful and involved young Christian is both a marginalized and marginalizing identity".[82] Trends towards secularism shape expectations of how young people behave, forcing them to carve out their own space between religious practices of their elders and dominant youth culture.[83] Religious behaviour and practices are not necessarily passed directly from one generation to another and there are gaps in understanding between adults and teenagers in religiosity as in many other aspects of life.

Despite the significance of birth and childhood to religious doctrine, children do not occupy a clear or consistent place within religious communities. They are often constructed in terms of future survival and where childhood identity is considered it is more for what it can reveal about adults and their development than specifically to provide a child's vision of religion. Wider constructions of religious children tend to see them as cause for concern; focusing on the counter-cultural nature of their appearance or conduct with little attempt to understand how they perceive their own identities.

3.3. CHILDREN AS CHILDREN: THE PLACE OF CHILDREN WITHIN THE FAMILY

3.3.1. *Reproduction*

Children are most comfortable when situated within families and their identity in that context is perhaps the most fully developed. But even within that familiar environment there are differing perceptions and the potential for contradictory construction of the child's identity. There must be few parents who do not hope that their children will inherit some, at least, of their own characteristics. There is an inherent desire and drive to see and recreate ourselves in our own children but modern conceptions of childhood and their reflection in family law increasingly shift the focus from the wishes or expectations of the parents to the needs of the children. Children are not the property of their parents and should not be considered as "instruments of our egotistical desires to ensure the world enjoys carbon copies of ourselves".[84]

---

81 See e.g. discussion in C. Shelley, "Beating Children Is Wrong, Isn't It? Resolving Conflicts in the Encounter Between Religious Worldviews and Child Protection" (2012) *15 Ecclesiastical Law Journal* 130.

82 G. Vincett, E. Olson, P. Hopkins and R. Pain, "Young People and Performance Christianity in Scotland" (2012) 27(2) *Journal of Contemporary Religion* 275 at 277.

83 P. Hopkins, E. Olson, R. Pain and G. Vincett, "Mapping intergeneralities: the formation of youthful religiosities" (2011) 36(2) *Transactions of the Institute of British Geographers* 314 at 317.

84 R. Ahdar, "The Child's Right to a Godly Future" (2002) 10 *International Journal of Children's Rights* 89 at 96.

Scots family law acknowledges the importance of children to parents by according them the privileged legal status of parenthood and giving them certain legal rights in respect of their children.[85] These rights, however, are secondary to the responsibilities owed by parents to their children and rights can only be exercised where necessary in order to fulfil responsibilities.[86] The children come first and their needs must be assessed according to the test of welfare. How well does this work, however, where parents want to create their children not only in their own image but also in that of their religious maker? In the context of Christianity, parents "care for their infants not just because these children are continuations of their own bodily substance" but because an "infant is also a child of God, made in the image of God".[87] Legal issues most often arise where religious parents want to care in a manner which conflicts with a secular and apparently objective assessment of what is in the child's best interests. From the perspective of the outsider, the identity of the child is of a child at risk whereas, from the perspective of the parent, the risk to the child is posed by the denial of an authentic religious identity. In such contests, it may be that "no resolution exists"[88] without significant compromise but greater attempts are nonetheless needed to try to understand the motivation of religious parents.[89] There will always be differences of opinion between religious and non-religious parents about how best to raise a child – as indeed there will be differences of opinion where no religious values are involved. There is a danger that if religious influence in childrearing becomes regularly associated with negative outcomes it will overshadow the fact that religion "can and usually does create and foster a culture of good parenting".[90]

3.3.2. Letting Go

While parents have a natural urge to reproduce and recreate in the form of their children, "good" parenting also requires the process of "letting go". Children have specifically designed rights and protections reflecting their care needs and dependent nature but they are also adult-becomers and, in order to develop, they require graduated and evolving versions of adult rights. Scots family law regulates the capacity of children and young people principally through the Age

85 Children (Scotland) Act 1995, s2.

86 Ibid., s1.

87 J. Witte Jr. and D.S. Browning, "Christianity's Mixed Contributions to Children's Rights: Traditional Teachings, Modern Doubts" (2011) 61 *Emory Law Journal* 991 at 1008.

88 A.D. Lederman, "Understanding Faith: When Religious Parents Decline Conventional Medical Treatment for Their Children" (1994) 45 *Case Western Law Review* 891 at 926.

89 C Shelley, "Beating Children Is Wrong, Isn't It? Resolving Conflicts in the Encounter Between Religious Worldviews and Child Protection" (2012) 15 *Ecclesiastical Law Journal* 130, particularly 139–141.

90 L. Wardle, "The Jurisprudence of Parenting and the Influence of Religion on Effective Parenting", available at http://ssrn.com/abstract=2061102.

of Legal Capacity (Scotland) Act 1991. It operates a distinction based on age: below the age of 16, children have no legal capacity and beyond that age they have full legal capacity.[91] This sharp distinction is, however, softened by various other provisions within the Act which acknowledge the process of evolution from childhood to maturity. Children, for example, are capable of entering into transactions which are age appropriate and, over the age of 12, they are also capable of taking certain actions including making a will and instructing a solicitor.[92] Making decisions about their own religion and in particular deciding to join or to leave a particular religious organisation are not specifically dealt with in the Act but an analogy might be made with the provisions relating to consent to medical treatment. A person under the age of 16 is treated as being capable of giving consent to medical treatment where he or she is assessed by the relevant medical practitioner as capable of understanding the nature and consequences of the proposed treatment.[93] It might be argued that a similar understanding test could be applied in the context of a child wishing to join a religious organisation.

The place of children within the context of family relationships has changed considerably in recent decades but, despite outwardly settled legal rules which establish clear familial relationships, attitudes towards parenting and the place of children remain contested. Perceptions of how identities are shaped and when they should be respected change depending on the construction of the child as dependent or autonomous and the parent as protector, facilitator or threat.

4. IDENTIFYING RELATIONSHIPS: A CASE STUDY

Outwardly, under international law, Scotland is committed to the UN Convention on the Rights of the Child. Internally, Scots family law has been substantially reviewed and reformed on several occasions in recent years, in line with the Convention, to create a statutory framework within which there appears to be space for the protection and accommodation of the child's identity. Conventions and enactments can establish principles but they show us little of what happens in practice. Martha Minow has suggested that greater insight might be gained from talking "more explicitly about how we all negotiate identities and make choices amid the constraints of relationships with others".[94] In the facts of a recent Scottish sheriff court decision in *S v S*,[95] and the narrative constructed by the parties and the judge, there is an excellent case study by which to consider that

91 Age of Legal Capacity (Scotland) Act 1991, s1(1).
92 Ibid, s2.
93 Ibid, s2(4).
94 M. Minow, "Identities" (1991) 3 *Yale Journal of Law and Humanities* 97 at 130.
95 2012 Fam LR 148.

process of negotiation and choice.[96] In this case, described below, the focus is much less on clear legal rules than on messy lived reality; less on individual rights and obligations than on relationships.

4.1. A HOLIDAY ROMANCE

For a Scottish woman and an Egyptian man, it all began with a holiday romance in Egypt in 1994. As often happens, although they kept in touch for a while when the holiday ended and the woman returned home, after a few months the letters stopped. Several years later the woman came across an old holiday souvenir, re-established contact with the man and after some time they married in Egypt. They moved to Scotland and had children but through time the relationship broke down and a divorce was sought. The children were to live with their mother and see their father regularly. By the time the divorce action came to court, there was one remaining issue to be resolved. The father, a Muslim, sought a specific issue order[97] to the effect that the three children, a daughter (aged six) and twin boys (aged four) should be brought up as Muslims. In deciding that no such order should be granted, the sheriff engaged in a relatively straightforward application of the well-established principle in family law to the effect that the welfare of the child is the paramount consideration.[98] Legally, it was not a difficult case: it concerned "a simple yet at the same time complex issue".[99] It was simple in that the words of statute are clear and the obligation on the sheriff is well understood. But it was complex both because the day-to-day living of family relationships is complex and because "identity ... is a contested and contextual concept".[100]

4.2. MULTIPLE IDENTITIES

The many different roles and identities that individuals play and hold in everyday life and relationships were highlighted in the narrative of this case, in the changing relationship between the couple and also in their relations with the woman's parents. The man and women, as children, grew up in their own religious families and, as young adults, they each to some extent rejected the restrictions of their parents' religious rules and asserted their independence. At the time

96 Three recent English decisions, raising similar issues, are discussed in M. Welstead, "The Battle for Children's Souls: The Role of Religion in Parental Disputes", in B. Atkin (ed.), *The International Survey of Family Law 2013*, Family Law 2013, pp. 91–117.

97 Children (Scotland) Act 1995, s11(2)(e).

98 In Scots law this familiar principle is encapsulated in the Children (Scotland) Act 1995, s11(7).

99 Official transcript at para. 122.

100 B.B. Woodhouse, "Are You My Mother? Conceptualizing Children's Identity Rights in Transracial Adoptions" (1995) 2 *Duke Journal of Gender Law and Policy* 107 at 110.

their relationship began, the picture painted of the man was of someone brought up as a Muslim but who did not "pray five times a day or adhere strictly to rules regarding such things as consuming alcohol. He did, however, always observe Ramadan."[101] The woman had been brought up in a strictly religious family, with parents who were members of the Brethren community[102] but as an adult she had left the church. Religion was not a major issue in their romance but an interest in religion was something which they shared and valued at a time when they were getting to know each other. He gave her an English version of the Koran and she told him that "she had no specific faith and was looking for the truth somewhere".[103] When they married in Egypt, the significance of religion was a matter of dispute. He claimed it was a religious marriage and that she had signed an agreement whereby any children would be raised as Muslim. She indicated a lack of clarity in the translation of the documents and some general confusion about the civil or religious significance of the Egyptian marriage ceremony. For both the Muslim man and his ex-Brethren wife, becoming parents brought new elements to their identity. As a father, and particularly as a separated father, his religious obligations towards his children became more pronounced. The mother, while denying any significant change in belief, did get into the habit of attending church and taking the children to Sunday school: an experience they enjoyed for the benefits of community, singing and social interaction more than the development of faith.

The wife's parents were Christian, members of the strict Brethren, and she herself had been brought up in that religious environment. Despite their personal beliefs and commitment to a particular lifestyle as members of a strong religious community, the wife's parents demonstrated significant flexibility in their different roles as parents and parents-in-law. The mother was said to have raised with her daughter the difficulties of marrying a Muslim man, but nonetheless went shopping with her for a wedding dress. After the wedding, when the young couple settled in Scotland, they lived for a while with the wife's parents. Putting to one side his very strong religious beliefs, her father played the role of a welcoming host and friendly father-in-law, even having amicable conversations with his Muslim son-in-law that sometimes involved politics and religion. In these very ordinary, everyday descriptions of behaviour it is clear that, despite the headline story of religious conflict and apparently incompatible religious rules, individuals have considerable flexibility to negotiate their various obligations and ability to make things work in the interests of maintaining good relationships.

---

101 This case is reported at 2012 Fam LR 148 and the full transcript is also available at www.scotcourts.gov.uk. References are to the online transcript which sets out the facts in full detail. Official transcript at para. 5.

102 A Protestant evangelical fellowship which emerged in the UK in the early 19th century: www.plymouthbrethrenchristianchurch.org.

103 Official transcript at para. 5.

4.3. RELIGIOUS IDENTITY: BORN OR BECOMING

"We know that children change dramatically between birth and adulthood, and we know they are subject to influence during the course of that development. We know much less, however, about how that development is influenced, let alone what the ideal outcomes of that development might be."[104] The key question in this case concerned the religious identity of three children and the rights and responsibilities of their parents in shaping this identity. For the father, and according to Islam, the children were Muslim from birth and he considered it his duty and responsibility as a Muslim man to raise them as Muslims. For the mother, the identity – religious or otherwise – of the children was something that would develop over time: they would grow into their own identities. In the facts of the case, as presented by the various witnesses, different understandings of religion and identity emerged. At birth, the father "said the call to Prayer in ears of each child"[105] and by so doing marked the child as Muslim. He accepted that when they grew up, they could choose for themselves but until that time they had been born Muslim and he was obliged to raise them accordingly. For the mother, she was happy for the children to be exposed to religion – by going to mosque, church or Sunday school, through watching and copying the behaviour of their parents, by reading stories and experiencing different traditions through food and festivals – but that did not mean they had a particular religious identity. From her perspective, "the fact that the children sing a hymn or say a prayer does not equate to understanding".[106] From the perspective of Scots family law,[107] the rights of the parents in respect of their children come second to their parental responsibilities and therefore the sheriff was not required to resolve direct conflict between the rights of the parents but rather to make an assessment of how best to promote the welfare of the children.

In the words of the various witnesses in this case – parents, friends, a religious expert, a child psychologist and a judge – the infinite complexities of religion and identity were clear. The one issue on which they might all be seen to agree was that challenges and differences can be accommodated without undue harm when good relationships are maintained. For the father, his need to "put more pressure on the children to become Muslim"[108] was linked to his separation from the mother and his fear that he could no longer trust her. On a more positive note, the mother tried to see what their separate religions had in common: "being a better person, knowing the difference between right and

104 E. Buss, "Allocating Developmental Control Among Parent, Child and the State" (2004) 27 *University of Chicago Legal Forum* 27.
105 Official transcript at para. 14.
106 Official transcript at para. 61.
107 Children (Scotland) Act 1995, ss1, 2 and 11.
108 Official transcript at para. 17.

wrong".[109] She emphasised the importance of raising the children to respect the different but equally valid beliefs of their parents; although of course it might be said that it was much easier for her to take that approach secure in her position as the resident parent. For the child psychologist, any risk to child development of religious confusion would depend on how the parents "manage the differences and co-operate".[110] In a similar vein, the sheriff concluded that it was for the parents to ensure that the children were not made to feel that they were part of a conflict. In the longer term it was the context of conflicted relations, rather than any conflict between different religious practices and beliefs, which would create "feelings such as discomfort, uncertainty or confusion"[111] and be likely to have most significant and harmful "impact on the personal identities of the children."[112]

5. THE LIMITS OF LABELLING

In contemporary "sound-bite" culture, slogans and mantras are created, repeated and proliferated sometimes before deeper reflection on what they mean has taken place. Ideas can become embedded through repetition and familiarity, without detailed substantive debate, and to some extent that might be said of rights language: bite-sized principles with immediate appeal, which enter our consciousness sometimes before their legal implications have been fully worked out. Their simplicity and self-evident rightness make them easy to adopt and to endorse but it is only in subsequent practice that their complexity emerges. In the words of Ann Laquer Estin: "[f]or children who grow up in closely knit communities, rooted in a particular place, the question of belonging is an easy one … for children in global families, the question of belonging raises many troubling questions".[113] It is very tempting to look back on apparently simpler times when perspectives were more commonly local and everyone knew where they belonged but changing patterns of migration within Europe together with a shift in perspective have contributed to increasing globalisation of outlook. A framework of international human rights, while intended to be inclusive and cohesive can instead have the effect of excluding and emphasising difference and conflict. While universal rights can be an empowering and effective tool, the sheer enormity of scale can also be overwhelming and to some extent demotivating. The complexities of meaning and the challenges of effective implementation at a global level increasingly make the tasks seem impossible.

109 Official transcript at para. 42.
110 Official transcript at para. 68.
111 Official transcript at para. 123.
112 Ibid.
113 A.L. Estin, "Where (in the World) do Children Belong?" (2011) 25 *Brigham Young University Journal of Public Law* 217.

One reaction to the increasing emergence of legal claims and public concerns about religious and identity rights is to return to the legal principles in an attempt to clarify them further and improve their application. Identity, however, is very rarely something fixed and certain: or at least that is the case with the complex notions of identity with which law is increasingly required to engage. "If lawyers and judges treat identity as something discoverable rather than forged or invented, they hide the latitude for choice and struggle over identity."[114] The ascription of legal identity tends to assume that such identity is clear and fixed rather than shifting and "fuzzy".[115] As issues involving children and religious identity become more prevalent in legal courts and academic discourse we should be wary of reacting too quickly. Perhaps it is not always a case of striving to do better in the development and application of law and policy but sometimes of acknowledging law's limitations. Fixing individual badges of identity and presenting them in the black and white language of law may distract attention from the real importance of lived relationships. Legal labels are static in contrast to the dynamic nature of everyday life. Parents of children usually realise quite quickly that they do not have unfettered power to control and shape their offspring and in the context of religion, as in many other aspects of personal development, it is well to remember that often religion "is 'caught' by the child as much as it is taught."[116] While boundaries must be set and they should be applied firmly and fairly, flexibility is essential and the aspiration of "perfect" often gives way to "good enough". There may be a lesson there for law. Law can create and apply labels but it is much less suited to the flexibility and compromise required in negotiating relationships. In the longer term, good relationships more than clear identities may be what matters most for everyone.

114 M. Minow, "Identities" (1991) 3 *Yale Journal of Law and Humanities* 97 at 111.

115 The "fuzziness" of religious identities of young people is highlighted in G. Vincett, E. Olson, P. Hopkins and R. Pain, "Young People and Performance Christianity in Scotland" (2012) 27(2) *Journal of Contemporary Religion* 275.

116 R. Ahdar, "The Child's Right to a Godly Future" (2002) 10 *International Journal of Children's Rights* 89 at 99.

STATE CURRICULUM AND PARENTS' CONVICTIONS UNDER THE EUROPEAN CONVENTION ON HUMAN RIGHTS

Sanna Mustasaari and Sanna Koulu

1. TRAVELLING WITH CHILDREN IN STRASBOURG

Anyone who has travelled with children – or observed these journeys as a fellow passenger – is familiar with the challenges and frustration that travelling with children may involve. Parents do, nevertheless, take their children to places far from home, and most of the time they do so willingly, as experiences and memories springing from such trips enrich the lives of children and adults alike. Using this as metaphor, we wish to begin our contribution by noting that for a lawyer too, "travelling with children", that is, going beyond national law with regard to children's legal rights, is both exhausting and rewarding. As the legal regulation concerning children is increasingly fragmented and internationalised, the applicable norms and principles are often found in transnational contexts, for instance in the case law of the European Court of Human Rights. While drawing interpretative guidelines from the case law of the Strasbourg Court may sometimes be challenging, there is no denying that the Court plays a crucial role in taking the rights of the children seriously and developing child-centred approaches to legal argumentation.

In this chapter we will discuss one specific issue with regard to the Court's case law and the rights of the child, namely the possibility for the child to be exempted from certain lessons or school activities on grounds of freedom of religion. The issue can arise for example in conjunction with music lessons, dancing as a part of physical education, or sex education. While the content of the lessons for which exemption is sought can vary, the common feature is the conflict between state-mandated curricula and the convictions of the parents. The position of the child is less clear, and it is not clear how the best interests of the child could best be safeguarded in these cases.

The European Convention on Human Rights,[1] like many other human rights conventions, stresses the role of the parents in bringing up children. The case law of the Court, however, supports the importance of state curricula. We argue that whichever side is emphasised, that of the parents or that of general society, more attention should be paid to the concrete circumstances of the child and the family as well as to the probable consequences for the child of allowing or denying the exemption.

2. RELIGION AND EDUCATION: BETWEEN PARENTAL AND STATE AUTHORITY

The issue of religious convictions and their impact on education is most often framed as a conflict between the family and the state.[2] In the most basic terms, it is a question of who has the right to decide how children should be brought up and what they should be taught. The religious freedom of the parents is weighed against public interest and, in the Nordic welfarist tradition, the state's central role in organising education.

Before turning to the question of exemption from certain lessons at school, it is important to draw attention to one well-established fact concerning the interrelationship of Convention rights and national law. The articles of the European Convention provide certain rights to individuals and establish core areas of those rights as autonomous orders that oblige all Member States. Still, to a large extent the protection provided by the Convention consists of the joint effects of national legislation and the Convention. The Convention might not oblige a state to grant a certain right or privilege to an individual, but if the state does provide for such rights, they will fall under the relevant norms of the Convention. So, when the national legislation provides an option for exempting a child from

1 European Convention for the Protection of Human Rights and Fundamental Freedoms, as amended by Protocols Nos. 11 and 14, adopted by the Council of Europe on 4 November 1950.

2 See also D. Archard, *Children: Rights and Childhood*, 2nd edition, Routledge 2004, p. 213.

certain lessons or activities at school, this opens up more space and more direct effects for human rights considerations than would exist if such exemptions were not granted in the national law.

The question of religious freedom in children's education is connected to several human rights provisions, but there are no directly applicable articles in the European Convention itself. Specifically, Article 9 on freedom of religion does not explicitly address the relationship between parents and children. The question falls instead into the scope of two other human rights instruments: first, the First Protocol to the European Convention,[3] and second, the UN Convention on the Rights of the Child.[4]

The most relevant article is found in the First Protocol to the European Convention. The First Protocol is almost as old as the Convention itself, and it entered into force in 1952. According to Article 2 of the First Protocol (P1–2), the state shall respect the parents' right to bring up their children as follows:

> "Article 2 – Right to education
> No person shall be denied the right to education. In the exercise of any functions which it assumes in relation to education and to teaching, the State shall respect the right of parents to ensure such education and teaching in conformity with their own religious and philosophical convictions."

Freedom of religion, provided for by Article 9 of the Convention, is also important for the issue of education and the convictions of the members of the family.[5] The right to education should be read together with Article 9 of the European Convention, according to which:

> "1. Everyone has the right to freedom of thought, conscience and religion; this right includes freedom to change his religion or belief and freedom, either alone or in community with others and in public or private, to manifest his religion or belief, in worship, teaching, practice and observance.
> 2. There shall be no interference by a public authority with the exercise of this right except such as is in accordance with the law and is necessary in a democratic society in the interests of national security, public safety or the economic wellbeing of the country, for the prevention of disorder or crime, for the protection of health or morals, or for the protection of the rights and freedoms of others."

---

3 Protocol to the Convention for the Protection of Human Rights and Fundamental Freedoms, signed in Paris on 20 March 1952.

4 Convention on the Rights of the Child, adopted by the United Nations General Assembly on 20 November 1989.

5 U. Kilkelly, *The Child and the European Convention on Human Rights*, Ashgate 1999, p. 72.

The UN Convention was adopted in 1989, but the provisions on freedom of religion are surprisingly reminiscent of the above quoted two articles of the European Convention and its Protocol.[6] Article 14 of the CRC states that:

> "1. States Parties shall respect the right of the child to freedom of thought, conscience and religion.
> 2. States Parties shall respect the rights and duties of the parents and, when applicable, legal guardians, to provide direction to the child in the exercise of his or her right in a manner consistent with the evolving capacities of the child."

The question, however, remains: where is the child in all this? Is the child only a pawn in the conflict of parents and the state, or is there a role for the child's rights and agency? To what extent can we focus on the perspective of the child, and what legal strategies can be employed to this end? It should be obvious that the question of exemption from certain lessons concerns the child most directly. If the exemption is not granted, he or she is the person most directly involved. He or she may have to decide whether to skip the lessons in accordance with her parents' wishes and risk not getting a passing grade. There may be social consequences that concern the child's identity or experience of belonging to her peer group. If the conflict between parents and school is acute enough, she might suffer from the conflict itself.

The implications of the issue for the child him- or herself are pertinent enough that the issue can be said to concern the child. One of the most enduring strategies in highlighting the child's role in legal and policy decisions is the emphasis on the best interests of the child. Its most prominent expression is found in the UN Convention, though the principle is much older.[7] This means that in addition to Article 14, we should pay close attention to Article 3 of the CRC:

> "Article 3
> 1. In all actions concerning children, whether undertaken by public or private social welfare institutions, courts of law, administrative authorities or legislative bodies, the best interests of the child shall be a primary consideration."[8]

---

6 The International Covenant on Civil and Political Rights (ICCPR), adopted by the United Nations General Assembly on 16 December 1966, also protects both equal freedom of religion of all human beings and the rights of the parents to follow their religious convictions in bringing up their children. According to Article 18 of the ICCPR: "1. Everyone shall have the right to freedom of thought [...] 4. The States Parties to the present Covenant undertake to have respect for the liberty of parents and, when applicable, legal guardians to ensure the religious and moral education of their children in conformity with their own convictions."

7 See for instance R.H. Mnookin, "Child-Custody Adjudication: Judicial Functions on the Face of Indeterminacy" (1975)39 *Law and Contemporary Problems* 226–293.

8 For some of the discussion on what it means that something is "*a* primary consideration" as opposed to "a paramount consideration" or "*the* primary consideration", see e.g. N. Lowe and G. Douglas, *Bromley's Family Law*, 10th edition, Oxford University Press 2007, pp. 451 ff.; and S. Choudhry and J. Herring, *European Human Rights and Family Law*, Hart Publishing 2010, p. 227.

In the system of the UN Convention, the principle of the best interests of the child is broadly applicable; the best interests of the child should be a primary consideration in all actions concerning children. According to the recent general comment of the Committee on the Rights of the Child, the principle of the child's best interests is a threefold concept.[9] It is firstly "a substantive right: The right of the child to have his or her best interests assessed and taken as a primary consideration when different interests are being considered in order to reach a decision on the issue at stake". Secondly, it is "a fundamental, interpretative legal principle: If a legal provision is open to more than one interpretation, the interpretation which most effectively serves the child's best interests should be chosen." Thirdly, it is "a rule of procedure: Whenever a decision is to be made that will affect a specific child, an identified group of children or children in general, the decision-making process must include an evaluation of the possible impact (positive or negative) of the decision on the child or children concerned".[10]

In contrast, the European Convention does not mention explicitly either the best interests principle or children's rights. This is partly due to the Convention's age, as its drafting dates from the late 1940s. In practice the Convention has evolved over time, and the principle of the best interests of the child was highlighted in the case law of the Court early on.[11] The European Court has reasserted several times that the Convention is a living instrument and should be interpreted dynamically and in compliance with provisions from other human rights treaties. However, just how far-reaching this emphasis on children's rights and the best interests principle is remains obscure.

The fact that the European Convention and the UN Convention partly overlap in issues concerning children does not mean that the best interests principle would operate in the same manner or be interpreted in the same way under the European Convention as in the UN Convention. Instead of being a general legal rule applied in all decisions concerning children, and at all stages of decision-making, as is the case in the UN Convention, the scope of the best interests principle is much more limited within the system of the European Convention.

Within the framework of the European Convention, the best interests of the child have mostly been assessed under Article 8 in the context of the alleged violation of the right to respect for private and family life.[12] The best interests principle has so far been scrutinised only after the Court has already found a particular situation to be an infringement of a right protected by the

9 General Comment No. 14 (2013) on the right of the child to have his or her best interests taken as a primary consideration (Art 3(1)), CRC/C/GC/14.

10 Ibid., p. 4.

11 For discussion, see U. Kilkelly, *supra* note 5, p. 252. See also *Keegan v. Ireland,* 26 May 1994, Application No. 16969/90, for an early example of the impact of the CRC on the Court's deliberations.

12 For discussion, see especially U. Kilkelly, *supra* note 5, p. 3, and S. Choudhry and J. Herring, *supra* note 8, pp. 223, 233 and 245.

Convention. The best interests principle forms a part of the assessment of whether the infringement is justified and proportionate. In contrast, the principle is not involved in the consideration as to whether a certain situation forms an infringement in the first place. The best interests principle has, however, evolved in the case law of the Court in accordance with the understanding that the Convention is a living instrument and subject to dynamic interpretation of the Court. In the future the principle of the best interests of the child may well take root also in the case law of the Court under other articles of the Convention.

3. THE EUROPEAN COURT ON A TIGHTROPE BETWEEN THE STATE AND THE PARENTS?

As explained above, the second sentence of Article 2 of the First Protocol aims at balancing between the rights of the parents to raise their child according to their convictions and the power of the state to determine the substance of obligatory education. The Court has explicitly stated that this provision is about the rights of the parents and not about the rights of the child.[13] Given the general attitudes regarding children's upbringing and education at the time when the Convention and the Protocol were drafted, nearly seventy years ago, it is hardly surprising that Article 2 is not framed as being about the rights of the child. Yet the question must be posed whether this precludes the rights of the child or approaches based on the best interests of the child from playing a role in the future interpretation of the Article. This question is especially timely now, as almost forty years have passed since the Court ruled in the landmark case of *Kjeldsen, Busk Madsen and Pedersen v. Denmark* (1976).[14]

In this case, the applicants claimed that their rights under Article 2 had been violated, as their children were not exempted from participating in their school's sex education lessons. The applicants considered these lessons against their religious views, asserting that the material used in sex education was vulgar

13 See *Eriksson v. Sweden*, 22 June 1989, Application No. 11373/85. The case concerned the taking of a child into public care and the efforts of the mother to have public care terminated. While mainly challenging the state on the basis of Article 8, the applicants also invoked the right to education. The applicants, mother and daughter, claimed that placing the daughter in public care and limiting the access rights of the mother prevented the mother from giving the daughter education according to the beliefs of the Pentecostal movement. According to the Court, the child could not claim be to be a victim of a breach that concerned the right of the parent to ensure that their convictions are respected in teaching. *Eriksson v. Sweden*, paras. 83 and 93. See also U. Kilkelly, *supra* note 5, pp. 84–85; F. McCarthy, "Prayers in the Playground: Religion and Education in the United Kingdom and Beyond", in J. Mair and E. Örücü (eds.), *The Place of Religion in Family Law: A Comparative Search,* Intersentia 2011, pp. 235–263; and M. Hunter-Henin, "Introduction", in M. Hunter-Henin (ed.), *Law, Religious Freedoms and Education in Europe,* Ashgate 2011, p. 6.

14 *Kjeldsen, Busk Madsen and Pedersen v. Denmark*, 7 December 1976, Applications No. 5095/71; 5920/72; 5926/72.

and contained inappropriate photographs. Mr and Mrs Kjeldsen had even taken the matter to the Danish Minister of Education, requesting an exemption for their daughter from sex education. Their request had been turned down on the grounds that for practical reasons such an exemption was not possible to arrange. Danish law did not provide for exemptions of this kind, although the parents did in principle have the option of schooling their children at home or at private (religious) schools.

The case of *Kjeldsen and others* is of particular importance as it was in this case that the Court laid down the general criteria for the assessment of whether the state has infringed its obligation to respect the right of parents to ensure that education and teaching is in conformity with their own religious and philosophical convictions. Having been called upon to ascertain whether or not Danish legislation contravened the Convention and the First Protocol, the Court held that in this case the moral underpinnings of the education in question were very general in character and did not go beyond of what a democratic state might regard as the public interest.[15]

The Court stated that Article 2 of the First Protocol does not prevent states from imparting information or knowledge of a directly or indirectly religious or philosophical kind in education, nor does it permit parents to object to the integration of such education in the school curriculum. The Court also noted that many subjects taught at school are necessarily based on some philosophical account of moral values. According to the Court, the obligation to respect the religious convictions of the parents means that the state is obliged to safeguard that information or knowledge included in the curriculum is conveyed in an objective, critical and pluralistic manner. The state is thus forbidden to pursue an aim of indoctrination that might be considered as not respecting parents' religious and philosophical convictions.

Since the *Kjeldsen* case, the Court has heard a few cases falling under Article 2 of the First Protocol.[16] For instance, in its Grand Chamber judgment in *Folgerø and others v. Norway* (2007), the Court found that emphasising Christianity in religious education whilst not granting an exemption for children from non-Christian families breached parents' rights under Article 2 of the First Protocol.[17] From our perspective here, however, the admissibility decision of *Dojan and others v. Germany* (2011),[18] proves more interesting. In this case, similarly to

15 Ibid., paras. 49, 53 and 54.

16 For discussion on the Court's case law on religious education, see P. Cumper, "Religious Education in Europe in the Twenty-First Century", in M. Hunter-Henin, *supra* note 13, pp. 207–227.

17 *Folgerø and others v. Norway*, 29 June 2007, Application No. 15472/02. The case concerned a refusal to grant an exemption from a compulsory subject called Christianity, Religion and Philosophy. According to the Court, the curricula emphasised Christianity in an imbalanced way.

18 Decision as to the admissibility of Application No. 319/08, *Willi, Anna and David Dojan v. Germany and 4 other applications*, 13 September 2011.

the *Kjeldsen* case, the applicants considered sex education to be against their convictions, claiming infringement of their rights, as the teaching staff of the concerned school did not exempt their children from sex education classes. The classes included events such as a workshop called "My body is mine", which was aimed to combat sexual abuse. Significantly, however, in this case the German legislation did provide for the possibility of exempting a student from a certain lesson. According to the Schools Act and the Compulsory Schooling Act, the principal of the school could exempt pupils from certain lessons at the request of parents. Since the exemption was not granted in the case at hand, the applicants kept their children away from school during the sex education lessons and were sanctioned with penal fines. The fines were upheld in the Court of Appeal, and later the Federal Constitutional Court refused to admit the complaints.

The application in the European Court of Human Rights was unfortunately declared inadmissible and did not proceed to full examination. The Court considered the application to be manifestly ill-founded because it had already previously solved similar issues. According to the Court, there was no genuine question about whether the state had exceeded its margin of appreciation. This decision is interesting in itself, as it circumvents the very question of the relation of national law and Convention rights. At the same time, the decision offers limited scope for analysis, as admissibility decisions do not generally provide conclusions over the substance of the Convention provisions.

In brief, there are noteworthy aspects to the approach adopted by the Court in the *Dojan* case. They concern the construction of the state's margin of appreciation in these cases along with the absence of an assessment of proportionality in the decision, and the interrelationship of national law and Convention rights. Two points are in order here. Firstly, the margin of appreciation in these cases is impacted by the phrasing of Article 2 of the First Protocol, according to which the state shall respect the *right of parents* to ensure such education and teaching in conformity with their own religious and philosophical convictions. Reasons for this are obviously historical; were the Protocol drafted today, Article 2 would presumably include a mention of the convictions of the child.

The Court has, rather consistently, approached value conflicts between school and families as matters of jurisdiction between state and parents. For example, in the case of *Campbell and Cosans v. United Kingdom* (1982),[19] the applicant mothers claimed that corporal punishment was against their convictions and thus in breach of the second sentence of Article 2 of the First Protocol. Ruling for the applicants, the Court made no explicit reference to children's rights or their particular situations.[20] Like in the Grand Chamber judgment *Folgerø v. Norway*, the rights,

19 *Campbell and Cosans v. United Kingdom*, 25 February 1982, Applications No. 7511/76 and 7743/76.

20 For discussion of the case, see F. Cranmer, "Beating People is Wrong: Campbell and Cosans, Williamson and their Aftermath", in M. Hunter-Henin, *supra* note 13, pp. 283–304.

interests and views of the children in question were completely left aside while the rights of the parents, e.g. their right to privacy, were thoroughly analysed.[21] This, in our opinion, marks a break with modern child law and discourse on children's rights where the child's perspective is considered paramount in all matters involving children.

The second point concerns the doctrine of the margin of appreciation, which is inseparable from the principle of proportionality.[22] This brings into the picture the issue of national legislation and its interrelationship with the Convention. In the numerous cases concerning abortion, for instance, the Court has confirmed that once a Member State adopts statutory regulations concerning an issue that in and of itself would not fall under the Convention, these regulations will be subject to an assessment of whether a fair balance has, in a particular case, been struck between different rights and legitimate interests.[23]

In this respect the two cases, *Kjeldsen* and *Dojan*, were significantly different. Even though the *Dojan* case does not elaborate on the role of national legislation, the very fact of it being an admissibility decision points to a certain lack of responsiveness to the interrelations of the Convention and national law. In the *Kjeldsen* case the question was merely about the acceptability of the national legislation of the state and the substance of the syllabus, whereas in the *Dojan* case the national law actually provided scope for situational consideration of the particular circumstances of the request. Thus the question was not only about the general acceptance of the substance of the sex education, but also about the procedure and legal reasoning in the case that concerned granting the exemption. To a lawyer used to reading the Court's case law under Article 8, the references to public interest and margin of appreciation alone seem inadequate. The fact that a state has acted within its margin of appreciation does not in itself determine that the means it has adopted are proportionate.[24] In this respect, the *Dojan* case

---

21 *Folgerø v. Norway, supra* note 17, for example para. 98.

22 For an exhaustive discussion on the margin of appreciation and proportionality, see for example A. Legg, *The Margin of Appreciation in International Human Rights Law,* Oxford University Press 2012 and, specifically in the field of family law, S. Choudhry and J. Herring, *supra* note 8, pp. 26–34.

23 In *A, B and C v. Ireland*, 16 December 2010, application 25579/05, para. 249, the Court stated the following: "As in the negative obligation context, the State enjoys a certain margin of appreciation (see, among other authorities, *Keegan v. Ireland*, 26 May 1994, §49, Series A no. 290). While a broad margin of appreciation is accorded to the State as to the decision about the circumstances in which an abortion will be permitted in a State (see paragraphs 231–38 above), once that decision is taken the legal framework devised for this purpose should be 'shaped in a coherent manner which allows the different legitimate interests involved to be taken into account adequately and in accordance with the obligations deriving from the Convention' (see *S.H. and Others v. Austria*, no. 57813/00, §74, 1 April 2010)". See also G. Puppinck, "Abortion and the European Convention on Human Rights" (2013) 3 *Irish Journal of Legal Studies* 142–193.

24 See for instance Court's argumentation in *Schneider v. Germany*: "Having regard to the foregoing, the Court, referring, mutatis mutandis, to the detailed reasoning in its judgment in the case of Anayo (§§67–73), therefore considers that the domestic courts did not fairly balance the competing interests involved in the decision-making process and thus failed to provide the

presents a missed opportunity to elaborate on the position of the child with regard to religious upbringing and state responsibility.

4. EXEMPTION FROM EDUCATION IN NATIONAL LAWS

In several national legislations, exemption from classes is made possible under certain conditions. For instance, according to the Finnish Basic Education Act, a pupil's education may be adjusted by special arrangements, if the completion of the basic education syllabus would in some respect be unreasonable for the pupil in view of her circumstances and prior learning.[25] The principal of the child's school has broad discretion in deciding upon matters of special arrangements, such as exemption from education.[26] An appeal against a decision on special arrangements may be lodged with the Regional State Administrative Agency, whose decision may be appealed to an administrative court of law.[27] It follows from Article 3 of the CRC that, in considering whether to grant the exemption, all of these authorities are under the obligation to have the best interests of the child as a primary concern.

Similarly, according to the Swedish Education Act, a pupil may be exempted from certain classes at a parent's request if special reasons for such an exemption are found.[28] In 2011 Sweden reformed its legislation on education and the new Education Act has applied since July 2011. According to the *travaux préparatoires*, the provision on exemption in the new Act is phrased in a more restrictive manner in order to emphasise the exceptionality of exempting pupils from classes.[29] The new Act explicitly states that the exemption has to be decided on individual basis in each case. A permit for home schooling, for instance, also requires special reasons. These restrictions would indicate that a general exemption from a certain subject would not be in accordance with the law.

In deciding upon the claims and wishes of the parents and the views and interpretations of education authorities, the courts are often faced with the difficult task of striking a fair balance that would enhance the rights of the child and the parents. *Johanna Schiratzki* discusses two Swedish cases from 1995 and 2003 where

applicant with the requisite protection of his interests safeguarded by Article 8. They failed to give any consideration to the question whether, in the particular circumstances of the case, contact between F. [the child] and the applicant would be in F.'s best interest." *Schneider v. Germany*, 15 September 2009, Application No. 17080/07, para. 104.

25 Finnish Basic Education Act, Section 18.2 (Perusopetuslaki 1998/628).

26 S. Hakalehto-Wainio, *Oppilaan oikeudet opetustoimessa* (translated from Finnish: *The pupil's rights in education*), Lakimiesliiton kustannus 2012, pp. 94–95.

27 Finnish Basic Education Act, section 42.

28 Swedish Education Act, section 19 (Skollag 2010/800).

29 Government Bill 2009/10:165, p. 523.

the courts had to consider requests for exemptions regarding music classes.[30] In the first case, the court affirmed an exemption from music classes for a child because playing and listening to music were against the religious views of the parent.[31] According to an expert witness (psychologist), taking part in these classes was harmful for the child, as the classes were so fundamentally against the convictions of the parent. Following the opinion of the expert witness, the court considered the exemption to be in the best interests of the child. Controversially, in the 2003 case an exemption was not granted, as the court was not convinced that taking part in the music classes was causing the child psychological harm.[32] In this case the court also considered other provisions of the UN Convention, and stated further that exempting the child from the music classes would breach Article 2 of the UN Convention (prohibition of discrimination).

The restrictions in the new Swedish Education Act, namely the requirement of special reasons, has led to some changes in municipal practices, especially regarding home schooling. In 2013, the Swedish Supreme Administrative Court ruled on a case that concerned four daughters of an Orthodox Jewish family, resident for many years in Gothenburg, Sweden.[33] Under the previous Education Act, Gothenburg Municipality had for years accepted that the children were home-schooled by their parents and attended a Jewish online school. After the new Education Act and the requirement of special reasons came into force, the municipality considered it no longer possible to grant the children an exemption from attending a school under the Swedish educational system, as no special reasons required by the law were present. According to the education authorities, questions of religious practices, rather than special reasons for home schooling, were matters of practicalities that could be arranged at school.

The parents claimed that the religious life of their family included many practices that simply could not be arranged in the Swedish school system, for example strict dietary rules and prayers thirty times a day. The parents also expressed worries that the school could not guarantee a safe environment for their children, who due to their religion (manifested, for example, in a special dressing code) would clearly stand out as different from other children and risk being attacked or bullied. The Swedish Supreme Administrative Court sided with the municipality, agreeing that the special needs of the children arising from their religion were to be handled in the framework of the general school system, not by home schooling the children. The court did, however, explicitly state that it

30 J. Schiratzki, *Barnets bästa i ett mångkulturella Sverige. En rättsvetenskaplig undersökning*, 2nd edition, Iustus Förlag 2005, pp. 159–163.

31 *Stockholms läns LR (first instance administrative law court), Ö18900-95*, according to J. Schiratzki, *supra* note 30, p. 163.

32 *LR i Hallands län (first instance administrative law court) 04419, 2366-03*, according to J. Schiratzki, *supra* note 30, p. 164.

33 *Högsta Förvaltningsdomstolen* (Swedish Supreme Administrative Court), *HFD 2013 ref 49*. See M. Jänterä-Jareborg in this volume, section 5.

was particularly important to pay heed to the children's circumstances. The case attracted a lot of attention in the media and stirred up discussion around home schooling, although some discussants pointed out that even with the increase in the number of home-schooled children (from 92 in 2006 to 239 in 2011), home schooling nevertheless remains a marginal issue.[34]

The examples of national legislation and decisions of national courts, on the one hand, and the case law of the European Court, on the other, evoke several thorny questions about the application of Convention rights and obligations. First, the question can be raised as to how, according to the Convention, the conflicting interests of the parents and the general school system, representing the public, should be balanced. Secondly, we need to ask what role, if any, the wellbeing of the child should be given in these situations. In the *Dojan* case, for instance, the applicants asserted not only that the educational material was pornographic and contrary to their religious and moral convictions, but that their children did not have the necessary maturity to receive the envisaged sex education. According to the parents, the children had been raised without the influence of the media and were used to modest and chaste sexual behaviour at home. In their view the approach to sexuality adopted in the education material would lead to premature "sexualisation" of the children.[35] It strikes us as odd that the Court seems to require no consideration of the wellbeing and interests of the particular child whose participation in or exemption from the education was at stake. Here a more substantive statement from the Court would have been welcome.

5. BEST INTERESTS OF THE CHILD: FROM UNIVERSAL RULES TO PARTICULAR CONTEXTS AND BACK?

The principle of the best interests of the child maintains that in all decision-making involving children their interests should be a primary consideration. While in general the law should take children's interests and needs into account, the principle obliges all courts to consider the decision they are about to make in the light of the best interests of the children affected by it. However, it is not too clear what actually is in the best interests of the child when considering religious freedom and the possibility of being exempted from certain lessons that are claimed to clash with matters of faith.

Publicly funded universal and free education is one of the cornerstones in the Nordic welfarist tradition. In addition to the general availability of schooling,

---

34 *Dagens Nyheter*, 2 January 2013 ("Ortodox familj vill undervisa hemma").

35 The question of children's right to sexual self-determination is a complex one, but it is clear that in order for the right to be effective, it presupposes a right to sex education. See D. Archard, *supra* note 2, pp. 105–111.

the contents of the education provided to all can be considered to be in children's best interests, at least to some extent. After all, it is usually in children's best interests to grow up to be independent adults, with several options for organising their own lives and with the capacity to choose among them according to their own inclinations and identities.[36] That is, the child's best interests are not only a question of providing sufficient care and protection during their minority, but also a question of providing for their future. The state-mandated public curricula thus generally aim at equality of opportunity through providing all children with the kind of learning considered essential for their future.

Orientation towards the future is present, moreover, in another aspect of the child's best interests, related to their cultural identity and heritage. It is considered good for the child to be brought up in accordance with his or her ethnic and religious background. This idea finds its expression for example in Article 14 of the CRC, according to which the state shall respect the rights and duties of the parents and, when applicable, legal guardians, to provide direction to the child in the exercise of their freedom of thought, conscience and religion in a manner consistent with the evolving capacities of the child. Article 29 of the CRC, in addition, mentions the importance of respecting the parents and the cultural identity of the child in education. National legislation furthermore usually echoes these ideas. However, while the statutory expressions of this thought rarely lay out the reasoning behind it, we find David Archard's proposal for such reasoning convincing. Archard has argued that "children have an interest in acquiring an identity which is not grounded in choice: this is valuable both instrumentally, because it enables them unselfconsciously to negotiate the conflicts within their culture, and intrinsically because it provides them with a sense of 'effortless belonging'".[37]

These two aspects of the best interests principle intersect as regards the question of education and religious freedom. Granting or not granting an exemption from specific school classes may not be a crucial issue, but it highlights the fundamental issue of who is entitled to determine the child's future: education can be highly charged both politically and morally. Both aspects, as well as argumentation based on the best interests in general, promote a universal understanding of the best interests, an understanding that is focused on the hypothetical adult that the child will become. According to this line of argumentation, while universal schooling may not constitute the absolute "best" education an individual child can receive, the best interests of each individual child are best served through universal rules. It is beneficial for all children that

36 See H. Brighouse, "What Rights (if Any) do Children Have?", in D. Archard and C.M. Macleod (eds.), *The Moral and Political Status of Children*, Oxford University Press 2002, especially p. 40. See also J. Mair in this volume, sections 2–3.

37 This succinct synopsis is from H. Brighouse, *supra* note 36, p. 49. For a more thorough discussion, see D. Archard, "Children, Multiculturalism, and Education" in the same anthology, pp. 142–159.

education is freely available, state-mandated and focused on teaching them a wide variety of necessary and useful skills and knowledge. However, from this perspective it can be difficult to identify and account for the individual interests of individual children. Bringing in the individual interests of the child as factors to be considered paramount in the argumentation may actually weaken the protection of the rights of the "universal" child.[38]

While there is nothing wrong with aiming to provide the best for all children, this universality highlights the political character of the best interests principle – a principle whose interpretation is remarkably open-ended and vulnerable to being co-opted for different agendas.[39] The question is then to assess what role is given to the individual wellbeing and the concrete circumstances of each child and family, in contrast to the more universal understanding of the principle of the best interests of the child described above. We argue that focusing on the situation of the individual child in question is a better way to account for his or her best interests, even though such an interpretation of the best interests principle is still prone to political agendas.[40]

So the question is, when the wellbeing and interests of the particular child should be taken into account in the legal argumentation of a given case. And conversely, when can the national courts rely on the notion of the universal interests of the children reflected by the law? The answer seems rather bleak at the moment. In the light of its case law on Article 2 of the First Protocol, the European Court does not appear to take the individual wellbeing of the particular child much into account, if at all. It might be argued, however, that there are already signs of an impending change, as the individual circumstances of the particular child are emphasised in other case law.[41]

---

38 See for example J. Schiratzki, according to whom the decision by the Swedish court in 1995, referred to above, was an example of how the principle of the best interests of the child might be used to trump her rights. Granting an exemption from music classes on the basis of the best interests of the child actually breached the rights of the child, especially the right to education. J. Schiratzki, *supra* note 30, pp. 159–163.

39 For critical viewpoints in the context of child custody, see the discussion on welfarism by S. Choudhry, J. Herring and J. Wallbank, "Welfare, rights, care and gender in family law", in J. Wallbank, S. Choudhry and J. Herring (eds.) *Rights, Gender and Family Law*, Routledge 2010, pp. 1–25. See also A. Charlow, "Awarding Custody: The Best Interests of the Child and Other Fictions" (1986–87) *Yale Law and Policy Review* 267–290, especially p. 267: "Because the 'best interests of the child' standard is more a vague platitude than a legal or scientific standard, it is subject to abuse both by judges who administer it and parents who use it to further their own interests."

40 It is worth noting again that our understandings and interpretations of a child's best interests do not take place in a vacuum. Instead, they are inevitably coloured by how we think of childhood and the child's place in the family and in society, and thus by our conceptions of which families are considered "normal" and "good". This ties into the notions of normativity and normalising (disciplinary) power developed by Michel Foucault. Unfortunately there is no room in this context for engaging this immense and fruitful theoretical tradition, but for brief discussion see e.g. S. Koulu, "Arranging Child Care: the Autonomy of the Changing Family" (2013) *International Family Law, Policy and Practice* 121–128.

41 See for instance *Schneider v. Germany*, discussed also *supra* note 24.

6. CHILD'S FREEDOM OF RELIGION OR PARENTS' CONVICTIONS?

This far we have proposed that the child's circumstances should be more thoroughly and transparently considered in making decisions on exempting her from certain lessons or activities. We have also noted that at the same time, it is not enough to draw upon the principle of the best interests of the child, as the principle can often be employed to support both sides of the debate in a normative and normalising manner. In this section, then, we will discuss how the picture changes when the request of exemption is grounded on the freedom of religion of the child instead of the convictions of the parent.[42]

Sylvia Langlaude argues that the right of the child to religious freedom ought to be reviewed through the question of what it means for a child to be religious.[43] Her answer, in brief, is that children's religiousness should not be viewed through an adult perspective on religion, as children are not religious on their own but as members of their families and religious communities. They "are socialised and nurtured into a religious faith, in connection to their family and religious community".[44] Langlaude's message is about how we should approach the conflicts between the state, the parents, and the children. It can be illustrated by an interesting Swedish case from 2013 that, in our view, might give us clues on how to navigate these often intricate issues.

The case can be summarised as follows. It concerned a claim for exemption on the grounds of the child's freedom of religion.[45] In this case a girl, a member of a Christian minority (Laestadians), refused to take part in dancing lessons, as dancing was in breach of her convictions. Stating that the principle of proportionality is the leading principle of the Swedish administrative law, the administrative appellate court (Kammarrätten i Sundsvall, second instance administrative law court) found it central to find a fair balance between the freedom of religion of the girl and her parents, on the one hand, and the aims of the curriculum on the other. Noting that dance was only part of physical education, and the school had not explored any alternative ways for the child to

---

42 For a provocative discussion about the child's right to religious freedom, see L. Papadopoulou, "Children and Religious Freedom", in P. Lødrup and E. Modvar (eds.), *Family Life and Human Rights. Papers presented at the 11th World Conference of the International Society of Family Law,* Gyldendal akademisk 2004, pp. 533–551. Papadopoulou argues that if we accept freedom of religion as a subjective right, we need to accept that children should not be indoctrinated into a specific religion at all. Thus, freedom of religion would best be realized if children have already enjoyed it "in its special manifestation as freedom from religion" (p. 551).

43 S. Langlaude, *The Right of the Child to Religious Freedom in International Law,* Martinus Nijhoff Publishers 2007, pp. 34, 249.

44 Ibid., p. 34.

45 *Kammarrätten i Sundsvall,* 4 July 2013, *Mål nr 1494-12.* We would like to thank Laura Karppinen for bringing this case to our attention.

demonstrate her competence in the topic, the court ruled in favour of the girl and her parents.

While the applicants in this case were the parents, the argumentation of the court is based on an understanding of the freedom of religion that does not strictly distinguish between the religious rights of the child and religious rights of the parent. In our mind, what is noticeable in this case is how the court bases its decision on Article 9 of the European Convention in a manner that subtly emphasises the girl's own convictions without constructing arbitrary positions of the members of the family as independent holders of rights. This approach accepts that the religious rights of the child and her parents are inescapably intertwined and yet places the child at the centre of the decision-making. The court thus seems to avoid the pitfalls that Langlaude identifies in the international protection of the child's freedom of religion, namely the failure to fully grasp what it means for the child to be religious.[46]

Furthermore, the approach adopted in this case also seems congruent with the structure of the CRC, which after all emphasises the role and autonomy of the family in a child's upbringing. In 2011, the UN General Assembly adopted the Third Optional Protocol to the UN Convention on the Rights of the Child establishing a complaints procedure for violations of children's rights.[47] It remains to be seen whether the Committee on the Rights of the Child, within the framework of the new mechanism, will adopt a similarly child-centred approach as that demonstrated by the Swedish court in this case. The Committee might also consider placing greater weight on the child's right to universal education. In the light of Langlaude's research on the work of the Committee the latter prognosis seems more plausible. Indeed, Langlaude's analysis indicates that the Committee's strong emphasis on the individuality of the rights of the child and the need to nail down their specific substance might in some cases create oppositional positions between the state, parents and child, thus failing to mediate them.[48] While Langlaude does not place much hope in the ICCPR, it should be noted, in all fairness, that the Special Rapporteur on Freedom of Religion or Belief has also recognised the need for a finer account on children's rights to education and religion and the important role of both state institutions and parents in promoting these rights.[49]

---

46 S. Langlaude, *supra* note 43, p. 198. According to her analysis, this failure results in children's problems in having their voice heard in the European Court; "[it] ignores children when they are applicants, and silences them when they are directly or incidentally affected".

47 The Protocol allows bringing complaints before the Committee on the Rights of the Child regarding the violation of individual rights of the CRC. The Protocol was published for signature and ratification in 2012 and entered into force in 2014.

48 S. Langlaude, *supra* note 43, p. 248.

49 See the UN Special Rapporteur's Digest on Freedom of Religion or Belief, p. 38 (10 March 2011). The Special Rapporteur is appointed by the United Nations Human Rights Council, which monitors the ICCPR. See also *supra* note 6.

7. PLANNING FUTURE TRAVELS

We shall conclude our contribution by citing the words of David Archard and Colin M. Macleod, who wrote some fifteen years ago:

> "It no longer seems possible to posit a simple harmony between the interests of children and those charged with the responsibility of rearing them, such that the exercise of authority over children during their development of maturity can be viewed as a fairly straightforward matter. Instead the challenge is to deepen our understanding of children's interests and to explore how the conceptualization of children's interests affects the character of the moral claims they have."[50]

In short, we need to strive for such a deeper understanding of children's interests and to steer away from assumptions of "simple harmony" – and, conversely, from simple black-and-white oppositions. It is worthwhile to look for a more neutral approach such as that promoted by Ayelet Shachar in another context. Drawing on her own comprehensive research on private law litigation in Canadian courts, Shachar examines how Canadian courts recognise and evaluate cultural claims emerging in family law cases.[51] She places the "demystifying approach" to cultural claims between two absolutist alternatives: the "culture-neutralizing approach" and the "culture override approach". The first allows no weight be given to culture or religion in the courtroom, whereas the latter treats culture or religion as the paramount concern, a factor that overrides all other considerations regarding the life of the family or the child. We suggest that a similar continuum between two absolutist oppositions can be traced in debates about religion, education and children's rights. As we noted at the beginning of section 2 of this chapter, far too often the questions concerning children's rights are equated with the question of who – the state or the parents – has the authority over children. Framing the issue this way, as a conflict between the parents and the public interest, means that it is easy to lose sight of the child.

The case law of the European Court of Human Rights under Article 2 of the First Protocol points to the potential conflict between the public interest as to the moral content of education and the religious convictions of individuals. This conflict is most acutely drawn between parental authority and public authority over the children in question. Hence, the rights of the children, their opinions (participatory rights), their freedom of religion or their individual best interests risk being rendered invisible by the Court.

In addressing the issues of state curricula and religious convictions, a focus on the rights and interests of the child might offer the demystifying approach,

50 D. Archard and C.M. Macleod, "Introduction", in D. Archard and C. Macleod, *supra* note 36, p. 4.

51 A. Shachar, "Demystifying Culture" (2012) *International Journal of Constitutional Law* 429–448.

the middle way between the two absolutes. It is crucial to aim for a fair balance between the interests of the "universal" child and the "particular" child in the value conflicts that escalate in educational contexts. This calls for a more nuanced evaluation of the rights of the child and of her circumstances and situation. A comprehensively child-centred approach ought to be adopted also in Strasbourg, so that on future travels the feelings and interests of any children on the trip would be considered alongside those of the adults.

CARE PLACEMENTS OF CHILDREN OUTSIDE THEIR PARENTAL HOME – CONCERNS OF CULTURE

Sanne HOFMAN and Kirsten SANDBERG

1. INTRODUCTION

As part of a larger project, entitled "From formal rights to real rights" at the Institute of Women's Law at the Faculty of Law, University of Oslo, the subproject "Cultural considerations – in the best interests of the child?" analysed Norwegian decisions on taking minority children into care. The research question was how the "cultural background of the child" had been used as an argument in such decisions.[1]

More specifically, the questions were, first, in what ways the cultural background of the child had been used in the assessment of the basic requirements for taking a child into care, and second, how it had been taken into account in the best interests determination which has to be undertaken once the requirements are considered to be fulfilled. The third issue that emerged from looking into the cases

1 The subproject was undertaken by the Dutch children's rights lawyer and at that time research assistant Sanne Hofman, under the supervision of Professor Kirsten Sandberg. The report has been published in Norwegian, see Sanne Hofman, "Hensyn til kultur – til barnets beste?", *Kvinnerettslig skriftserie nr. 84/2010*, Department of Public and International Law, Oslo, available at www.jus.uio.no/ior/forskning/omrader/kvinnerett/publikasjoner/skriftserien/dokumenter/84-sanne-hofman.pdf.

was the consideration of culture in deciding where the child should be placed, that is, in what kind of a foster home.

In this chapter, a "minority child" is understood as a child with an ethnicity and cultural background other than Norwegian, and who may have a different language and/or religion (that is, not belonging to Norway's majority church, the Church of Norway). The term "cultural background" is used as the short form of "ethnic, religious, cultural and linguistic background", as in Article 20(3) of the Convention on the Rights of the Child.

Taking as a starting point the legal rules and their interpretation through the use of authoritative legal sources, not least by the Supreme Court of Norway, the project examined decisions from the county boards and the courts of first and second instance to see how the law was applied in practice. The county board is the competent body to decide that a child is to be taken into public care, whether or not with the consent of the parents or the child. It is an administrative body; however, it resembles a court in its independence and procedural safeguards to the extent that it is considered as a "court", e.g. under the European Convention of Human Rights. Its decisions may be brought before the court of first instance, the County Court, whose decisions may in turn be appealed to the Court of Appeal.

Searching for decisions in the database *Lovdata*, which is the official database containing sources of law in Norway, 75 decisions of interest for the project were found during the period 2000–2009. *Lovdata* is gradually becoming more comprehensive in its coverage of decisions made by courts and other bodies. For the relevant period, it covered practically all decisions from the Courts of Appeal, many decisions from the County Courts and a varying number of decisions from county boards. The interesting aspect of this research is not the figures, but the contents of the decisions. As it is partly up to the judges and the county board chairpersons what decisions to submit to *Lovdata*, there is reason to believe that the more interesting decisions have actually found their way there.

Out of the 75 decisions found, seventeen decisions were selected which explicitly mentioned the cultural background of the child. These consisted of seven decisions on immigrant children, five on refugee children, two on Sami children,[2] one on Roma children, and two decisions in which it was unclear whether the children were immigrant or refugee children.

An analysis of the cases revealed that the child's cultural background is an issue which decision-makers assess and evaluate in very different ways, without always making it clear what is considered and whether "culture" is in the best interests of the child and why it is or is not. The decisions seem to take either too much or too little account of the child's cultural background.

2 The Sami are an indigenous group in Norway, Sweden, Finland and Russia. The largest number of Sami people live in Norway, probably around 40,000 in a population of around 5 million.

2. THE LAW

The cultural background of the child has a strong position under Norwegian law. Through the incorporation of the Convention on the Rights of the Child (CRC) into the Human Rights Act of Norway in 2003, the Convention obtained the formal status of legislation but with precedence over other legislation in case of conflict. Article 20(3) of the CRC provides that due regard shall be paid to the child's ethnic, religious, cultural and linguistic background, which is repeated in the Norwegian Child Protection Act section 4-15 in order to make the child protection authorities aware of this obligation. In addition, Article 30 of the CRC gives minority and indigenous children the right to enjoy their culture, practise their religion and use their language in community with other members of their group. This does not, however, mean that harmful practices may be exercised; see Article 24(3).

The Supreme Court of Norway has made it clear that the child's cultural background has to be taken into account in the best interests consideration, and that it may override other important elements in that consideration. In the Supreme Court judgment in *Rt. 1997 p. 170*[3] a Pakistani boy aged six who had lived with a Norwegian foster family for almost five years was returned to his biological parents. According to the Supreme Court it was in the child's best interests to grow up with his biological parents and their way of life, culture and religion, even though he was a vulnerable boy who could only speak Norwegian whereas his parents did not speak Norwegian well. He had been raised as a "Norwegian" boy and had a very strong attachment to his foster parents.

Both the taking into care of the child and the actual placement afterwards must be in the child's best interests, according to the CRC and the Norwegian Child Protection Act. However, there are strict requirements in the Child Protection Act which have to be fulfilled before the best interests consideration may be undertaken. The best interests assessment cannot stand on its own, but is the final consideration to be carried out after the legal requirements are found to be fulfilled. The cultural background of the child is one of the elements in the best interests assessment.

Taking a child into public care means that the parents lose the right to have the child living with them and that the child is moved out of their home. The parents may no longer take decisions related to the daily care of the child. Legally under Norwegian law they still have parental responsibility for the child, but it is very limited once the child is taken into care. It is not clear from the law what the remaining responsibility encompasses. With regard to religion or culture, in practice the parents only retain the right to decide that the child shall still belong to their religion,[4] but they may not oblige the foster parents to practise the religion or culture in the daily life of the child. It is the foster parents who decide whether

3 *Rt.* is short for *Norsk Retstidende*, which is the Norwegian collection of Supreme Court judgments.

4 Provided the child is below 15 years of age. Above that age, he or she may decide for him/herself.

it suits them in their everyday life to, for example, serve halal food to the child, or whether to celebrate the holidays of the child's religion or culture.

According to the Child Protection Act section 4-12, the requirements for taking a child into care are: serious neglect of the child's physical or mental needs, failure to follow up a child's special need for health care or training, violence or sexual or psychological abuse, or risk of severe damage to the child's health or development because the parents are unable to take sufficient responsibility for the child. In addition, it must be necessary to take the child into care, meaning that preventive measures must have been tried or at least considered and found to be insufficient. Finally, it has to be determined whether it is in the child's best interests to be taken into care.

The legal requirements entail an assessment of whether the parents are able to provide the care that the child needs. What a child needs is to a certain extent culturally determined. The term "caring ability" implies a cultural and normative perspective of care. What is to be the norm for good enough care is a general question, but it stands out more sharply in relation to groups with a different way of life. A particular challenge of the county boards and the courts is to assess whether the care situation of the child is acceptable even if the way the child is raised is different from what is usual in the wider culture, or whether it is unacceptable and thus fulfils the legal requirement for taking the child into care.

Taking a child into care means that the child will live somewhere else than his or her parental home. There are several alternatives, but our project was limited to placement of children in foster homes. In the placement of minority children, according to Article 20(3) CRC, the Child Protection Act section 4-15 and the regulation on foster homes, due regard shall be paid to the child's ethnic, religious, cultural and linguistic background. The county board may include in its care decision a condition regarding the placement, e.g. that the child is to be placed in a foster home belonging to the same ethnic group as the child or in a family where at least one of the parents speaks the mother tongue of the child. When a child is placed outside his or her parental home by the authorities, the state has a strong obligation to go a long way to place a minority child in the culture where the child belongs or to ensure that the child has the possibility of retaining his or her cultural identity. That is true not least because of the right given to the child under Article 30 CRC to enjoy his or her culture, practise his or her religion and use his or her language in community with other members of his or her group. Taking the child into public care does not render this right invalid.

The right to practise one's culture and religion is not absolute. Cultural practices, whether majority or minority, must be in accordance with human rights, and no culture or religion is exempted from this limitation. The state has an obligation to actively combat harmful practices. However, the best interests of the child is the overarching principle, and as long as it is in the best interests of the child, the child has the right to enjoy his or her culture.

3. CULTURAL BACKGROUND IN THE CONSIDERATION OF SERIOUS NEGLECT

When the courts or the county boards consider whether the threshold of serious neglect has been reached, based on the lack of caring ability of the parents and the care needs of the child, the culture of the child in some cases is taken as the starting point. One case[5] concerned a Vietnamese mother with three children aged five, seven and twelve. The mother had been arrested thirteen times for theft and three times for driving without a licence, and she involved the children to a great extent in her criminal activities. In addition, there were many other problems and great doubt as to the emotional care she could provide for her children. After a series of voluntary measures had been undertaken for several years the County Board decided that the children were to be taken into public care. According to the Board, the insufficient emotional care she gave her children was not due to culture but to her lack of universal parenting abilities and her personality.

However, the County Court overturned the care decision because, in the court's view, the care situation in the family should not be viewed through Norwegian eyes. The Court of Appeal agreed with the child protection authorities that the mother did not show the physical, emotional signs of caring which have become common in this country, but according to the appointed cultural expert her caring ability was entirely in line with Vietnamese culture. The mother was not different from other Vietnamese mothers. The children were returned to the mother. It is worth noting in this case that the children's needs had changed from that of a better anchoring in Norwegian society to a better anchoring in Vietnamese culture.

4. REFUGEE CHILDREN

In other cases the cultural background of the child was not mentioned at all in the consideration of the basic requirements for taking a child into care. As it turned out these were mainly cases concerning refugee children. In these cases the focus was on the refugee background of the parents, in particular their psychological problems and traumatic experiences. It may seem that the latter determined the care needs of the children, rather than the care needs being the central issue. For example, in one case[6] a mother and her nine-year-old daughter had experienced horrible events before moving to Norway five years earlier. The mother suffered from memory problems due to a metal splint in her back, did not manage the activities of daily life, and had problems learning Norwegian and making herself

5 *FNV-2005-178-ROG* and *LG-2006-155198.*

6 *FNV-2006-203-OST.*

familiar with Norwegian society. In addition she had had several fits of psychosis. Nobody could tell whether she would be stable after her last serious fit. The child had been placed in a temporary foster home as a matter of urgency, was later returned and was now placed in a children's home. She did not want to return to her mother until her mother had recovered.

The care needs of the child were not visible in this case. The County Board only stated that the child's role as her mother's helper, interpreter and guide to Norwegian society was not as much of a strain on her as the Child Protection Services thought, because for the child this was only a matter of course – it had to be that way. The mother got her child back. However, pointing to the girl's role as being just a matter of course and a necessity under the circumstances does not explain what the child might really need. To all children their situation is as it is, but that does not mean it is acceptable. As it turns out, refugee children must apparently tolerate neglect to a greater extent than other children. It seems as if the care situation must be worse in these cases before the decision-maker agrees to placing the child in public care. The parents' background as refugees functions as an excuse for bad care.

5. PHYSICAL VIOLENCE

The study further showed that physical violence has a special position in the consideration of whether the basic requirements of the Child Protection Act section 4-12 have been fulfilled. While in some of the cases concerning emotional or psychological neglect the child's culture was taken as a starting point, that was not so in the cases regarding corporal punishment. In most of those cases the consideration of the parents' caring ability was based on what is common in Norwegian culture, first and foremost Norwegian society's zero tolerance approach to corporal punishment. In the cases where violence had been used against children, whether as a means of disciplining them or not, the parents' caring ability was generally considered to be insufficient, without regard to culture. True, the country boards and the courts did look at the cultural background of the parents, but the reasoning for the decision was that this kind of "care" is not accepted in Norway.

The fact that the parents used the same methods to raise their children as many others in their culture did not make a difference as regards violence. Whereas the way the Vietnamese mother treated her children was accepted because it was similar to what other Vietnamese mothers (allegedly) did, this way of thinking is not to be found in cases regarding physical violence. It seems to be more difficult to state that forms of maltreatment of children other than physical violence, such as emotional neglect, are unacceptable in Norway. It is an interesting question why emotional neglect is not treated in the same way as corporal punishment. Corporal punishment is not tolerated in Norway even if everybody else in that minority culture does the same thing. Nor is emotional neglect tolerated in general. However, when everybody else within a certain culture treats their children the same way, it is tolerated.

The reason for the difference may be that the law, psychology and society are less explicit as regards emotional neglect. The norms and the impact on children are less clear, which makes it more difficult to set the limits. The difference may also be due to it being more problematic to say that some culture-specific aspects of child-raising are not allowed, without running the risk of generalising it to the whole group or culture. Since there is zero tolerance of corporal punishment, we consider it different from continuous nagging and scolding the child, strict rules that are not in line with what is commonly accepted as being in the child's best interests and development, a lack of positive feedback or affectionate emotional expressions towards the child, spending the time cooking instead of being together with the child, etc. These ways of acting may be due to culture, but they may just as well be due to personal characteristics, or both.

6. THE BEST INTERESTS ASSESSMENT

The assessment of the child's best interests, which has to take place once the basic requirements for public care are fulfilled, is done in different ways. First, in half of the cases examined the county board or the court did not undertake a best interests assessment at all. Even if the child as a rule is taken into care when the basic requirements are fulfilled, i.e. when the child experiences serious neglect or abuse at home, a best interests assessment must be undertaken in each case in order to ensure that public care is actually in the child's best interests. Secondly, it was just as surprising to see that when the requirements were not fulfilled and a best interests assessment thus was not necessary, it was still undertaken, probably to underline that it was correct not to take the child into public care.

The best interests assessment in practice takes into account four main issues: the biological principle, stability and continuity, the needs and interests of the child, and the child's own views. In analysing the significance of the child's cultural background in each of these aspects, the most striking was that the cultural background seemed to strengthen the biological principle. Continuity was related to the original culture of the child, including cases where the child had never lived with his or her parents. The child's own views were mainly absent. The child was rarely asked about his or her wishes in relation to culture, religion or language, neither with regard to being taken into care nor in the choice of placement.

Culture as an element of best interests was viewed differently in different types of cases. In almost all cases the child's cultural background was considered to be an important point of departure, but for certain children it was easily outweighed by other considerations. This was true for immigrant children, children of minorities and Sami children, particularly in cases about corporal punishment. For refugee children, however, where the cultural background was generally not mentioned in the assessment of the basic requirements for placing a child into care, it was given great weight in the best interests assessment, against taking the child into care.

For example, in a case concerning a refugee family,[7] the parents were so traumatised that they did not at all manage to give their ten-year-old son sufficient care. The child protection services had tried all possible preventive measures for years. The County Board found the legal requirements of section 4-12 to be clearly fulfilled, as the boy was exposed to serious physical, psychological and emotional neglect. All the same, the child was not taken into public care because, in the Board's view, it was in the child's best interests to remain in the culture he knew and belonged to.

In another case,[8] two sisters of twelve and fourteen years of age from an Iraqi refugee family had independently of each other contacted the child protection authorities, because they could no longer stand their father's strict cultural and religious rules. Yet the decision to place the children in public care was annulled by the County Court in respect of one of the girls. Besides considering her to be a robust child who had demonstrated that she could state her own views, the Board also found it to be in her best interests to take part in her culture of origin to which her whole family belonged.

Even where the board or the court finds "the cultural background of the child" to be important to the child, they very rarely look more closely at the content of this concept in the best interests assessment, and *why* it is important for the child. Taking part in his or her culture of origin is considered to be valuable for the child, without any further elaboration of its value for this particular child in his or her concrete care situation.

7. THE PLACEMENT

One would expect that the cultural background of the child would be given great attention in the decision of where to place a child once it has been decided to take him or her into public care, especially as the Child Protection Act explicitly states that due regard is to be given to the child's cultural background in such decisions. This rule was adopted when in 2003 the CRC was integrated into the Human Rights Act, with reference to Article 20 CRC. However, in most county board decisions the placement issue was only summarily dealt with in a statement such as "the child is to be placed in an authorised foster family". The best interests of

7 *FNV-2005-67-AGD.*
8 *TRYFY-2006-4525.*

the child and the child's cultural background mostly were not discussed in that respect.

Whenever the care situation of the child is found to be below an acceptable level, it is understandable and consistent with the law that the cultural background of the child does not have a prominent place in the assessment of the child's best interests regarding whether or not to take the child into care. It is taken into consideration, but could hardly be decisive since all children have the same right to protection and to appropriate care above a minimum level. The issue of where to place the child once the decision to take the child into care has been made, however, is a different matter.

The decision on which specific foster home the child is to be placed in is not considered to be the type of formal decision where all the requirements of the Public Administration Act have to be met. It cannot be the object of a complaint to the county board or a lawsuit on its own but only as part of a lawsuit regarding the decision to take the child into care, and only where it does not fulfil a condition set by the county board in the decision to take the child into public care. If the county board did not set a condition other than the child being placed in a foster home, there is no possibility of appealing against the concrete placement. The problems that this may give rise to will be illustrated by one of the cases, concerning a Sami child, but in the material examined the same issue arose for immigrant children and children of national minorities as well.

In this case[9] the condition with regard to the concrete placement of the child was set by the County Court, which was of the opinion that this should have been done by the County Board. However, as we shall see, the Court did so unsuccessfully.

As soon as he was born, the Sami boy in the case in question was placed by the local Child Protection Services with his father's sister. Following the formal decision by the County Board to take the child into care, however, the Child Protection Services moved the child to a Norwegian foster family. The parents brought the case to court because they disagreed with the choice of foster home.

In the question of taking the child into care the court found that the parents were not capable of providing the child with acceptable care, and accordingly upheld the decision to take the child into care. In this care situation, the court would not place decisive weight on the child's cultural and linguistic background. Subsequently, the court considered the best interests of the child and the cultural argument with regard to the actual placement. The court wished to review whether the Child Protection Services had had due regard to the child's cultural and linguistic background in their choice of foster home, even though the County Board had not made a separate decision on the specific placement or set a condition in this regard. The court was of the opinion that in certain cases, in particular when the child's cultural background is not Norwegian, the type of foster home may be of fundamental importance to the child. With reference to, among others,

9 *TINFI-2006-154927.*

the Supreme Court decision in *Rt. 1997 p. 170* (section 2), the court found that it should have the option to review the choice of foster home.

Concretely, the court made an overall assessment of the best interests of the child and found that in the choice of foster home the Child Protection Services had not paid due regard to the cultural background of the child. In the Court's view, the arguments against placing the child with the father's family were not strong enough. The Court set as a condition for upholding the care decision that the child was placed in a foster home with the father's family, where at least one of the foster parents would speak Sami to the child.

This, however, was not the final word in the case. The Court of Appeal set aside the County Court's judgment, saying that the choice of foster home cannot be tried by the courts unless the County Board has made a decision in that regard, even if there are particular cultural and linguistic issues in the case.

What happened to the best interests of the child in the Court of Appeal is unclear. Strikingly, the child is invisible in its decision; the decision is all about procedural errors with great impact on the future of the child.

This underlines how important it is that the County Board, in cases where cultural considerations may be of particular significance, makes requirements as to the concrete placement of the child, which usually does not happen. Then there is no possibility of monitoring or reviewing whether the Child Protection Services have had due regard to the child's cultural background in the best interests assessment of the concrete choice of foster home.

The case was appealed to the Supreme Court, but unfortunately only with regard to a procedural issue. It would have been interesting to have a statement from the Supreme Court as to whether it agreed with the County Court or the Court of Appeal regarding review of the choice of foster family in cases where particular cultural or linguistic concerns are at stake.

Incidentally, the Court of Appeal judgment was set aside by the Supreme Court on the grounds that the County Court judgment had not been lawfully appealed. In a later decision by the Child Protection Services the case was withdrawn from the courts, and thus the County Court judgment became legally valid. However, the Sami boy did not move back to his Sami foster family. The Child Protection Services maintained that no one in the boy's family was capable of giving him appropriate care. We do not know how the case has further developed.

In the decision on where to place a child who is taken into alternative care, the consideration of the child's cultural background seems to have become the responsibility of the Child Protection Services but with no legal possibilities to monitor whether they have actually taken it into due account, unless the county board has set conditions in this regard. What is in the child's best interests in this respect is in most cases invisible. The same used to happen in relation to the issue of contact with the biological parents after a placement of a child. This issue was decided by the Child Protection Services, and the parents had no right to appeal the decision. The visibility of the right to contact, and its significance as a separate legal phenomenon, has increased over the last two decades. The choice of placement and its significance as a distinct legal phenomenon, especially whether due regard is paid to the child's cultural and linguistic background, still is not visible in decisions from courts and county boards. Thus, the legal consideration of the child's cultural background is not a reality in the choice of placement in practice. This also affects the right of the child under Article 30 CRC to enjoy his or her own culture in community with other members of his or her group. In our view the legal safeguards for the child's rights in this respect are not sufficient, and the actual placement is not necessarily in the best interests of the child. The law is there, but it needs to implemented in practice.

8. OVERALL EVALUATION

Decisions about taking a child into care, as well as considerations of the best interests of the child in general, have to be made according to the specific situation of the individual child. Yet under the Convention and Norwegian law due regard shall always be paid to the child's cultural background, both in respect of the question of taking a child into care and in the choice of actual placement. "Due regard" does not mean that it is always in the best interests of the child to remain with the biological parents or to be placed in a family of the same culture. Nor does it mean that this is the only relevant aspect of the child's care situation. It is the whole child and the entire care situation that are under consideration.

"Due regard" for the child's cultural background is about not paying too much or too little attention to it. More importantly, it is about asking the right questions of what culture means in this situation and how important it is for this individual child. If "the cultural background of the child" is given a more specific content, it is easier to decide how much weight is to be attached to it, and whether it actually is in the best interests of the child. It is possible to identify cultural characteristics which we consider negative or positive in the care situation, without attributing them to whole groups of children or parents. The same is true for "refugee background". One has to define what it means and what effects it has on the needs of the individual child and the care that the parents can provide.

Realising this gives us an opening to discuss what counts as good enough emotional care in our society, just as we have had a discussion on corporal punishment. This would make it easier to focus on the care needs of the child and how regard for the child's cultural background fits into this picture. It is not the other way round, making the cultural background the starting point and then seeing how the child's needs fit into that.

Yet it is important to remember that even if the child's cultural background is not always the decisive element in the best interests of the child with regard to taking a child into care, the child still has the right to enjoy his or her culture after placement. The degree to which this is possible depends on whether or not a foster home with the same cultural background is found for the child. There is a lot to be said about the recruitment of foster homes of different cultural backgrounds which we will not go into further here. If the foster home does not have the same background, it can still, to a certain extent, be required or expected to support the child in practising his or her own culture. In addition, the child's rights in this respect may at least partially be realised through contact with the biological family, a support person and/or a weekend home with the same cultural background.

CHILD MARRIAGES AND THE LAW – WITH SPECIAL REFERENCE TO SWEDISH DEVELOPMENTS

Göran LAMBERTZ

1. INTRODUCTION

1.1. THE PROBLEM

Almost everyone will agree, regarding child marriage:

- that it is wrong,
- that it robs far too many children of their chance to a life of their own choice,
- that we need to protect children against it, and
- that society should be more active in trying to do something about it.

The difficulties arise when we start considering concrete measures. What should in fact be done, and how forcefully should we react? Is it enough to try to change long-term attitudes of some parents and relatives? Or must we change the law to make it quite clear to everyone that child marriages are never acceptable? But do we really mean "never"? What if a girl becomes pregnant and her religion prohibits her from giving birth without first getting married? Should there not be an exception for at least those cases?

What makes these questions particularly difficult is the fact that even if most of us agree that it is wrong for children to get married, there are many who believe that it is not necessarily so. The issue at stake is to a great extent a cultural phenomenon. It is a fact that in certain cultures child marriages are accepted, and even common. What conclusions should be drawn from that? Should we disregard those who have an "unacceptable" view from a majority standpoint? Or should we treat their view as equal to ours and refrain from intruding? Is it in fact discriminatory to interfere with "the view of other cultures"? Or should we act firmly based on majority values only? If we do, how do we show others the necessary respect? Or is there no need for that?

These questions touch on a legislative issue which is nowadays topical in Europe to a much greater extent than before: should the legislator take into consideration the fact that society is multicultural and that values are not as homogeneous as they used to be? Some say that "here we are all governed by the law of this country, no matter what we believe and what our values are, and the law should be the same for all of us". Others say that "the legislator must respect minority values at least to the extent that those values do not hurt people outside of the minority". Which view is right and which is wrong? The answer is perhaps not self-evident, at least not from the outset.

Whatever position we take, it seems we are facing a double problem of a kind which is rather unusual when it comes to legislation:

(a) We need to protect children against getting married much too early. How can this be done efficiently, with acceptable legislative and/or other measures?

(b) In giving children the protection they need, to what extent should we give consideration to the fact that in many cases their families and relatives believe this to be an unjust intrusion into their lives and values?

1.2. THE AIM AND FOCUS OF THIS CONTRIBUTION

The aim of this contribution is to analyse and try to answer the difficult problems of child marriages and the law. And it is to take a standpoint, from a reasonably informed background, on the issue of what legislation should be passed, if any. The focus is in particular on Sweden, but the analysis and conclusions are in principle valid for all Europe and many other parts of the world.

If any measures should be taken against child marriages, it is not necessarily legislation. It could be more important that we try to make sure, for example,

- that schools and authorities understand the problem;
- that they can identify the problem and take appropriate measures;
- that there is a well-established method for family contacts in acute situations;
- that there is a central national body which can lead, coordinate and support;
- that there is a respectful but efficient dialogue with the adults concerned; and
- that religious leaders are persuaded to speak up against child marriage.

In this contribution, however, I will only deal with the issue of legislation: what should the legislator do, if anything? I will not deal with all possible legislative measures, but only those which would probably be most important. It so happens that those measures are at the same time the most controversial ones.

The problem is of a particular nature if the child is induced to marry against her or his own will. From a legislative standpoint those situations are easier to deal with than those which involve children who do not oppose to getting married. Here, in principle, I only deal with those child marriages where it cannot be proven that the parents or relatives have forced or even put pressure on the child to marry.

The vast majority of children who marry are girls. To make the discussion less complicated I will limit myself to talking about girls only.

1.3. OUTLINE

In section 2 I briefly describe the problems with child marriages. My focus will be on Sweden, but most of what I say is valid for most parts of Europe and many other countries of the world. In section 3 I discuss, from a general standpoint, whether legislative action is justified and whether the gains will exceed the losses. After that I focus more closely on two possible legislative solutions. In section 4 I discuss whether all child marriages should be banned, or whether an exception should be available in special cases, due to particular concerns. In section 5 I discuss the issue of criminalisation. If child marriages should be criminalised, who would then be seen as committing a crime? What, more precisely, constitutes the criminal offence? And should we also criminalise those "marriages" which are not formally marriages (by law) but have in practice the same effects? In section 6 I look at the important question of how we could mitigate the negative effects of a prohibitive legislation, should it be passed. And in section 7, finally, the conclusions are summarised and to some extent further reflected on.

1.4. MY OWN ROLE AND ENGAGEMENT

A few words should be said about my own role in this. Between 2010 and 2012 I acted as the chairperson of a legislative project, initiated by the Swedish Government, concerning forced marriages and child marriages. The project involved experts with different professional backgrounds and a full time secretary. In this contribution, I refer to the project as the FCMP (Forced and Child Marriages Project). We produced a report which was handed over to the Cabinet of Ministers in May 2012.[1] In the report we made some proposals regarding both new legislation and other measures.

In March 2014 a government bill was presented to Parliament including most of the proposals in our report and some more.[2] The bill was passed and the new legislation entered into force on 1 July 2014.

2. SOME POINTS OF DEPARTURE

2.1. CHILD MARRIAGES: THE PROBLEM AND ITS SCOPE

What is the problem of children getting married? Is it not evident that parents normally know what is best for their child and act on the basis of this knowledge? Whatever the case may be, if the parents have made a decision and the child has accepted it, why is it a problem for society and the legislator to be concerned about?

The problem is, in short, that children are deprived of their right to decide for themselves what to do with their lives. The relevance of this is considerable. Most children trust their parents to know what is best for them, and do not question the decisions that the parents make for them. They do not do so until many years later, when it is often too late to make changes. Early marriage often leads to schooling

---

1 English title: *Strengthened protection against forced marriages and child marriages*, 665 pages, Statens Offentliga Utredningar (SOU) 2012:35, Stockholm 2012, summary in English on pp. 37–51. A list of literature etc., in Swedish, is included in pp. 561–573. The English summary is included as an Annex to this book.

2 Government Bill (prop.) 2013/14:208.

being discontinued. Lack of education can result in long-term alienation and major difficulties in getting into the labour market and earning a living. This risk is amplified by the fact that the girl becomes closely linked to the husband and his family. This happens not only due to the marriage itself, but because of the common children and through financial ties.

It is an important principle that human beings should not be deprived of their right to make the important decisions for their own lives. That is what child marriage does to girls.

There are numerous examples of very young girls who marry much older men. This is much less common in Europe than in some other parts of the world, but with migration it occurs also in Europe. The girls are mostly not forced to marry, at least not in the strictest sense of the word. But it is seldom something they choose of their own volition. It must be remembered that most children are not capable of making sensible choices when it comes to matters which will affect the rest of their lives.

It is not possible to give any exact figures on how common child marriages are. The main reason is that many of these relations are legally not marriages. The reason for this is they are not entered into according to the law of the state, but according to the rules of religions or traditions. And yet they are quite problematic in the sense that we are discussing here, because the "spouses" themselves and their relatives and friends look upon them as married. The reason is that they have been through a marriage ceremony of a kind which causes the ties between them to be strong. For one thing they cannot break up the relationship without going through certain dissolution procedures imposed by the culture or faith.

It is very important that these "informal marriages" are taken into account when the problem of child marriages is discussed. And they should be characterised as child marriages in a broader sense, because they carry with them the most important characteristics of "normal" marriages and appear to be just as problematic.

In the project mentioned above (FCMP) we tried to get hold of figures which would give us a reasonably accurate picture of the number of child marriages in Sweden. We learned that in December 2011 there were thirteen children in Sweden aged 15–17 who were registered as married. In that same year the Swedish Migration Board handled eleven cases which involved a child marriage in matters concerning residence permits. And in the year 2011 the Swedish Tax Agency, i.e. the Swedish authority in charge of registration in population records, handled a total of seventy cases regarding national registration of a child marriage concluded abroad. In all those cases, at least one of the partners was, at the time of the marriage, either a Swedish national or a resident of Sweden. The number of children living in informal marriages is thought to be several times higher than these figures on formal child marriages indicate.

On top of this are those relations which in many ways cause the most serious concerns. By this I mean the girls who are sent to the countries of origin of their families to marry there, often a much older man, and to stay with the husband in that country, at least for an interim period. Swedish schools report on such cases every year.

I think it is fair to estimate that 400–500 girls living in Sweden who are still children, i.e. below 18 years of age, are either married or about to get married. This estimation includes informal marriages. Sweden (2015) has a population of approximately 10 million inhabitants.

On a global basis the problem is of course much greater. In a report published in 2012 from the United Nations Population Fund (UNFPA), it is estimated that one out of every three girls in developing countries (excluding China) will be married before they are 18 and one out of nine before 15. Most of these girls are poor, less educated, and living in rural areas. In 2010 over 67 million women aged 20–24 had been married before they turned 18. It is estimated that in the next decade 14.2 million girls under 18 will be married every year. That translates into about 39,000 girls every day. And the numbers are rising.[3]

Even if quite a few girls are directly affected by the problem of child marriage, it is certainly much more than a matter of quantity. It is the stories that these girls tell that makes one understand the depth and the seriousness of the problem. While I worked on FCMP, new cases popped up on a regular basis, each girl having a narrative of her own: the 15-year-old who was persuaded to travel to Iraq for the summer holidays, and was left there to be married to her 28-year-old cousin; the 16-year-old who, after a similar experience, left her husband, also in Iraq, and had a child with her beloved one, with the result that the baby was killed by her relatives. And so on. Hearing these narratives, one is easily persuaded to believe that it is absolutely necessary to do something about the practice of child marriage.

Child marriages are often connected with non-Western cultures which – as far as Europe is concerned – have found a place in Western societies during the last few decades. Such marriages are also often connected with honour-related violence and oppression. This knowledge is important in order to understand the core of the problems. At the same time it is essential to take the starting point from a human rights perspective, which gives rise to the following question: is it a human right not to be married off as a child? Most of us would, I think, say that it ought to be. We will return to this issue in section 3.

The questions are there to be answered: is this a problem for the legislator to handle? What consideration should be given to the fact that to some people child marriage is not necessarily bad, or at least not so bad that the parents should not have the right to decide? Remember that we are not talking about forced marriages. We are discussing the situation of girls who feel they should do what their parents ask them to do and may well agree to that. Should we legislate against that?

---

3 UNFPA Report, *Marrying too young*, 2012, p. 6.

2.2. THE CURRENT LAW

Most countries have a *fixed minimum marriage age*, i.e. an age below which people are not allowed to marry. In Sweden, as in most countries in Europe, the age is 18. In the United Kingdom it is 16.

But the laws of most countries also provide a possibility for children to marry under that age, in exceptional cases, after a *special permission* has been granted by the competent authority. The reason for granting a special permission is often that the situation for a girl would be very difficult if she would not be able to marry. Often it is because she is pregnant and because it is shameful or against the family's religion or culture to give birth to a child without being married.

I know of no country where child marriage is *criminalised*. And there are obvious problems with criminalising it. Firstly, who is the criminal, i.e. the person committing the criminal offence? Is it the man who marries the girl, the parents or the person performing the wedding ceremony? What about the girl herself? Secondly, how do we deal with the fact that a large number of the marriages are entered into abroad, where a different law applies? Thirdly, how do we handle the informal marriages? Criminal law must be reasonably clear. People should know, at least in principle, when they risk facing criminal punishment. If we want to criminalise informal marriages, how do we separate them from relationships where the couple is just living together?

Some countries have laws whereby child marriages concluded abroad are normally *not recognised*. That means that the "spouses" are not registered as married and that the "marriage" does not carry with it the legal consequences of a marriage. Normally, according to an established position of private international law, a marriage entered into abroad is valid in other countries if it is valid in the state of celebration. In Sweden, however, since 2004, a marriage entered into abroad is not recognised in Sweden if at the time of the wedding it would not have been possible for the couple to marry according to Swedish law, due to a marriage obstacle such as the lack of the required age to marry.[4] This applies on condition that at least one of the two was a Swedish citizen or had habitual residence in Sweden. This provision normally prevents foreign child marriages from being recognised in Sweden. There is, however, also a clause of exception here. The marriage is to be recognised if there are "special reasons" to do so. One such reason could be that the marriage was celebrated many years ago and it would be unreasonable not to recognise it in the circumstances.[5]

I do not know of any other kinds of protection for children, directly by law against the practice of child marriage, than the ones mentioned above. And the most important of them is of course the stipulation of a minimum marriage age.

4 See Act (1904:26 s. 1) on Certain International Legal Relations regarding Marriage and Guardianship, Ch. 1 §8 a.

5 See Government Bill (prop.) 2003/04:48 p. 56.

One other possibility of protection directly by law would be a *prohibition on performing* wedding ceremonies concerning children. Such a prohibition could include both such ceremonies where a legally binding marriage is intended to take place and those which result "only" in an informal marriage. Another alternative is to limit it to covering only legally binding marriages. There could also be a rule in migration law whereby a child can never be granted a permanent residence permit based on marriage if the marriage took place when one of the two was still a child, from the point of view of the granting state. Other measures could also be considered. In section 3 we will look at some possible additions or changes in the law.

In many countries there is a kind of protection against child marriage which could be labelled as taking place "indirectly" by the force of law. One example is rules whereby it is a duty for social services to take actions to prevent children from getting married, and for schools to report cases where pupils are at the risk of being married off. Another example is laws which make it compulsory for immigrants to learn about family laws and customs of the host country.

3. LEGISLATION OR NOT?

3.1. QUESTIONS TO BE RAISED

When you ask the question whether a law should be enacted to solve a certain problem, you always need to judge whether legislation is justified in the first place. But you also need to give thoughts to the possibility that legislation may not be the best tool to achieve the effect you want, and to the possibility that the drawbacks of a new law may be greater than the gains.

In dealing with child marriages, as we have seen, one more consideration needs to be included: is the drafting of legislation an appropriate measure when some groups have reason to feel that this legislation is to a certain extent aimed at them? This consideration is particularly sensitive if the groups concerned are vulnerable. And that is to a large extent the case when it comes to the practice of child marriages.

3.2. GENERAL CONSIDERATIONS

It is fundamental for all legislation that new laws should be passed only when the matter is:

(a) important enough, and
(b) of concern for the legislator.

Laws are normally not passed regarding how people dress or the colour of cars. Nor do we legislate to tell people how to bring up their children[6] or to tell churches what to preach. Laws should be efficient, or at least have the potential to be efficient. And they should be as clear as possible, fair and understandable. The negative effects of the law should not outweigh the positive. New legislation regarding child marriages should meet all these requirements.

The legislator must always make sure that national laws are consistent with international conventions and other supranational legislation by which the state is bound. When it comes to child marriages, the UN Convention on the Rights of the Child is of particular interest.[7] According to this Convention the best interests of the child should always be a primary consideration (Article 3(1)). The states which are parties to the Convention shall undertake appropriate measures regarding children's economic, social and cultural rights to the maximum extent of their available resources (Article 4). States shall also ensure, to the maximum extent possible, the development of the child (Article 6(2)) and protect children against all kinds of sexual abuse (Article 34).

Whether these provisions in the Children's Convention require states to prevent child marriages is an interesting question which, as far as I know, has not been subject to a legal analysis to any great extent. It falls outside the scope of this contribution to enter into such an analysis. But it is, to my belief, quite possible to consider that the provisions by which states have a duty (a) to ensure the development of the child to the maximum extent possible, and (b) to protect children against all kinds of sexual abuse carry with them an obligation for the state to prevent child marriages, and to do so efficiently.

Marrying much too young deprives the girl of her right to decide for herself what to do with her life. Early marriage often means that the girl leaves school, which in turn means lack of education, often long-term alienation and severe difficulties in getting into the labour market and earning a living. All these effects are extremely important in someone's life. Stopping child marriages should therefore be a serious concern for those states where the practice exists. This means the problem is important enough for the legislator, and something which is certainly the legislator's responsibility.

That being said, it must be underlined that other kinds of measures could also very well be needed. It seems very important, for example, to train teachers and other professionals who meet the child to see the signs that a child marriage is likely to take place, to act on these signs and to act properly. Equally important

6 One exception from this principle is the prohibition on spanking of children introduced in Sweden in 1979. Laws of the same nature have since then been enacted in almost forty countries.

7 The 1950 European Convention on the Protection of Human Rights and Fundamental Freedoms does not include any provision which concerns child marriages specifically. It is possible however, that Article 8, regarding the right to protection for private life and family life, could be invoked by a woman married off as a child against her State for not protecting her against early marriage. So far no such case has been tried by the European Court of Human Rights.

could be to create a national body with the knowledge and resources to educate, give advice and help in acute situations, etc. And a third very important measure could be the promotion of knowledge on how to act efficiently but respectfully towards parents who are about to marry off their young daughter. In this contribution, however, I only deal with legislative measures.[8]

As stated above, no legislation should be enacted unless there is reason to believe that it can achieve its goals. This requirement is extremely important where child marriages are concerned, as we shall see in sections 4 and 5. There are different ways to avoid the law for those who are determined to circumvent it. But that does not necessarily mean that the law has not been efficient. What really counts is if the law changes people's behaviour so that there are considerably fewer child marriages with the assistance of the law than before it was passed. This is of course difficult to estimate. But if the law is successful in sending a clear signal that society does not accept child marriages, this should be sufficient.

The last question to ask in these general considerations is whether the drawbacks of legislation will outweigh the gains. This is a difficult question to answer because it is not easy to know what the effects will be. And yet, this is something that must be analysed carefully before any decisions on legislative measures are taken.

3.3. DIFFERENCES IN CULTURE AND VALUES ARE INVOLVED

One issue of particular interest concerning possible legislation against child marriages is the fact that such marriages are, in European countries, to a large extent a practice which exists in immigrant and minority groups only. This is not true, of course, from the perspective of some of the countries where the practice is common. In my contribution, however, the issue is discussed from a European and, in particular, from a Swedish perspective.

Why should such an insight matter? Why should we take into consideration the fact that child marriages exist in certain groups and not in others? The reason is that it complicates any legislative measure, and does so in at least three different ways:

(a) *The group/culture problem.* We must ask the question whether it is reasonable for the legislator to take the majority standpoint only, and to disregard the

8 Anyone interested in a discussion relating to other measures is advised to read the English summary of the FCMP Report, *Strengthened protection against forced marriages and child marriages*, Stockholm 2012, pp. 47 ff. For a more detailed text, however only in Swedish, see chapters 20–22. The English summary of the report is included as an Annex to this volume.

view of the groups affected that some child marriages are acceptable. To what extent should the legislator take into consideration the fact that society is multicultural and that values are not as homogeneous as they used to be? Is it in fact discriminatory, or an intrusion into the freedom of some groups or cultures, to interfere with their view? That is sometimes the standpoint of the legislator. One example is the freedom of religion argument which is often invoked for allowing, under certain circumstances, the practice of circumcision of boys.

(b) *The family/privacy problem.* We must also ask whether the problems of child marriages are of a kind that should be left to the families concerned to solve. If it is the opinion of the parents that marrying is best for the girl, why should the legislator know better? How far should the legislator go in interfering with people's views regarding issues that are to a great extent of a private or family nature?

(c) *The negative effect problem.* If we pass stricter legislation against child marriages to the effect that some groups feel attacked by the majority of society, how can we counteract this negative effect? And how can we counteract the reaction, which may seem logical, that the legislator is acting in a xenophobic way? How can we make sure that legislative measures will not create more difficulties than they can solve?

How should we deal with *the group/culture problem*? Is it acceptable for the legislator to disregard the views of minorities, or does disregard amount to discrimination? This is not an easy question. If it has been a strong custom for centuries in a group that young people "marry" in a traditional way, and this is believed to be both natural and right, then it is clearly not obvious that society should interfere. Some Roma groups could be mentioned as an example. Among some Roma in Sweden it is not uncommon for children at the age of 16–17 to move in with each other and are – at least by some – considered "married".[9] The Romas have been discriminated against for a very long time in Europe, Sweden included. Should society then interfere with a tradition of theirs which the Roma groups themselves might not see as particularly problematic?

Would one possible solution to the group/culture problem be to give scope for exceptions in the law? Could we, for example, make an exception for Roma groups from a law prohibiting child marriages? I think that this is not a road to be chosen. I would not entirely rule out the possibility of sometimes having separate laws governing certain groups, but it is clear that exceptions for groups from specific obligations would create great consequential problems: who belongs to the group? Should an exception also be made for other groups? It would also be very difficult to explain group exceptions like this to the public. And what about the efficacy of

---

9 This information was given by Swedish Roma representatives at meetings within the Forced and Child Marriages project mentioned earlier.

law? If we leave out the groups where an unwanted practice exists, then who will at all be caught by the law?

So the question remains: should we legislate even though it can be seen as a measure directed against the group? This boils down, I believe, to the question of whether regard for the interests of the children concerned is more important than regard for the interests of the group. To this many would respond that "the interests of the individual must outweigh the interests of the group". But it is clear that this is not always the case. If the individual's interest is a rather weak one and the group's interest is of the utmost importance to the group, then the group interest should normally prevail. Let us take an example from mosques. If some individuals want to wear shoes there and the congregation says no to this, then it is obvious that the legislator should not support a plea from the individuals to give them the right to wear shoes.

So we need to weigh the interests in the particular case. Does the interest of girls not to be married while they are still children outweigh the interest of the group – for example a Roma or a Muslim group – that this practice will continue to be allowed and that the group is saved from the stigmatisation and xenophobia to which legislation risks contributing? I believe that it does. The freedom of girls to make decisions regarding their own lives is certainly an interest of the utmost importance. And the big decisions – with whom you will spend the rest of your life, when you will have children, whether you should get an education or not, etc. – should at least in principle not be taken while you are still a child, but wait until you are an adult. Therefore it is very important to stop a practice which in fact prevents a girl from postponing the most important decisions in her life. Furthermore, a fear of xenophobia or stigmatisation cannot be allowed to result in a lack of attention on the part of society to the individual's exposure to harmful practices. Instead measures should be taken to prevent any xenophobia and stigmatisation that may arise. It cannot be accepted that children from minorities are refused the protection considered self-evident for children belonging to the majority in society.

In my opinion the interests of the individual in this case clearly outweigh the interests of the group.

Is it acceptable, then, for the legislator to interfere with *the view of the girl's family* that it is in her best interest to marry early, and to the man the family has chosen for her? Should this be for the parents to decide? Why should society know better, particularly if it is a society which is not familiar with the traditions and views of the family? To what extent should the legislator intrude at all in rather private matters? It is true that in European countries the law normally prohibits the parents to assault the child, and it requires the parents to put the child in school, bring up the child in reasonably safe surroundings, etc. But should the law also require the parents to see to it that the child does not marry before a certain age?

These are basically the same questions as the ones mentioned above, concerning legislation "against a group". The problem in principle is this: are the interests of the child more important than the interests of the family?

It is clear that sometimes the interests of the child are more important, and sometimes the interests of the family. The legislator will not tell the family what food to put on the table for the child to eat. But the legislator will certainly interfere with the question of whether the child should be taken to hospital when seriously ill. So, here too the question must be answered for the specific issue.

Does the interest of girls not to be married while they are still children outweigh the interest of the family to be able to make decisions of that kind for her? In my mind it is quite clear that it does. Again, the freedom of girls to make decisions regarding their own lives is an interest of great importance. The really big decisions in her life should not be taken while she is still a child, when it can normally be expected that she does not understand the real impact of them. The interest of the family, of privacy in matters of this kind, should therefore not prevent the enactment of legislation against child marriages.

Yet another aspect should be considered: could the girls themselves perhaps be put at risk if laws are introduced to stop them from marrying young in their home country, i.e. the state where the family is habitually resident? The risk to be taken into account is that some girls might be sent abroad to marry. If that is the case, nothing has been gained for those particular girls. However, legislation in one country cannot reasonably be stopped because of a risk that some people will avoid the law in that country by leaving.

The *conclusion* is that legislation should be enacted in order to protect children from child marriages. Having established this, we need to return to the earlier discussion on how differences in both culture and values can be taken into consideration. It is of the utmost importance that legislation against child marriages *does not cause unnecessary harm*. Therefore it needs to be considered how this can be achieved. Could any particular measures be taken to alleviate the possible reaction among the groups affected that the legislator is acting against them and to prevent xenophobic attitudes in society from gaining ground? We will come back to this question in section 6.

3.4. POSSIBLE LEGISLATIVE MEASURES

I cannot discuss in detail all possible legislative measures against child marriages. However, it is certainly of some interest to envisage what kinds of measures could be contemplated. I will therefore start by listing those which I can think of, and explain them very briefly.[10]

10 The listing of the possible legislative measures is done from a Swedish perspective. It may be that in other countries some of the measures mentioned have already been taken or would be

(a) *Licence to perform marriages.* Not just anyone is allowed to perform legally valid marriages, but only persons who can do it in a particular capacity (e.g. ministers of a state church, judges in some legal systems, etc.) and persons who are given a specific licence, normally by a state body. To prevent child marriages – including so-called informal marriages – we could put some special requirements on those who already have the required licence or are applying for it. It could for example be required for religious communities and wedding officiators who have received permission to perform marriages that they do not carry out any child marriages at all, or otherwise they will lose their permission. Since there is a marriage age requirement, this measure would in practice be directed only against informal marriages, i.e. those "traditional marriages" which do not result in a legally binding alliance but have the same effect in practice (see section 5.2).
(b) *Stricter rules for recognition of child marriages abroad.* As was mentioned before, in section 2, Swedish private international law contains rules which in principle prevent the recognition of child marriages entered into abroad, if at the time of the marriage there was a close link to Sweden. This is very important, since a prohibition to marry as a child would otherwise be almost an empty letter. As it is today, the limits to recognition only apply to persons who have a strong connection to the country in which recognition is sought. There are also exceptions which will prevent refusal to recognise in cases where there are strong reasons to accept the marriage, for example if it was performed many years earlier. It could be discussed whether these rules should be made stricter, for example to the extent that no exceptions are made to the rule that child marriages will not be recognised.
(c) *Stricter rules on proxy marriages.* In some countries and some cultures it is accepted that the marriage is concluded on behalf of the spouses-to-be in the absence of them or one of them. In these "proxy marriages" it is common for a relative to present a written authorisation from the party not present, and for the marriage to be registered based on this. A possible legislative measure could be to never recognise such marriages where the parties have not both been present at the wedding, and maybe even to make it a crime to induce or allow a proxy marriage.
(d) *Making it more difficult to obtain residence permit.* If the woman (or the girl) is a citizen or has a permanent residence permit in a certain country, her husband will normally also be granted a permanent permit to live in that country, due to the marital bond. But if the marriage is not recognised, he will not be granted such a permit. If special interviews are conducted by the migration authorities, as is the case in Sweden, the results of the interview

---

regarded to be irrelevant, because of the legal surroundings. In the Report of the FCMP, all the measures mentioned above are discussed, and some of them proposed. For a short version in English, see pp. 49–51 of the Report.

will therefore often be important for him. The question for the authorities in Sweden will be whether there are "special reasons" to recognise the child marriage (see section 2.2). The woman (or girl) may be secretly against the marriage and against the man getting a residence permit. To get truthful answers from her, there could therefore be reason to interview her without anybody from the family listening. But then there is the dilemma that if she answers truthfully, it could put her at danger. Therefore, a possible legislative measure could be to allow for her answers to be kept secret even though they will play a role in the decision of the authorities.

(e) *No exceptions to the marriage age rule.* The minimum age for marrying is, in most Western countries, 18 years. This is the case in Sweden. But in most countries, it is also possible to marry below the minimum age in exceptional cases. In Sweden, before the 2014 law reform the exception was usually granted if the girl would soon be 18 and was pregnant, if it was very difficult for her – because of her religion and family tradition – to give birth to the child without being married. Should this possibility of granting an exception to the rule be abolished?

(f) *Criminalisation.* Finally, a possible legislative measure to prevent child marriages is criminalisation. Parents who initiate marriage for their underage daughter would be performing a criminal act. The same could apply for others who actively take part in arranging the marriage.

In my opinion, it is clear that of all these possible legislative measures, the last two have the most potential to make a difference, that is (e) a fixed marriage age without exception, and (f) criminalisation. These two are at the same time those possibilities which are, in my experience, the most controversial ones in the sense that people have very different views regarding their appropriateness. In sections 4 and 5 I will discuss these two measures in more detail.

3.5. CONCLUSION

It is clear that the issue of child marriages is per se a matter for the legislator. It is important enough and it concerns matters which belong in the legislative sphere. Whether the positive sides of legislation outweigh the negative is a question which cannot be answered without first analysing the cultural and family aspects of it, and without analysing the drawbacks and gains of each specific measure.

The reason for legislation – to protect girls – in my opinion clearly outweighs the interests of those who may regard themselves as being attacked by legislative measures against child marriages. But if measures are taken, the legislator should also make efforts to alleviate any negative effects for those groups and families concerned.

4. NO POSSIBILITY OF EXCEPTIONS TO MARRIAGE AGE?

4.1. THE QUESTION

As mentioned, most countries have a stipulated minimum marriage age. In Sweden it is 18, which is also the age when a person goes from being a child to becoming an adult. But most countries also have, by law, a possibility for children to marry in exceptional cases, after special permission from a competent authority.

Is it necessary, or at least well founded, to keep a possibility for children to marry in special cases? Or should this possibility be abolished so that there is no way of legally getting married in the country concerned below the age limit set by law? Let us look at the arguments for and against.

4.2. THE ARGUMENTS FOR KEEPING THE POSSIBILITY OF EXCEPTIONS

The main arguments for keeping a possibility for children to marry in exceptional cases, after special permission, are as follows:

(a) The state should not unnecessarily interfere with people's private lives. If a girl who is very mature for her age wishes to marry, knows very well what she is doing and gets the "blessing" of everyone around her, it could be claimed to be strange that the state should forbid her to.
(b) Sometimes it creates great difficulties for a girl and her family if she is not allowed to marry until she has reached a certain age. In some groups it will be very unfavourable for both the mother and the child if the child is born out of wedlock. In some religious surroundings it is just not accepted. If a girl becomes pregnant there may be in practice, from the family's deeply felt point of view, only one alternative: that she gets married to the father of the child. Abortion may, from a religious or cultural point of view, be just as unacceptable as the alternative of giving birth to the child outside of wedlock.
(c) If the couple cannot marry in Sweden, there is always a possibility for them to marry abroad in a county permitting the marriage. Why then prevent them from getting married in Sweden, where they live?

4.3. THE ARGUMENTS FOR A CHANGE

The arguments for abolishing the possibility of exceptions are of a somewhat different nature. Whereas the arguments for keeping the possibility focus on the situation of the specific girl and her family, the arguments against are in principle about the protection of girls in general and about the need to treat all children equally.

(a) It is questionable whether old-fashioned rules and traditions of a group should ever be allowed to outweigh the protection that the child is given by law. Neither law, nor society in general (in Sweden) make any distinction between children born inside or outside of marriage, and it is certainly not obvious that the legislator should accept it as an argument that some people still make such a distinction. By leaving scope for an exception, the legislator contributes to preserving old-fashioned and discriminatory norms about children.
(b) If the exception is retained because girls who become pregnant need protection against reprisals in their own group, it could likewise be claimed to be an unacceptable kind of support for norms implying that extramarital sexuality is shameful and prohibited. Even if people who believe in those norms should be respected, the reprisals do not belong to any reasonably modern society.
(c) In practice the possibility of an exception means that legislation does not provide the same protection for children from religious, cultural or ethnic minority groups as for children of the majority of the population. An important point of departure must be that all children should be given the same protection by law.
(d) The fact that the possibility of an exception exists may sometimes put pressure on girls to marry. If the exception is abolished, young people who do not wish to marry will be given better opportunities to follow their own preferences. The same is true for parents who want to stand up to pressure from relatives or others to marry off a child.
(e) It may be that families are so anxious that their underage daughters marry a person selected by the family that the girls are pressured into becoming pregnant, possibly after the conclusion of an informal marriage, if this will increase the chances of receiving permission to marry. This amounts to forced parenthood, and must, naturally, be counteracted. Early parenthood increases the risk of negative consequences for the girl, such as lost educational opportunities and alienation.
(f) The exception possibility does not only give a girl the right to enter into matrimony, but also excludes her from the protection that the age limit provides.
(g) It could be questioned whether it is acceptable under any circumstances for children to take decisions with such far-reaching consequences as those involved in entering into marriage.
(h) If the legislator believes it to be a serious matter to stop the custom of child marriages, then the signal needs to be clear and strong. The signal effect of legislation will certainly be much stronger if there is a total prohibition on children marrying.

4.4. DISCUSSION AND CONCLUSION

The arguments for keeping the possibility of an exception are strong. In some cases, given the circumstances, it will seem almost inhuman that the girl is not allowed to marry. After all, it could be argued, marriage is not much more than a formality, if a pregnant girl will give birth to the child anyway, and live together with the father. Why not let them marry if it makes the life of the girl much easier? Why force them to go abroad if they "must" get married? And why interfere with the wishes of a girl who may very well know what is best for her?

But the arguments against the exception are also strong. Without such a possibility there will be much less pressure on the girl. It will be settled once and for all that she cannot marry as a child, at least not in her home country, and no discussion needs arise. In the long run this should help in modernising views on sexual habits and on children born outside of marriage. And maybe the most important argument of all: girls belonging to immigrant and minority cultures will have the same protection by law as girls of the majority population. Society will show clearly that all children are expected to have the same chances of making decisions regarding their own lives.

Striking a balance between the arguments for and against is not an easy task. In the report of the legislative inquiry that I mentioned earlier (FCMP) we came to the conclusion that the arguments for abolishing the exception possibility outweigh the arguments against. So we proposed a change in the law. And I believe this to be the right solution. It certainly serves girls best in the long run. It is true that some girls will probably suffer as a result, but the practice on permissions was already very restrictive in Sweden.[11] My conclusion, therefore, is that the possibility for children to marry in exceptional cases should be abolished.[12]

5. CRIMINALISATION?

5.1. GENERAL REMARKS

As I have mentioned earlier, I know of no country where child marriage is criminalised today. It is true, of course, that some child marriages are against the child's will, forced by the parents or other relatives. In those cases the situation can sometimes be dealt with through other provisions in criminal law. But one of the delimitations of this contribution (see section 1.2) is that we are only dealing

11 In 2008–2010 a total of 58 girls applied for marriage exemption in Sweden. Three of them were granted the exemption, all of them 17 years of age. The remaining 55 applications were denied.

12 The Government was of the same opinion and passed on this proposal to Parliament, see Government Bill (prop.) 2013/14:208, pp. 22–25. As mentioned in section 1.4 the bill was accepted and the new legislation entered into force on 1 July 2014.

with those child marriages which are of the child's free will, or where it cannot be proven that the child has been forced or even pressured into marrying. The question now is whether those child marriages should be criminalised. What, exactly, should then constitute the crime? And who should be punished?

It is fair to say that European legislators in general nowadays try not to criminalise unnecessarily. If possible we try to deal in other ways with phenomena which we do not like. This is, however, by no means without exceptions. And the general principle must be said to be that an act by a person should be made a crime by law if it is serious enough to be judged as a crime. If the action is thought to deserve imprisonment, it is normally no doubt worth criminalising. Criminalisation, however, involves difficulties which other kinds of legislation do not entail. First and foremost there is the aspect of legal certainty. Something should not be made a crime if it is almost impossible to describe or delimit it. People must know, at least in principle, if they are threatened by criminal punishment when doing something (e.g. marrying off a child) or abstaining from doing something (e.g. preventing the child from marrying).

5.2. WILL ANY CHILD MARRIAGES BE CAUGHT BY CRIMINALISATION?

One important and obvious complication of criminalising child marriages is that they are prohibited in most countries. They cannot therefore, in principle at least, be entered into lawfully. And if the exception possibility is removed, then there is no way for a girl to marry lawfully as a child. So what is there to criminalise, if it cannot happen?

Unfortunately it is not that simple. We cannot get rid of all child marriages by just abolishing the possibility of exception. There will still be some. In fact there will be many, and probably not considerably fewer than before. There are two reasons for this.

Children are firstly to be protected by the legal system in the country where they live, for example Sweden. But what happens if those who have their background in another country are *taken to their country of origin* to be married? Child marriages are sometimes prohibited there too,[13] but in fact such marriages happen anyway and not seldom. So when the children come back for example to Sweden, they will be married. Whether we will acknowledge these marriages in our countries is a question in itself. Sometimes we will, sometimes not. But whatever the case is, these girls will be considered married by their families and relatives, and the couples will act as if they were married and in fact be bound to each other

13 For an overview of marriage age rules in Islamic and contemporary Muslim family laws, see A. Büchler and C. Schlatter, "Marriage Age in Islamic and Contemporary Muslim Family Laws – A Comparative Survey" (2013) *Electronic Journal of Islamic and Middle Eastern Law* 37–74.

as such. So those children need the protection. Criminalisation is one possible way of providing it.

The second reason why child marriages will also continue to take place after the exception is abolished is the existence of so-called *informal marriages*. Many children enter into alliances similar to marriage in a religious or traditional order. These alliances do not become legally valid, but in practice the couple is considered to be married in their own community. The "spouses" cannot freely leave the relationship, but often have to abide by a strict traditional regime to do so. In reality, this is often just like being formally married.

5.3. DISCUSSION

One of the most difficult questions concerning the possible criminalisation of child marriages is whether so-called informal marriages should be included, and thus criminalised. If they are to be included, there will be major delimitation difficulties and therefore a lack of legal certainty. How do we, for example, define a "marriage" if it is not a legally binding one? How do we define those relationships which we want to criminalise? Is living together enough to constitute an "informal marriage"? No, that can hardly be the case. How about if, as is the case in Sweden, living together constitutes, by law in the state concerned, almost the same legal effects as marriage? What if there is a religious ceremony or the signing of a document before someone who has the legal capacity to perform a marriage? If relations entered into through such a ceremony would be treated as equal to marriages, when would the act be "ceremonial enough"? As a part of criminal law the delimitations that will be needed may appear artificial, and they are often not clear and precise, the way one would normally expect criminal law to be.

As we can see, criminalisation becomes very difficult if informal marriages are to be included. But at the same time, if they are not included the law will fall short in efficacy.

Before assessing the issue of criminalisation we should take a look at the very serious cases and decide whether they justify a penalty of a criminal law nature.

Take the example of a very young girl, say nine years of age, who is married off to a 28-year-old cousin and expected to give birth to the couple's children as soon as her body is ready for it. Those cases happen,[14] also to girls living in European countries. I believe it is evident that measures must be taken to prevent them. It is also clear, I believe, that the person arranging such a marriage – for example the girl's father – deserves a rather severe penalty. And that is, in my mind, the case even if the girl says that "she is not opposed to the marriage as long as her parents want it".

[14] For examples in actual life, see the UNFPA Report, *Marrying too young*, 2012, pp. 1, 20 and 76.

In my opinion, the arguments for criminalisation in a case like the one just mentioned are so strong that arranging such a marriage should be made a crime of its own, provided that the law can be drafted in a clear manner and can be expected to be sufficiently effective in its application in practice. The decisive argument, in my opinion, is that there are, no doubt, children in great need of such protection by the legal system. So the question is then how should a child marriage crime be construed and delimited in order to be clear and effective enough?

5.4. WHAT IS THE CRIME AND WHO COMMITS IT?

So how could the legislator construe a "child marriage offence"? Who should be penalised and who should not? Should only legally binding marriages be included, or also "informal" ones?

In the FCMP report, a provision was proposed of the following wording:

> "If someone induces a child to enter into matrimony, or takes an initiative for, or arranges a child marriage, then it is a criminal offence."

The proposed sanction is imprisonment for two years or less, or a fine.

I believe that this proposal deserves further analysis.

In this proposal the crime would in principle be to be "involved actively" in the marriage, either by inducing the child to marry or by initiating or arranging the marriage. Anyone who induces, takes an initiative or arranges the marriage would be committing a crime. The child herself would not. But the other spouse could be, provided he takes active part by inducing it, or as an initiator or organiser. I believe this to be a reasonable delimitation. It could be argued that it is better to make it a crime for the caretakers (i.e. legal custodians or other persons caring for the child) to "let a child marriage happen". That would make it easier to find those responsible and at the same time create better legal certainty. But a caretaker who really has no power over the situation should not reasonably be punished.

It should be clear that a proposal like this will also include among those liable to be sentenced for the crime for example a mother who loves her daughter dearly and believes it to be an excellent opportunity for her to get married to a caring man who has asked for the girl's hand. Criminalisation applies even if the marriage could be believed, in the specific case, to be in the best interests of the girl. If the mother induces her child to marry, or initiates or arranges the marriage, then she is committing a crime. This may sometimes seem unreasonable. But it must be remembered that the law will be drafted in the interests of all children, with the idea that marrying at a much too early age is in most cases detrimental for the child's personal growth and development. It will seldom be of any harm to the girl to wait until she is 18.

One possibility could be to criminalise only those marriages where the child is a lot younger than the stipulated marriage age, for example 16 or younger. This solution would have the advantage that only those cases which are clearly worth punishing would be caught by the law. However, it is difficult to decide where the age line should be drawn. Also, such a solution would make the law less consistent. A child is a child, and there is much to say for the principled approach that the law should protect not only some children, but all.

We then come back to the difficult question of whether a child marriage offence should include informal marriages or not. The proposal in the FCMP report is that they are included. The main reason for this is the fact that they deserve to be criminalised just as much as formally binding marriages. Then there is also the efficacy argument. If those alliances are left out, many "actual" child marriages will continue to take place and in reality have the same negative impact on children as legally binding marriages.

In the law proposal we describe an informal marriage as:

> "an alliance which is equal to marriage in the sense that it is binding under an established system of norms which includes special requirements for dissolution of the alliance and is entered into in accordance with that system of norms."

It is obvious that the difficulty with this proposal has mainly to do with the delimitations and, as a consequence, insufficient legal certainty. When is, for example, a system of norms "established", and when are there "special requirements" for dissolution? This of course needs to be reasonably clarified, either in the law itself or in the preparatory works, so that the courts will have some guidance in applying the law.[15] Uncertainty cannot be excluded altogether. This should not, however, be much more of a problem than otherwise when a new criminal law provision is introduced.

As was noted earlier, there will not be much room for child marriages in a country where there is a minimum marriage age and no possibility of exceptions from this age. If criminalisation is to be effective it therefore needs to include marriages entered into abroad. It should not be possible to avoid the law by taking the child to some other country where she is allowed to marry. It will of course not be possible to punish, under Swedish law for example, someone who initiates or arranges a marriage in for example Iran and where there is no connection to Sweden. A prerequisite must be, as is mostly the case, that the crime has been committed in the country where the act is penalised, in this case Sweden. This means that the inducing, initiating or arranging must take place in that country.

Considering that I was the chairperson of the FCMP, it may not come as a surprise that I find the proposal acceptable. If we want to criminalise child

15 The different issues are to some extent discussed in the FCMP Report, pp. 552 f.

marriages, then the proposed way of doing it seems to be a good one. Furthermore, the responses to the proposal in Sweden were mostly very positive.

5.5. CONCLUSION

My conclusions regarding criminalisation of child marriages are as follows:

(a) Those child marriages which the child enters into of her own free will should also be criminalised. The law should include all children, i.e. persons under 18 years of age.
(b) Criminalisation should include "informal marriages". These could be described as "alliances which are equal to marriage in the sense that they are binding under an established system of norms which includes special requirements for dissolution of the alliance and are entered into in accordance with that system of norms".
(c) Criminalisation should also include marriages entered into outside of the country, provided that the criminal act is taking place in the country of criminalisation.
(d) The law should be drafted such that the criminal act consists of either inducing the child to marry, or initiating or arranging the marriage.

5.6. THE SWEDISH GOVERNMENT BILL AND THE 2014 LAW AMENDMENTS

The Swedish Government was of a different opinion and did not pass on the report proposal on criminalisation to Parliament. The main argument against the proposal was that criminalisation of child marriages will not be needed when other protective measures are taken, among them criminalisation of forced marriages including such marriages where someone "uses an exposed position" to make her or him accept the marriage.[16] The protection for children abroad is also strengthened to some extent by a stricter qualification of those exempt situations where a child marriage can be recognised in Sweden; there will be a need for "extraordinary" reasons instead of the earlier "special". Another argument was that the FCMP proposal lacked the necessary precision and that the effects of it would sometimes seem unreasonable or had not been carefully analysed.

However, one important part of the proposal was accepted: the introduction of the concept of "informal marriages". The proposal in the report to criminalise forced marriages, including marriages where an exposed position has been used, contained informal marriages, and they were defined in the same way as in the

16 "Exposed" (*utsatt*) is a higher requirement than "vulnerable"; the latter would apply to almost every child.

proposal regarding child marriages. The definition was somewhat changed in the bill compared to the report, but in principle is the same. The new law defines an informal marriage as:

> "a marriage-like alliance entered into according to rules which are binding for a group and which
> 1. entail that the parties are regarded as spouses and are considered to have rights and obligations in relation to each other, and
> 2. include the issue of dissolution of the alliance."[17]

A very important and interesting question is whether children will have sufficient protection if the law – like the new law in Sweden – criminalises the act of a person who *by using an exposed position induces* a person to marry. In the Swedish bill[18] this is further developed on p. 141 (my translation):

> "When adults on whom the child is dependent put pressure on the child to marry against her own will or arrange a marriage without consideration to what the child wants, it could [therefore] be a case of using the child's exposed position. This is true not only for younger children but can also be the case when the child is getting close to 18. In general, however, children are less independent and more dependent on adults the younger they are. […] A child in its early teens can still be dependent on its parents to such an extent that even relatively mild prompting from the parents can be enough for the child to find it useless to try to oppose the marriage."

This must mean, for example, that it is still not a crime in Sweden to tell your 15-year-old daughter to marry (religiously if not legally) an older man whom she does not mind marrying, or whom she will marry because she would never even consider opposing the will of her parents. And it is not a crime to arrange the informal marriage of your 12-year-old daughter to a boy whom she really wants.

There could of course be different opinions on whether these cases need to be dealt with by law or not. I believe that they do, and that it is important. These girls are much too young to marry. And therefore the legislator, I believe, is letting girls down by putting decisive weight on whether they were in fact forced, pressed or prompted. Whether they oppose it or not, children are too young to marry, period.

By accepting that the individual needs to be protected not only from legally binding marriages but also from informal marriages, Sweden has, however, come halfway. I hope that other countries will follow this example. And I hope that governments will eventually be persuaded that child marriages need to be ruled

---

17 Compare with the wording in the report proposal, section 5.4 above. The new provision is found in the Swedish Penal Code (*Brottsbalken*), Ch. 4 §4c para. 2, in force since 1 July 2014.

18 Government Bill 2013/14:208.

out completely. The law should be drafted in the interests of all children, based on the knowledge that marrying at a much too early age is detrimental to the child's personal growth and development.[19]

6. HOW SHOULD WE COUNTERACT NEGATIVE EFFECTS?

It is clear that there is a danger of negative effects of new laws such as those proposed above. I have come to the conclusion, in section 3, that this danger should not prevent legislation. But that does not mean that the problem should be left without further analysis and consideration. On the contrary: if legislation may create problems it is a matter for society to take the risk seriously and try to prevent or at least alleviate such problems. So we should ask how this could be done.

What possible negative effects are we talking about? There could of course be difficulties in the application of the law, etc. But the legislator is used to handling difficulties of that kind. They are normally taken care of within the law proposal, for example in the form of clarifying statements and examples *in the proposed legislation's travaux préparatoires*. The effects that definitely justify some serious thought outside the law proposal itself are those which we touched upon in section 3, those which have to do with the problem that legislation may be felt as an attack on certain groups in society. It could go so far as to stigmatise the groups concerned and even have the effect of supporting xenophobic forces. Right-wing nationalist forces could try to use legislation against child marriages for their own purposes, trying to show that the groups concerned do not belong in our democratic and equal societies. If society, through its laws or otherwise, points at immigrant or minority groups as representing negative behaviour and opinions, such a risk must be taken into account.

In all legislation which may be perceived as directed against a certain group, it is important to underline one thing: all groups, cultures and people deserve basic respect even if their traditions and approach include values that are unfamiliar to the majority in our countries. It is clear that basic respect of this nature can never be allowed to mean any departure from fundamental rights and freedoms. But it should mean that amendments to laws that may be perceived to be directed against the group or tradition be implemented in a tone of voice and with an approach in general which do not create unnecessary confrontation.

So, showing respect, using the right tone of voice and having a general approach of non-confrontation are crucial in respect of legislation of the kind we are discussing. But it is not enough. It is important to also make it clear what

19 From earlier experience of the legislative process in Sweden I would predict that the Swedish legislator will take the final step quite soon. I believe that child marriages as a crime of its own will be criminalised in Sweden in 10–15 years.

the real reason for legislation is. Therefore, it must be emphasised that legislation against child marriage is intended to protect children and to safeguard equal human rights for all, not to attack or accuse particular groups. It is also important to be very open about the dangers of negative effects and to initiate a dialogue with those groups that may feel under attack. Those groups should be asked to give their reactions to the law, and their representatives should be given the opportunity to suggest measures to avoid problems. Such suggestions should be taken seriously. And at the same time, if possible, a dialogue could be introduced to increase the will of any directly concerned group to accept the law.

To conclude, when legislating against child marriages states should take measures to counteract the difficulties which certain groups may experience because of the new law. This is not only a matter of respect, tone of voice and non-confrontation, but also a matter of clearly explaining the intent of the law, of openness, dialogue and a willingness to respond to needs expressed.

7. CLOSING REMARKS

There is no doubt that the practice of child marriages can be extremely harmful for the girls at risk. They lose their right to make decisions regarding their own way of life and they lose the chance for an education and for growth and development. It is therefore very important to try to stop this practice. It is so important to protect these girls that states should be prepared to consider actions which they would normally rule out in their legislation.

Child marriages involve, however, problems of an unusual kind. This has to do with the fact that many groups and individuals do not share the view of the majority of our societies that child marriages are necessarily wrong. It has also to do with the fact that legislation may harm those groups and individuals to an extent that is clearly unwanted.

We need to have the individual child in focus, and we need to legislate against child marriages. At the same time we need to take the sensitive situation for the groups concerned into consideration. That makes the drafting and enforcement of legislation against child marriages unusually difficult.

Most important of all is for society to give a strong and persistent signal that child marriages will not be accepted. Hopefully in the long run this signal will convince everyone that the biggest decisions of a person's life should be taken by that person herself. And they should be taken only when the person is mature enough to have reasonably clear and well thought-out views on what is best for her.

CIRCUMCISION OF YOUNG BOYS: A CONFLICT BETWEEN PARENTAL AND CHILD RIGHTS

The Swedish Experience from a Medical Point of View

Staffan JANSON

1. INTRODUCTION

Male circumcision is practiced all over the world by approximately a billion Muslims, three hundred million Christians, at least sixteen million Jews and an indeterminate number of animists and atheists. It involves, all in all, about

30% of the world's male population.[1] Circumcision is performed for three main reasons.

(a) Circumcision is regarded to be an important cultural tradition and initiation rite. The background is undetermined, but may have to do with hygiene or sexual reasons.
(b) Religious reasons, prescribed in Judaism and Islam are decisive. References are made mainly to the old testimony in the Bible. Male circumcision is, nevertheless, an older practice, even if its origins are obscure.
(c) Circumcision is a non-religious, routine operation. This is the case mainly in the United States of America, where it has been widely practiced since about 1870, initially to prevent a number of alleged diseases such as epilepsy, enuresis, impotence and a variety of psychiatric diseases. It was also meant to prevent masturbation, which at the time was thought to give rise to a number of severe diseases. These circumcisions are usually done while the mother is still at the maternity ward. In 2010 about 60% of all infant boys in the US were circumcised at a total cost of 800 million dollars per year.[2]

Male circumcision of small boys, unable to personally consent to the operation, has been debated for several hundred years. The principal debate has been about the parents' rights to decide about the intervention, contra the young boys' right to bodily integrity. Over the last two decades, probably due to the immigration of hundreds of thousands of Muslims to the Scandinavian (Nordic) countries, often as refugees, this topic has gained renewed interest in Sweden and the other Nordic states.

The current discussion, in the Nordic countries, is mainly centred on four topics:

(a) medical reasons in favour or against circumcision, including risks of side effects;
(b) parental rights versus children's rights and the importance of informed consent;
(c) respect for children's bodily integrity and autonomy;
(d) cultural and religious aspects.

These topics have also been intensively discussed in most of Europe and the United States, and the prominent *British Medical Journal* included a thorough discussion of the above-mentioned points in a 2010 issue of the journal.[3]

1 S.A.A. Abu-Sahlieh, "Male and female circumcision; our sex between the hammer of the gods and the anvil of customs", Colloque sur les mutilations sexuelles, Bellagio Study and Conference Centre, Italy, 2012.

2 W. Dekkers, "Routine (non-religious) neonatal circumcision and bodily integrity: A transatlantic dialogue" (2009) 19(2) *Kennedy Institute of Ethics Journal* 125–146.

3 See, in particular, S. Arie (2010) *British Medical Journal* 341 (21 Aug), pp. 370–371.

For a number of years the present author has been heading the Swedish Paediatric Society's Advocacy Committee, i.e. the Committee on Ethics and the Rights of the Child. In 2010 the Committee was asked to give a statement on non-medical circumcision of small boys, which later was discussed at the Paediatric Society's national meeting in the spring of 2011 and approved by its board in the autumn of 2011. In this chapter, a brief historic background will be given on the practice of male circumcision, after which attention will be given to the factors leading to the Swedish Paediatric Society's statement (section 3.2), the following debate in Sweden illustrating several controversies on male circumcision, the 2012 statement by the American Pediatric Association and its critique in Europe and, partly, in the US too. Finally, the joint statement in 2013 by the Nordic Ombudsmen for Children and the Nordic Paediatric Societies will be touched upon. The chapter approaches the topic in particular from a medical point of view, relating the analysis to the rights of the child, as established in particular in the United Nations Convention on the Rights of the Child (CRC).

2. THE PRACTICE AND ITS HISTORIC BACKGROUND

Male circumcision consists of cutting off a smaller or bigger part of the foreskin of the penis. Historically, this has been performed without anaesthesia. The practice of performing male circumcision without anaesthesia is still probably the most common around the globe. There are 4,500-year-old paintings from Egypt showing young males being circumcised. The origin of the practice of circumcision can be traced to the Bronze Age period – an era where superstition reigned, harmful propitiations were the norm, and women and children were considered chattel.[4] The custom's origin is not known, but it has been speculated that it may have been connected with the prevention of disease or a method of decreasing male sexuality. It has been speculated that the Jews probably brought this tradition with them when they emigrated from Egypt. Among Jews circumcision consisted initially in cutting a minute part of the skin, primarily to get a drop of blood from the penis (blood of alliance).[5] The present Jewish double practice of cutting the majority of the skin (*milah*) and pulling the skin between the incision and the glans with a sharp fingernail (*periah*) was introduced in the 2nd century AD by rabbis, in order to prevent Jews from hiding their religious mark, when faced with Greek-Roman hostility, by pulling the skin of the penis above the glans. But there is also a tradition among the Jews called *Brit Shalom* which means "covenant of peace",

4 R.S. Hendel, "That old time religion: the Bible preserves hints of Stone Age rites that retained their holiness for millennia" (2002) 18 *Biblical Archaeology Review* 1–5.

5 B.D. Earp, "The ethics of infant male circumcision" (2013) 39(7) *Journal of Medical Ethics* 418–420.

aimed at intervening in a looser and less harmful manner.[6] Among Muslims, many jurists are of the opinion that a round cut of a small part of the foreskin is sufficient, while others believe that the whole foreskin should be excised.[7]

Circumcision among Jews is generally performed on the eighth day after birth, but can be delayed in case of health problems. The child can also be spared if the mother has lost two other sons because of circumcision. Among Muslims, circumcision must preferably be done at an early age, and inevitably before puberty. Circumcision among Jews is accompanied with a religious ritual. Among Muslims, there is less ritual, but some classic Shiite texts prescribe the recitation of a religious formula.[8]

A common argument among Jews is that circumcision is prescribed by their religion and, accordingly, has to be obeyed. Over the centuries, however, Jews, as well as Muslims and Christians, have abandoned a number of customs and adapted their religious practice to a more modern and humanitarian thinking. Examples in Judaism are the abandonment of other biblical norms, such as the law of "an eye for an eye" (Deut 19:21) and the stoning of the adulterer (Deut 22:23). The practice of circumcision has also been debated several times in history. In modern times, the debate against male circumcision started in the aftermath of the French revolution in 1789. The goal was to create a secular society where religious communities were to be replaced by national cohesion. In 1842 in Frankfurt, Germany, a Jewish group proposed the suppression of circumcision and its replacement with an egalitarian religious ceremony for boys and girls, without the drawing of blood. In 1866 in Vienna, sixty-six Viennese Jewish physicians signed a petition against the practice. It is notable that the founder of the Zionist movement, Theodore Herzl, was influenced by this debate and did not circumcise his son at birth, although this was performed later during the son's adolescence. In more recent years this debate reached Israel where in 1997 human rights activists created an organisation to fight sexual mutilation. Dozens of parents, in spite of the opposition of their families, refused to circumcise their children, a practice they considered to be contrary to the Israeli legislation that forbids the abuse and maltreatment of children.[9] Among Muslims the origin of the custom is likewise unclear, as the Koran, the primary source of Islamic law, mentions neither male nor female circumcision. Due to the lack of statements in the Koran, modern Islamic authors resort to the statements of Prophet Mohammed, indicating that circumcision is obligatory.[10]

The historical notes given below are partly from a presentation delivered in 2002 by the Christian Palestinian doctor of law, active at that time at the Swiss Institute of Comparative Law in Lausanne, Dr Sami A. Aldeeb Abu-Salieh. In

6 Ibid.

7 W. Dekkers, *supra* note 2.

8 S.A.A. Abu-Sahlieh, *supra* note 1.

9 On the recent Israeli developments and case law, see Marie-Claire Foblets in this volume, section 1.4.

10 S.A.A. Abu-Sahlieh, *supra* note 1.

his paper on male and female circumcision[11] he emphasised certain fundamental points, presented in brief below.

(a) The principle of physical integrity: according to Abu-Salieh, one cannot be against female circumcision and in favour of male circumcision unless you want to convince others that your culture is better than that of others, that your religion is better, that your sacred books are superior to those of others and that girls have the right to protection, but not boys.
(b) Differences: one can admit that female (Pharaonic) circumcision is more harmful than male circumcision. However, similarly, one can admit that the amputation of the little finger is less harmful than amputation of the whole hand, but this does not give us the right to cut off the little finger of others without their consent and without medical causes.
(c) Medical benefits: it is difficult to believe that nature committed such a severe mistake that it requires a surgical intervention on a mass scale.
(d) Respect of others: if we respect children, we must wait and let them decide on their own until they are 18 years old.

As we will see later in this chapter, Abu-Salieh's line of argumentation is essentially shared by the Scandinavian Ombudsmen for children[12] and the Scandinavian Paediatric Societies, in their joint statement from 2013.

3. THE SWEDISH SITUATION

3.1. THE 2001 ENACTMENT

In 2001, Sweden adopted specific legislation on the topic, the Act (2001:499) on the circumcision of boys, which is among the first in the world. The background to this enactment was the large influx of refugees from Muslim countries from about 1985 and on, and the need to handle requests for circumcision of small boys.

According to this enactment parents have the right to have their small boys circumcised even if it is not medically motivated. The prerequisites are:

(a) circumcision shall not be performed against the boy's will;
(b) the parents should be informed about pain relief, hygiene and possible side effects of the operation by the medical staff in charge of the operation;

11 S.A.A. Abu-Sahlieh, *supra* note 1.
12 Each of the Scandinavian states has established a special government body, called the Children's Ombudsman, to control and supervise how society respects the rights of children, in particular as established by the CRC. Norway was the first country in the world to establish a national ombudsman for children in 1993 and Sweden followed next in 1998.

(c) the operation shall be performed with proper anaesthesia and with sufficient hygiene. This requirement is considered by the Swedish state to be consistent with Article 24 CRC, which states that a child should not be subjected to unnecessary pain or risk for complications. The surgeon is responsible for giving proper information; and
(d) regarding circumcision of boys younger than two months old, the Swedish National Board of Health and Welfare can authorise others than licensed surgeons to perform the surgery, for instance rabbis of the Swedish Jewish communities.

From a medical point of view, it is immediately obvious that the Swedish law on circumcision of boys includes contradictory positions. In particular, the following questions must be raised:

(a) How can it be possible for infants or other small boys to consent to an intervention of which they do not understand either the immediate or long-term consequences?
(b) Why is it less important to have licensed surgeons to perform circumcision on boys younger than two months of age? Is there an underlying assumption that the intervention has fewer consequences or is less painful for the youngest children?

The National Board of Health and Welfare which, inter alia, also gives recommendations to the Swedish health care system then suggested in a report of 2005[13] that there should be a *right* for boys to be circumcised within the public health care system of Sweden, even if there are no medical reasons for it. As a consequence of this recommendation, in October 2009 the Association of Swedish Health Care Owners (SKL)[14] asked the public hospitals to enforce this as a policy. However, on a regional level, namely the county councils, who operate the majority of the hospitals in Sweden, roughly one third of the councils have rejected this appeal for ethical reasons. The Swedish debate has, as a result, come to focus primarily on two issues:

(a) circumcision as a custom and tradition, i.e. an expression of cultural and religious identity; and
(b) the performance of circumcision within the Swedish public health care sector.

The *first concern* is a question of balance between the right of the child not to be subjected to unnecessary risks and the right to the best possible health care

13 Report from the Swedish Board of Health and Welfare, SoS 2005/7490/SK.

14 SKL is an abbreviation for the common group of Swedish county councils (27) and municipalities (290). The county councils own the national and regional hospitals as well as the primary health care centres, while the municipalities are in charge of the care of the aging people, normally in their homes.

according to Article 24 CRC, as well as the child's right to cultural and religious affiliation, generally protected by the CRC (see in particular Article 20(3)). Article 12 is also important in this context as it concerns the right of the child to be properly listened to, with due regard for the child's age and maturity. As mentioned above, the age for circumcision is not fixed within Islam, though most interventions are performed on small boys, while within the Jewish tradition it is supposed to be done on the eighth day after birth. The normative problem is whether the parents' religious freedom should overrule the child's rights to bodily integrity and to his or her own religious beliefs. Seen from a historical context, when circumcision was performed without anaesthesia, it is understandable that the intervention was performed when the child was so small that the child would probably not have any painful memories. In modern times, with a widespread humanitarian view about children, there should however be a good opportunity for society and religious groups to reconsider their current standpoints on circumcision.

The *second concern* is whether non-medical circumcision has a place in a publicly funded health care system, like that in Sweden. Arguments in favour are the high hygienic and anaesthetic standards of public hospitals in Sweden, decreasing the risks of the operation. The Swedish National Board of Health and Welfare has reported a number of cases where operations performed *outside* hospitals resulted in severe medical complications for the child.

3.2. THE 2009 STATEMENT BY THE SWEDISH PAEDIATRIC SOCIETY

In 2009, against the background of diverging opinions and practices related to the circumcision of small boys within the Swedish health care system, the Swedish Paediatric Society felt obliged to make a statement. After lengthy discussions within the Swedish Paediatric Society's Committee on Ethics and Children's rights (see above section 1), the board of the Swedish Paediatric Society gave its view of this topic, which in summary consists of the following:

(a) The value of the operation for the future health of the boy cannot, with the present knowledge, be thoroughly estimated. Circumcisions of boys on a routine basis cannot therefore be medically motivated.
(b) It is important from a long-term perspective to work against a custom that is a violation of the child's integrity and child's right of self-determination over the body, having regard to the states' obligations to take measures to abolish traditional practices prejudicial to the health of children, according to Article 24(3) CRC.

The Swedish Paediatric Society therefore made the following recommendations:

(a) all parents who want to have their baby boy circumcised should receive proper information about current Swedish law, the rights of the child and the risk for complications;
(b) parents should also be made aware of the fact that circumcision is a non-reversible intervention;
(c) the Swedish state is urged to initiate a discussion with the concerned religious communities about the desirability and *possibility of a symbolic form of circumcision*, without any surgical intervention, until the child is old enough to decide for himself; and
(d) if the parents after receiving information stressing the boy's own right to decide over his body still want to have the operation performed, the operation should be carried out under the best hygienic circumstances and with guaranteed anaesthesia.

The Paediatric Society also proposed that Sweden should consider creating regional centres with specific competence for circumcision, as it is known that side effects are less common in medical units with high competence.

Finally, in the opinion of the Paediatric Society, governmental bodies and associations with a child rights agenda should work towards a situation where circumcision of boys for non-medical reasons will be an intervention that the older boy or young man can decide on himself. The Society proposed, furthermore, that Swedish public authorities initiate discussions on the topic with representatives of religious communities and other advocates of infant circumcision, in order to investigate whether it could be possible in the long term to change the tradition to a more human and symbolic intervention.

Even though the Swedish Paediatric Society did not propose any prohibition on circumcision, its statement gave rise to an outraged debate in the Swedish mass media, mainly accusing the Society of being religiously and culturally insensitive. Others took the opposite standpoint and unfortunately the statement was also used in racist propaganda. The mailboxes of members of the Society's Committee on Ethics and the Rights of the Child (see section 1) were full of upset and hateful communications. Religious people (and some others), with whom the Society has normally had sensible discussions, either thought that the Society was insensitive and ignorant or that it should be held responsible for unforeseen consequences of its statement. The Swedish government remained silent.

What the Swedish Paediatric Society had actually stated was that the intervention should be performed under safe circumstances and that society should work for a long-term abolishment of this custom.

The cultural or religious line of defence was that Swedish society performs other interventions on small children, such as vaccinations, so why condemn circumcision of boys. My personal view on this is that vaccinations are given in order to prevent severe diseases or death and, as far as I understand, this is not the case with circumcision. The other main line of criticism is that society does not have any right to interfere with old customs or religious views. In my opinion, this objection is more understandable, but one should keep in mind that circumcision was practiced long before the Muslim or Jewish traditions were established. As mentioned earlier, circumcision is documented in Egypt as far back as 2,500 BC. We do not know for sure why this custom arose more than 4,500 years ago, most likely in North Africa or in the Middle East, nor whether the justifications behind it can still be regarded as valid in modern times and in other countries. So many other customs based on non-scientific views have slowly been eradicated. It is also well known that religious beliefs and customs have changed substantially over time and adapted to current demands. An understanding of this can be gained from reading the works of any religious historian, like Karen Armstrong for instance.[15]

A well-known book on paediatric ethics is *Clinical Ethics in Pediatrics* by Diekema, Mercurio and Adam, published in 2011 by Cambridge University Press.[16] In this book there is a specific chapter on male circumcision and although the three authors are all American, the manner in which they discuss the problems is very close to the viewpoints given by the Swedish Paediatric Society.

4. THE 2012 STATEMENT BY THE AMERICAN PEDIATRIC ACADEMY

The American Academy of Pediatrics (AAP) had given a statement in 1999 that was overall against circumcision of small boys. However, in the autumn of 2012 the Academy issued a new statement which was principally in favour of the practice for medical reasons.[17] This gave rise to a strong reaction from European paediatricians, doctors of forensic medicine and sexologists. In the spring of 2013, forty European physicians (including myself) wrote a response pointing at the cultural bias in the AAP's 2012 technical report and policy statement on male circumcision.[18]

An important point that was overlooked by the APP was that preventive medical procedures need more and stricter justification than medical procedures as such, as they are aimed at people who are generally free from medical problems. Even stricter criteria apply for preventive medical procedures regarding children, who cannot weigh the evidence themselves and cannot legally consent to the

---

15 K. Armstrong, *A history of God – the 4000 year quest of Judaism, Christianity and Islam*, Vintage 2004.

16 D.S. Diekema et al., *Clinical Ethics in Pediatrics*, Cambridge University Press 2011.

17 American Academy of Pediatrics Task Force on Circumcision, "Circumcision Policy Statement" (2012) 130(3) *Pediatrics* 585–586.

18 M. Frisch et al., "Cultural bias in the AAP's 2012 Technical Report and Policy Statement on Male Circumcision" (2013) 131(4) *Pediatrics* 796–800.

procedure. The most important criteria for the justification of medical procedures are (a) necessity, (b) cost-effectiveness, (c) subsidiarity, (d) proportionality, and (e) consent. For preventive medical procedures this means that:

(a) the procedure must lead to the prevention of a serious medical problem, where no less intrusive means exist for reaching the same goal;
(b) the risk of the intervention is proportional to the intended benefit; and
(c) when performed during childhood, it needs to be clearly demonstrated that it is essential to perform the procedure before an age at which the individual can make his or her own decisions about the intervention.[19]

4.1. GROUNDS FOR CRITICISM

With the above-mentioned factors in mind, the AAP's statement was criticised for the following reasons.

4.1.1. Urinary Tract Infections

About 1% of boys will develop a urinary tract infection (UTI) within the first year of life. The evidence of circumcision preventing UTIs is clinically weak and there are no randomised controlled studies. Although 60% of American boys currently are circumcised, UTIs are not less common in the United States than in Europe.

4.1.2. Penile Cancer

Penile cancer is one of the rarest cancer forms in the western world (~1 case per 100,000 men per year) and almost always occurs at an older age. It is also remarkable that penile cancer is just as common in Europe as in the United States, where almost 75% of the current non-Jewish adult population is circumcised.

4.1.3. Traditional Sexually Transmitted Diseases

There is no convincing evidence of circumcision providing protection against sexually transmitted diseases (STDs), except maybe for genital herpes and genital warts. Responsible use of condoms, regardless of circumcision status, will provide an almost 100% reduction risk of any STD. In addition, STDs occur only after sexual debut, which implies that the decision of whether to circumcise or not can be postponed to an age when boys are old enough to decide for themselves.

[19] S.A.A. Abu-Sahlieh, *supra* note 1.

4.1.4. *HIV and AIDS*

Three randomised controlled studies, conducted in Kenya, Uganda and South Africa, suggest that circumcision in adulthood may lead to a noticeable reduction in the risk of heterosexual HIV acquisition in areas with extremely high HIV prevalence. The studies in Africa indicate that circumcision halves heterosexual men's (but not women's) risk of HIV infection in the first years after the operation, in high endemic areas where viral transmission occurs mainly through heterosexual intercourse. There is, however, no evidence that circumcision, whether in infancy, childhood or adulthood, is effective in preventing heterosexual transmission in countries where HIV prevalence is much lower and routes of transmission are different, as in Europe and the United States. Sexually transmitted HIV infections in the West occur predominantly among men who have sex with men. Interestingly, the United States combines a high prevalence of STDs and HIV infections with a high percentage of circumcision. The situation in most European countries is the reverse. Other factors like consistent use of condoms, safe sex programmes, easy access to antiretroviral drugs and clean needle programmes seem to be more effective. As with other STDs, small boys are not the ones transmitting HIV.

4.1.5. *Complications*

There is a relatively small but still significant risk of complications in the circumcision of small boys, such as infections, bleeding, strictures, incident deaths and penis amputation. A study from the State University Hospital of Copenhagen published in 2013 in the *Danish Medical Journal*[20] showed a much higher rate of complications than reported earlier, even within a hospital with highly qualified surgeons. The reason for this is probably that the follow-up period in this case was longer than in earlier studies. In this study, 2.9% of those operated on by skilled paediatric surgeons had acute complications after circumcision and an additional 2.2% had late complications during a 8–15-year follow-up period. Excessive bleeding was most common with 1.6%, an expected rate. Of the late complications, skin bridges and insufficient removal of the foreskin were the main complaints. Another common side effect was a fibrotic ring causing phimosis, just giving a narrow passage for urination.

Longitudinal studies on psychological, sexual or urinary problems are lacking, but there are increasing reports of circumcised men who claim that they have decreased sensitivity in their penis and less enjoyment of the sexual act. This is probably a result of the eradication of a highly innervated organ that is also protecting the glans. Later studies have indicated that circumcision has a risk of de-sensitising the penis.

---

20 J. Thorup, S. Thorup and I. Botjer Rasmussen Ifaoul, "Complication rate after circumcision in a pediatric surgical setting should not be neglected" (2013) *60(8) Danish Medical Journal* 1–3.

4.2. CHILDREN'S PERCEPTION OF PAIN

Children's experience of pain has always been underestimated. There is practically no documentation at all about pain relief and children before the 1960s, and the common myth, which still exists to a great extent, is that children experience less pain and forget about pain more or less instantly. In the 1970s, it was noted that children got just a small fraction of pain relief compared to adults, and current international studies still report that almost 50% of nurses specialised in paediatrics believe that children exaggerate their pain.[21]

Pain is a complex stressor in children, who find themselves in a state of physiological, social, cultural and developmental dependence on adults. Pain suffered by a child can have significant consequences for the child's future experiences of, and reactions to, pain. Pain has always stressed children and it has been calculated that 50–70% of all children at hospitals waiting for surgery have severe anxiety regarding pain. It is also known that children with severe pain before operations are more stressed post-operatively and heal more slowly.[22] It is therefore of great importance to find ways to relieve children from any anxiety related to pain.

It is even more difficult to estimate pain perception in the neonatal, infant or pre-verbal child. For these young children pain can be estimated by experienced professionals by observing the pitch, duration and intensity of crying, facial expressions and physiological changes in blood pressure, oxygen saturation and cortisol levels. Commonly used analgesics and local anaesthetics usually provide some level of pain reduction, but not freedom from pain. EMLA anaesthetic cream, for example, provides insufficient pain reduction during circumcision, and subcutaneous anaesthetics, such as Lidocaine, fail in up to 10% of the time. Breakthrough pain is also common in the aftermath until wounds have healed.[23]

4.3. US CRITICISM

The 2012 statement by the AAP has not been free from criticism in the US, either. Indeed, US attorneys have found reason to criticise it, i.e. with reference to the rights of the child.[24] In their opinion, the AAP document fails to engage with several critical issues, such as:

---

21 J. Olmstead, S. Cott and W. Austin, "Unresolved pain in children: a relational ethics perspective" (2010) 17(6) *Nursing Ethics* 695–704.

22 W. Fincher, J. Shaw and A. Ramelet, "The effectiveness of a standardised preoperative preparation in reducing child and parent anxiety: a single-blind randomised controlled trial" (2012) 21(7–8) *Journal of Clinical Nursing* 946–955.

23 M. Frisch, personal communication. Morten Frisch is a Danish forensic medical doctor at the National Hospital of Copenhagen, who specifically has studied the anaesthetic effects of different medicals when given at circumcision. He has also studied the long-term effects of circumcision on male sexual function.

24 J.S. Svoboda and R.S. Van Howe, "Out of step: fatal flaws in the latest AAP policy report on neonatal circumcision" (2013) 39(7) *Journal of Medical Ethics* 434–441.

(a) the anatomy and function of the foreskin and the harm caused by its removal: the AAP document omits that the foreskin is a complex, erogenous, specialised, junction structure that has important sexual, immunological and protective functions for the intact male as well as for his female sexual partners;
(b) basic principles of medical ethics and how they bear upon the permissibility of the procedure in the first place: studies showing pain and changes in infant behaviour after circumcision are not mentioned to any great degree; and
(c) fundamental issues regarding human rights and children's rights and their relevance to the surgical infringement of bodily integrity.

In many ways this criticism is similar to that of European physicians. Therefore, it will not be recapitulated here in detail. An important element to point out is, however, that the AAP admits that the true incidence of complications after newborn circumcision is unknown and yet manages to conclude that current evidence indicates that the health benefits of newborn male circumcision outweigh the risks. The AAP has also failed to cite that cost-benefit analyses have found that circumcision was much more costly than condoms and antiretroviral therapy in preventing HIV infection in Africa. The AAP has also referred to the relative risk reduction in the African studies on HIV prevention, while the absolute risk reduction is only 1.3%. Given the numerous sources of biases in the studies, this absolute risk reduction is probably not valid.

5. THE STATEMENT OF THE SCANDINAVIAN OMBUDSMEN

In September 2013 the Nordic Ombudsmen for children and the chairmen of the Nordic Paediatric Societies met in Oslo, Norway, to discuss circumcision of young boys and thereafter gave a common statement (in Nordic languages only) under the heading "Let boys decide for themselves if they should be circumcised".

The statement commences by saying that circumcision carried out without medical reasons in a human being who cannot consent is an infringement of fundamental principles of medical ethics, particularly as the intervention is non-reversible, painful and may cause severe complications. The statement continues by pointing out that circumstances that may be important for adult men are not relevant for young boys in the Nordic countries. Circumcision of young boys is, on the contrary, in direct conflict with Article 12 CRC on the child's right to be heard in matters of relevance for the child and Article 24(3) obliging states to protect children from traditional rituals that can damage their health. This statement is in line with the 2013 statements by the UN Council of Human Rights and the 2013

Recommendation by the European Council.[25] Hardly surprisingly, the Nordic statement has been criticised in various ways and by various organisations and bodies, mainly with reference to the same arguments that were raised against the Swedish Paediatric Society's statement some years earlier (see above, section 3.2). The most notable element is, however, that the critics in practically all instances take the view of the adult, or sometimes of the family, but not of the child.

6. CONCLUSION

At the time of writing, Sweden faces the following situation. The legal system permits parents to circumcise their young boys for religious and cultural reasons, on the condition that the operation takes place within the health care system. Public authorities in charge of the country's public health care system have consequently urged county councils, which operate the majority of Swedish hospitals, to expedite the operations. On the other hand, the Swedish Ombudsman for Children and the Swedish Paediatric Society have consistently argued that any circumcision of small boys for non-medical reasons is a violation of children's rights and against the spirit (essence) of the CRC. Debate on the issue will in all certainty go on for many years and a profound change will probably only be possible if it is supported by representatives of the religious communities concerned.

[25] Parliamentary Assembly, Council of Europe (PACE), Resolution 1952: Children's right to physical integrity, 1 October 2013. See Marie-Claire Foblets in this volume, section 1.3.

THE BODY AS IDENTITY MARKER*

Circumcision of Boys Caught between Contrasting Views on the Best Interests of the Child

Marie-Claire FOBLETS

* I would like to thank Dr Monica Sandor for her most valuable help with the editing of this contribution, as well as Mareike Riedel and Jonathan Bernaerts for their stimulating comments.

1. INTRODUCTION

1.1. A TOPIC THAT DIVIDES OPINIONS AND COMMUNITIES

The subject of this contribution is a limited one, but one that is closely linked to very topical issues, as I will seek to demonstrate. It must however be placed in the wider context of contemporary plural societies, where debates on what are considered fundamental values and the way in which respect for those values may be ensured are increasingly frequent giving rise to disputes between individuals and/or communities that are often extremely difficult to resolve. These debates revolve around the question of how to accommodate diversity in a way that is compatible with democracy and the protection of fundamental rights and liberties for all. There is no shortage of illustrations ranging from inheritance rights that are discriminatory toward certain relatives, especially women, through marriage practices stemming from patriarchal values, to restrictive dress codes, to mention but a few.

In Europe in particular, the tensions that accompany these debates are often the direct or indirect consequence of the presence of recently established communities within a country, i.e. migrant communities, although they are not exclusively the result of such cross-border movements. Secularisation, as well as the individualisation of lifestyles in contemporary society, likewise give rise to new tensions between values that are perceived or experienced as clashing. One need think only of recent debates in France about the legalisation of gay marriage and in Italy about the display of the crucifix in state schools. Each of these cases has in its own way revealed a profound division within public opinion as regards rights that are deemed essential to the smooth functioning of a democratic society, while having nothing to do with the arrival of new communities. In France, it was the right to choose one's partner and the protection of privacy that were at issue, and in Italy, the right of parents to claim for their children the protection of the freedom not to believe.

The debate on which I will concentrate in this chapter focuses on the practice of infant and young boys' circumcision, and on the opposition that it has brought to light between two contrasting interpretations of the child's interests: on the one hand, an approach that links these interests to the incorporation of the child within the religion, tradition and group to which his parents (or one of them) belong and, on the other, a more individual conception of those interests that would endow the child with the right to make his own decision as soon as he has attained the necessary maturity to do so. No fewer than three recent debates, as I will show, illustrate these differences; the virulent terms in which they were (and to some extent still are) conducted show the extent to which commitments are strong on all sides of the question. There is every indication that the opposing views around this issue have touched a nerve among the participants in the debate.

The first of these debates was probably the most closely followed in Europe, namely the one that led in Germany to a court decision handed down in 2012 by a court in Cologne and that was widely discussed in the media over several weeks. It ended – provisionally – with a vote in the German Parliament for a legislative solution, a topic I will return to below. The second debate is the one conducted at the Parliamentary Assembly of the Council of Europe (PACE) and which resulted in the adoption of a resolution that called into question, as non-medically justified violations of children's physical integrity, a number of practices including, notably, the circumcision of young boys. Finally, more recently, it was Israel's turn, where a judgment handed down at the end of 2013 by a rabbinical court sparked off a public debate. On 29 June 2014, the High Court of Justice ruled on the case. Its decision had been eagerly awaited, judging by the reactions that during the months before filled not only the press but also the internet, which in Israel as elsewhere nowadays offers a platform of exchange that is particularly popular whenever a subject causes agitation.

1.2. OUTLINE

This chapter is divided into two sections. In the first part, I briefly summarise the essence of the three debates referred to above, with particular attention to the arguments – both in favour and against boys' circumcision – put forward in each of them. The aim here is not to analyse each argument in depth – such an analysis having already been made in various other fora and publications. Rather, the aim here is to provide the information necessary to serve as background for the second part, which will emphasise certain factors that explain why the different positions on what constitutes the best interests of the child when it comes to the practice of infant and young boys' circumcision, and on how best to protect those interests, are so difficult to reconcile. An examination of these factors indicates that a different approach is needed than simply asserting that one group is right and the other wrong, if we are truly to speak of sustainable accommodation of these differences.

Among the steps that I suggest may be useful for devising forms of sustainable accommodation is to draw upon anthropology and more particularly legal anthropology, which focuses on the impact various (including religious) norms and standards may have on human behaviour within particular contexts. I will first explain the anthropologist's intellectual and methodological approach, in order to then explore the insights one may gain from drawing on this discipline in a debate as vehement as the one on boys' circumcision – in particular when performed on infant boys – and, more generally, in other debates where profound values are at issue and where the objective is to build a bridge, as far as possible, between radically opposing positions.

Before ending on a few reflections of my own, I will briefly outline, in section 2.3, the three positions that can on the whole be identified throughout Europe today, either from the case law or from legislative initiatives, and that each seek to set limits on non-medically justified modifications of children's bodies.

1.3. CHANGING PERSPECTIVES ON CIRCUMCISION

Male circumcision is a surgical removal of some or all of the foreskin (or prepuce) from the penis. It is probably the oldest identified and most frequently performed optional surgical procedure for males throughout the world.[1] Circumcision of infants or young boys may be performed for medical, cultural or religious reasons. It is a widely observed practice performed almost universally in Jewish and Muslim communities.[2] Until recently, it has been largely uncontroversial, as compared to the practices of excision – in various forms – of young women, which has been the subject of vehement controversy for several decades: excision is considered by an ever increasing number of its opponents as a mutilation of the woman's body, as is clear from the unequivocal generic terms "female genital mutilation" or "female genital cutting" by which it has come to be known.[3]

It would seem, however, that a new wave of protest has recently emerged against the acceptance of male infant circumcision. This should hardly be

1 D. Gollaher, *Circumcision: A History of the World's Most Controversial Surgery*, Basic Books 2000; E. Wyner Mark, *The Convenant of Circumcision: New Perspectives on an Ancient Jewish Rite*, HBI Series on Jewish Women, Brandeis University Press 2003; M. Chebel, *Histoire de la circoncision des origines à nos jours*, Balland 1992; S.A. Aldeeb Abu-Sahlieh, *Male and Female Circumcision Among Jews, Christians and Muslims: Religious Debate*, Riad El-Rayyes Books 2000; L.B. Glick, *Marked in Your Flesh: Circumcision from Ancient Judea to Modern America*, Oxford University Press 2005; H. Lightfoot-Klein, *Children's Genitals Under the Knife: social imperatives, secrecy and shame*, Booksurge Publishing 2007.

2 S.A. Aldeeb Abu-Sahlieh, *supra* note 1; see also: Explanatory memorandum by Ms Rupprecht, rapporteur, Resolution 1952 (2013), Parliamentary Assembly; Council of Europe, Report (Doc. 13297; text adopted on 1 October 2013).

3 The rhetoric in the case of anti-female-circumcision campaigns is at times very strong, accusatory and emotional even, using concepts ranging from "female castration", through "sexual blinding" or "torture", to "war against women". See: "Mutilations sexuelles", special issue of *Droit et Cultures. Revue semestrielle d'anthropologie et d'histoire*, 1990, no. 20, pp. 146–270; E. Gruenbaum, *The Female Circumcision Controversy*, Philadelphia, University of Pennsylvania Press 2000; E. Dorkenoo, *Female Genital Mutilation: politics and prevention*, Hurst 2010; A. Macklin, "The double-edged sword: using the criminal law against female genital mutilation", in R. Mustafa Abusharaf (ed.), *Female Circumcision: multicultural perspectives*, University of Pennsylvania Press 2006, pp. 207–223; R.A. Shweder, "What about female genital mutilation? And why understanding culture matters in the first place", in R.A. Shweder et al. (eds.), *Engaging Cultural Differences: the multicultural challenge in liberal democracies*, Russell Sage Foundation 2002, pp. 216–251; S.M. Robleh, "A review of female genital mutilation (FGM): background, consequences and politics", in *Variations on the Theme of Somaliness*, Proceedings of the EASS/SSIA International Congress of Somali Studies, Turku, Finland, August 2001, pp. 91–110; A. Rahman, *Female Genital Mutilation: A guide to laws and policies worldwide*, Zed Books 2001.

surprising, as Ally Fogg remarks in his blog: "as awareness grows of the risks of adverse consequences and complications, as religious devotion slides and appreciation of individual human rights to bodily integrity grows, and as claims for health benefits from routine ritual circumcision are increasingly shown to be arguable, if not downright spurious".[4] Fogg does not claim that this is an exhaustive list of the factors that explain the growing opposition to the circumcision of boys, but be that as it may, evidence shows that these various factors do not have the same role or the same intensity everywhere. His diagnosis is corroborated by at least three recent debates: circumcision of boys has become a topic that divides opinions and communities, and not just in Europe.[5]

1.3.1. "Oho, also die Medizin ist jetzt unsere neue Religion":[6] Circumcision under Attack in Germany

The first debate to be discussed here is also the one that, in Europe to date, has given rise to the most turmoil on this question: in a judgment handed down on 26 June 2012, the Cologne Regional Court (*Landgericht*) held that "circumcision changes the child's body permanently and irreparably", adding that "[t]his change runs contrary to the interests of the child in deciding his religious affiliation independently later in life."[7] The German court was ruling on a case involving a family physician who had circumcised a four-year-old boy at the request of his parents, who were devout Muslims. A few days after the procedure, however, the boy had to be taken to the emergency room because of bleeding. From what the mother said there, the doctor inferred that she had not fully consented to the procedure, and informed the police. Based on this information, the public prosecutor of the city of Cologne launched proceedings against the physician who had performed the circumcision. The Cologne District Court (*Amtsgericht*) acquitted the doctor of the charge of grievous bodily harm. But on appeal, the Cologne Regional Court reviewed the ruling and handed down a strikingly different judgment: in the opinion of the appellate judge – whose ruling is the one that caused the uproar – the principle must be that the right of a child to his bodily integrity takes precedence over the rights of the parents. And even though the doctor who performed the circumcision was himself acquitted,[8] the ruling gave rise to a veritable clash of values regarding the relationship between religion and society.

4 A. Fogg, "Courts must not rule on circumcision, even in Israel", *Heteronormative Patriarchy for Men*, 3 December 2013, at http://freethoughtblogs.com/hetpat/2013/12/03.

5 See among others: G.C. Denniston et al. (eds.), *Circumcision and Human Rights*, Springer 2009.

6 This somewhat cynical reflection was made by Rabbi Tovia Ben-Chorin, cited in D. Graumann, "Etwas ist zerbrochen", *Die Zeit*, 13 September 2012, p. 10.

7 Landgericht Köln, *Beschneidung*, Judgment of Monday, 7 May 2012, No. 151 Ns 169/11; English translation by the ILM Website at Durham University Law School, available at https://www.dur.ac.uk/resources/ilm/CircumcisionJudgmentLGCologne7May20121.pdf.

8 In the opinion of the court, the doctor had acted to the best of his knowledge within the law; he could not have known that what he was doing was punishable by law.

The judgment outraged Muslims and Jews in the country and sparked an extremely emotional debate. The Central Council of Jews in Germany responded vigorously, considering that this was "unprecedented and interference with the prerogatives of religious communities" in Germany.[9] For Jews and Muslims, circumcision is more than just a pious custom: "Circumcision of newborn boys is an inherent part of the Jewish religion and has been practiced worldwide for centuries", noted the Council's president, Dieter Graumann, in an interview published in the daily *Frankfurter Allgemeine Zeitung*.[10] Although the ban which – at least indirectly – resulted from the judgment applied only to the Cologne region, doctors across the country refused from then on to carry out circumcisions because of what they saw as a risk of legal action, leaving it up to the legislators to come up with a decision regarding the right to circumcise. German paediatricians in particular applauded the position taken by the court, speaking of a legal decision that is "extremely important for physicians, since for the first time they have legal grounds which they can invoke". Embarrassment on the part of the authorities – Pinchas Goldschmidt, the president of the Conference of European Rabbis, called the verdict the "worst attack on Jewish life since the Holocaust" – probably explains why a legislative solution was agreed upon as early as the autumn of 2012.[11] The new law (20 December 2012)[12] protects the right to circumcise, provided that the operation takes place with the most effective pain relief possible and only if the

9 *"[B]eispiellosen und dramatischen Eingriff in das Selbstbestimmungsrecht der Religionsgemeinschaften"* [unprecedented and dramatic intrusion in the right to self-determination of religious communities], *Frankfurter Allgemeine Zeitung*, 27 June 2012.

10 *Frankfurter Allgemeine Zeitung*, 27 June 2012. See the English text in the press release of 27 June 2012 by the Central Council of Jews in Germany, available at www.zentralratdjuden.de/en/article/3706.on-the-decision-of-the-district-court-of-cologne-concerning-circumcision-of-boys.html.

11 www.circinfo.org/doctors.html.

12 Now incorporated into Article §1631d of the German Civil Code (BGB), the law provides, as regards neonatal circumcision: "*Beschneidung des männliches Kindes: (1) Die Personensorge umfasst auch das Recht, in eine medizinisch nicht erforderliche Beschneidung des nicht einsichts- und urteilfähigen männlichen Kindes einzuwilligen, wenn diese nach den Regeln der ärztlichen Kunst durchgeführt werden soll. Dies gilt nicht, wenn durch diese Beschneidung auch unter Berücksichtigung ihres Zwecks das Kindeswohl gefährdet wird. (2) In den ersten sechs Monaten nach der Geburt des Kindes dürfen auch von einer Religionsgesellschaft dazu vorgesehene Personen Beschneidungen gemäss Absatz 1 durchführen, wenn sie dafür besonders ausgebildet und, ohne Arzt zu sein, für die Durchführung der Beschneidung vergleichbar befähigt sind.*" ["Circumcision of the male child. (1) The care for the person also encompasses the right to consent to a medically unnecessary circumcision of the male child incapable of insight and decision, if it is to be performed according to the rules of medicine. This does not apply if the circumcision endangers, even in light of its purpose, should endanger the child's welfare. (2) In the first six months after the birth of the child, persons delegated for that purpose by a religious body may also perform circumcisions in accordance with paragraph 1 if they are specially trained for that purpose and, though not physicians, are comparatively qualified for performing circumcisions."] (http://last-conformer.net/2012/12/28/its-official/). For more detailed comments, see i.a.: M. Germann, "Die Verfassungsmässigkeit des Gesetzes über den Umfang der Personensorge bei einer Beschneidung des männliches Kindes vom 20.12.2012", *Medizinrecht*, July 2013, 7, pp. 412–424; T. Walter, "Der Gesetzentwurf zur Beschneidung – Kritik und strafrechtliche Alternative", *Juristen Zeitung*, 2012, pp. 110–117; J. Isensee,

parents have been fully informed about the nature of the procedure. Generally it ought to be doctors who perform circumcision, but if a boy is less than six months old it can also be performed by another qualified person, such as a *mohel*, a Jewish individual specially trained in circumcising.

The emotions triggered by the circumcision ruling in Germany were all the stronger on the part of Jews – but also Muslims – since, in their view, this ruling illustrated not so much the importance of physical integrity to the individual development of children regardless of their parents' freedom of religion, but instead a more general tendency to restrict the rights of religious minorities.[13] Moreover, they were of the opinion that isolating newborn boys' circumcision as an issue on its own is a highly selective – and thus unfair – way to address the overall question of how to achieve the right balance between protection of freedom of religion (*in casu* of the parents) and concern for the best interests of children. Parents continuously consent to practices that have an irreversible impact on their children's souls and bodies, whether by the choice of schooling, or vaccination or orthodontic work; and the ruling on circumcision was therefore perceived as an eclectic misapplication of the principles of individual freedom of religion and the right to control one's physical integrity.[14]

This is not a minor accusation; it echoes a reproach already voiced on several occasions in recent years in many other European countries as well: certain minority groups (mainly religious minorities) protest against what they perceive as a selective policy of intrusion in their traditions and practices that seeks, in the name of (the protection of) human rights and fundamental freedoms, to restrict certain rights in particular while ignoring the fact that these had historically been granted precisely in the name of religious freedom.[15] In their perception, these intrusions – whether formulated in court decisions or in legislation – have more to do with an increasing uneasiness in Europe about the presence of growing Jewish and Muslim communities in particular and their continued practices than with views about how to consistently protect individuals against infringements of their basic rights.

"Grundrechtliche Konsequenz wider geheiligte Tradition", *ibid.*, 2013, pp. 317–327; T. Hörnle and S. Huster, "Wie weit reicht das Erziehungsrecht der Eltern?", *ibid.*, 2013, pp. 328–339.

13 For an earlier critique of this tendency, see among others: A.M. Viens, "Value Judgement, Harm and Religious Liberty" (2004) 3 *Journal of Medical Ethics* 242; more recently: A. Bodenheimer, *Haut Ab! Die Juden in der Beschneidungsdebatte*, Wallstein Verlag 2012.

14 On this inconsistency, see: G.B. Levey, "Thinking about Infant Male Circumcision after the Cologne Court Decision" (2013) 3(2) *Global Discourse: An Interdisciplinary Journal of Current Affairs and Applied Contemporary Thought* 326–331; R.A. Shweder, "The Goose and the Gander: the genital wars", *ibid.*, pp. 348–366.

15 Recent attempts both in the courts and in the national legislation of various European countries (e.g. the Netherlands, Belgium and Denmark) have also targeted the Jewish method of slaughtering meat known as Shechita. See among others: M.-C. Foblets and J. Velaers, "Recent Discussions in Belgium and the Netherlands on Religious Freedom and the Slaughter of Animals without Prior Stunning", in B. Schinkele et al. (eds.), *Recht, Religion, Kultur. Festschrift für Richard Potz zum 70. Geburtstag*, Facultas 2013, pp. 67–86.

It may be hoped that in practice the new German law will succeed in offering the comfort necessary to those who were concerned about the legal void left by the circumcision ban of the Regional Court of Cologne and in particular to those who will henceforth be called upon to apply the law. However, symbolic wounds may unfortunately remain. To some, the weight of German history regarding the question of bodily integrity needs to be brought into the picture here since it may help explain a number of arguments that have played both in the reasoning of the court and in the background of the debates that broke out after the judgment of the appeal court was made public: "Strange as it may seem, the court based its decision on principles of individual freedom and physical integrity that make sense only as products of Germany's particular reckoning with its past, from the Nürnberg trials to the present", Kristen Loveland noted drily.[16] Some people have spoken out on this issue to remind anyone who would listen that the Jewish community does not need lessons from Germany when it comes to respecting the bodily integrity of minors.

Implicit in the Cologne court's reasoning is the view that ultimately it is the child who should decide whether to be circumcised, and whether to affiliate with the religion of his parents, after he reaches the (legal) age to make decisions and to consent. In practice, postponing the decision until the individual is able to make his own decision will most probably also mean that the pain, the discomfort and also the anxiety of the operation increases, but that seems to be a lesser evil compared to the paramount concern to safeguard bodily integrity in the absence of the child's consent. Yet to some, this approach is at the same time extremely disquieting, albeit from another point of view: it deprives parents of their capacity to make decisions in what they believe to be the best interests of their own children on the grounds that their view differs from a majority standard or convention. Such reasoning offers a clear illustration of an approach against which Mathias Rohe, a German expert in issues of accommodation of Islamic law in Europe, has vehemently warned: "Naturally, freedom of religion also has its limits, but these must not be drawn up according to majorities and minorities".[17] The decision of the Cologne court obliquely demonises the practice of non-medically justified circumcision of boys and, whether intentionally or not, its reasoning also proclaims the moral superiority of the judge's own view on how to best protect the interests of children.

Rohe's appeal for prudence applies all the more to the initiative taken by the Parliamentary Assembly of the Council of Europe (PACE), which also voted on a resolution against circumcision of children, including the circumcision of young boys. Rohe's warning was too late, however, as the resolution was passed with a very large majority, as I explain briefly in what follows.

---

16 K. Loveland, "The Circumcision Ban. Physical Integrity and Individual Dignity", www.dissentmagazine.org/online_articles/the-circumcision-ban.

17 M. Rohe, "Sharia Law in Europe" (interview L. Mudhoon), Qanatara.de – Dialogue with the Islamic World, 5 March 2008, http://en.qantara.de/The-Idea-of-Plural-Jursidiction-Is-Highly-Problematic.

1.3.2. The Parliamentary Assembly of the Council of Europe Speaks Out

On 1 October 2013 the Parliamentary Assembly of the Council of Europe (PACE) passed a (non-binding) resolution calling circumcision a "violation of the physical integrity of children".[18] The resolution also applies to circumcision of boys, calling it a human rights issue. The Council, a pan-European intergovernmental organisation, based its initiative on a report drafted by the Commission on Social Affairs, Health and Sustainable Development led by the German rapporteur Marlene Rupprecht.[19] The resolution passed by a vote of 78 in favour and 13 against, with 15 abstentions. The resolution also calls on contracting parties (states that are members of the Council of Europe) to "adopt specific legal provisions to ensure that certain operations and practices will not be carried out before the child is old enough to be consulted" (7.7) and "to initiate a public debate, including intercultural and interreligious dialogue, aimed at reaching a large consensus on the rights of children to protection against violations of their physical integrity according to human rights standards" (7.4). Practices covered by the resolution include female genital mutilation, the circumcision of young boys for religious reasons, early childhood medical interventions in the case of intersex children and the submission to or coercion of children into piercing, tattoos or plastic surgery. No fewer than five amendments sought to remove from the list the circumcision of young boys, but they were rejected. Moreover, an amendment that removed a reference to the "religious rights of parents and families" was supported by a large majority.

The resolution adopted by PACE does not stand on its own. In recent years, qualified medical staff elsewhere in Europe have also expressed concern about the harm that they consider newborn circumcision inflicts on the physical integrity of boys. Because of the lack of reliable scientific evidence demonstrating any decisive benefit, circumcision of infants has been condemned by the Royal Dutch Medical Association (KNMG),[20] the German Paediatric Association[21] and the Swedish Paediatric Society (BLF).[22] An increasingly widespread position among physicians in Europe thus seems to be that although circumcision of infants and young boys

18 Parliamentary Assembly of the Council of Europe, Resolution 1952 (2013) final version, p. 2, http://assembly.coe.int/nw/xml/XRef/Xref-XML2HTML-en.asp?fileid=20174&lang=en.

19 "Children's right to physical integrity", Report, Committee on Social Affairs, Health and Sustainable Development, Council of Europe, Doc. 13297 of 6 September 2013.

20 *Niet-therapeutische circumcisie bij minderjarige jongens* (non-therapeutic circumcision of minor boys), 2010, www.knmg.nl/jongensbesnijdenis.

21 Deutsche Gesellschaft für Kinderchirurgie, http://dgkic.de/index.php/presse/204pressemitteilung-oktober2012.

22 In 2001, Sweden enacted restrictive legislation: for boys less than two months of age it could be performed by appropriately trained non-medical practitioners using topical anaesthesia, but for boys over two months it had to be performed in hospital under general anaesthesia. In 2012 however, the Swedish Paediatric Society called for a complete ban on ritual circumcision (see also *infra* section 2.3) and Staffan Janson in this volume.

is widely performed in both medical and religious contexts, it constitutes a human rights violation against children. This amounts to an affirmation that the physical integrity of children takes precedence over religion.[23] The resolution voted for by PACE is thus grounded in arguments *against* male circumcision that sound very familiar to those promoting ever more fervently the rights of children in Europe, and it does no more than corroborate these arguments.

Yet it would be an exaggeration to state that PACE voted for an immediate ban on the circumcision of young boys; instead it called on the Council of Europe's contracting parties to "clearly define the medical, sanitary and other conditions to be ensured for practices which are today widely carried out in certain religious communities, such as the non-medically justified circumcision of young boys" (7.5.2). Even if the concern is in the first instance based on medical concerns and not targeting religion *per se*, undeniably given the context within which it was adopted, the resolution is to be interpreted as a disapproval of non-therapeutic body modifications performed involving children and that are grounded on religious beliefs.

Some years ago, the American anthropologist Zachary Androus, in a contribution on genital modification of children, reported a Somali immigrant in Italy remarking: "Europeans seemed to care more about the clitoris of African women than they cared about the women themselves".[24] The passage may appear overstated, but there is undoubtedly some truth in it. Although the adoption of Resolution 1952 (2013) by PACE is non-binding, it clearly confirms the Assembly's readiness to align itself with the view that the physical integrity of children is a value that should not easily be undermined, even if in the name of their religion. In other words, religion should end where it collides with the physical integrity of a child. To date, PACE has generally speaking been a strong supporter of religious rights,[25] but in the case of non-medically justified genital modifications, including the circumcision of young boys for religious reasons, it has given precedence to the rights of children.

---

23 In the United States, by contrast, the opinion of doctors seems to run in the opposite direction: according to the evaluation by the American Academy of Pediatrics (AAP) Task Force on Circumcision in 2012, "the health benefits of newborn male circumcision *outweigh* the risks". This opinion though is phrased in a nuanced way: "but the benefits are not great enough to recommend universal newborn circumcision" (American Academy of Pediatrics Task Force on Circumcision, Male Circumcision (abstract), National Center for Biotechnological Information, United States National Library of Medicine (Pubmed), 2012, www.ncbi.nlm.nih.ogv:pubmed/22926175).

24 Z. Androus, "Cultural Relativism at Home and Abroad. An American Anthropologist Confronts the Genital Modification of Children", in G.C. Denniston et al. (eds), *Circumcision and Human Rights*, Springer 2009, pp. 33–41 at 36.

25 See G. Gonzales (ed.), *Laïcité, liberté de religion et Convention européenne des droits de l'homme*, Bruylant 2006; J.-F. Flauss (ed.), *La protection internationale de la liberté religieuse/International Protection of Religious Freedom*, Bruylant 2002.

Criticism of PACE[26] for including in the list of violations the circumcision of young boys for religious reasons has come from those who interpret the best interests of the child more broadly, taking into consideration religious rights and practices as well, and refusing to concede that circumcision performed at a (very) young age – provided it is carried out according to the highest medical and hygienic standards – would cause major harm to children's health. In the critics' view, the priority should be respect for a ritual that has been performed for centuries and is an integral and indispensable part of certain religions. They see the recent inversion of priorities, whether by the medical profession or by PACE, as yet another in a long list of disapprovals attacking the religious identity of certain minority groups and even their very presence in Europe. In order to enable the debate to continue and to have as open a debate as possible between the different viewpoints on this highly sensitive issue, a parliamentary hearing on boys' circumcision took place in Strasbourg on 28 January 2014 on the margins of the plenary session of PACE. It brought together medical experts, including those representing the Jewish and Muslim communities. A record of the testimonies is available on the website of the Assembly.[27] The debate did not succeed in closing the gulf between the positions; several Jews and Muslims who participated in the discussion spoke about how important circumcision is to their religion, way of life and existence; they denied that the practice caused any irreversible harm and argued, on the contrary, for its health benefits. Many of them were outraged, reminding the audience of the Jewish experience of the Holocaust, and insinuating that the debate was motivated by anti-Semitism.[28] They expressed the fear that the 2013 PACE resolution would pave the way for bans to be put in place in various European countries.

1.3.3. Balancing Religious Rights with Child Protection

Yet some have also expressed a more moderate opinion on the issue, arguing that a more nuanced approach is also possible, without necessarily running counter to the spirit of protecting young children. In an article published in the *Helsinki Times* in December 2013[29] there was discussion of a decision handed down by the Helsinki Court of Appeal, which, after meticulous examination of the specific circumstances of the case before it, concluded that instead of convicting the

---

26 In one of her comments, Liliane Maury Pasquier, chair of the Parliamentary Assembly of the Council of Europe's Committee of Social Affairs, Health and Sustainable Development, even spoke of "vilification".

27 For a full record, see: http://clients.dbee.com/coe/webcast/index;php?id=20140128-5&lang=en.

28 In the same vein: T. Gold, "A ban on male circumcision would be anti-Semitic? How could it not be?", *The Guardian*, 11 October 2013.

29 K. Markkanen and A. Teivainen, "Court: Circumcision of Muslim Boys not an Offence", *Helsinki Times*, 12 December 2013. The judgment was delivered on 5 December 2013, *Case No 3184, R 12/705*. For a more detailed description of this judgment and Finnish case law on the issue, see Maarit Jänterä-Jareborg in this volume, section 8.

defendants in question, it would be far better to pass legislation that, within the domestic legal order, would clarify the conditions to be met when performing circumcisions on infants and young boys in order to be perfectly legal.

The court acquitted both the person who had performed the circumcision of two Muslim boys and had subsequently been charged with assault *and* the parents of the boys, charged with incitement to assault. "The decision marks a fundamental shift in Finnish judicial practice concerning the issue of boys' circumcisions", the authors of the article commented.[30] In this case, the same person who performed the operations with a cautery in the homes of the boys had already performed several circumcisions in both Turkey and Iran. However, the incision of one of the boys became infected, forcing the boy to miss school and seek medical assistance. The infection had been caused, the court found, not by the operation itself, but by insufficient after-care. The person who performed the circumcision used surgical gloves, sterilised the instrument used, applied local anaesthesia and provided the parents with instructions for after-care, the court added.

Interestingly, in its ruling, the Helsinki Court of Appeal also refers to the Council of Europe's Convention on Human Rights and Biomedicine[31] but it rejects the argument that this text could serve as justification to declare circumcision unlawful. In the opinion of the court, the Convention applies only to organ transplants, not to circumcisions. In addition, the court held that Finnish law does not prescribe that circumcisions must be performed by licensed medical practitioners and that the person who performed the operations had acted with due diligence. Finally, the court recommended that laws on male circumcision be drafted in order to eradicate any judicial ambiguities.

This court decision thus shows that it is possible to adopt a reasoning that is slightly different from that of PACE, upholding the general principle while still allowing for a result that accommodates the demands of the different parties involved. But be that as it may, there is no assurance that the position taken by the

---

30 The Finnish Supreme Court had, nevertheless, already ruled on circumcision of boys in a judgment of 2008, *KKO 2008:93*. In that judgment, the defendants were freed of the criminal law charges on the basis that the act (of circumcision) had been motivated on justifiable personal and religious grounds. The same position was taken in a later judgment by the Helsinki Court of Appeal, No 940, 30 March 2011. In the even more recent (appealed) judgment of the Helsinki Court of Appeal No. 12, 10 January 2014, regard was given to the circumcision's purpose of integrating the child in the Nigerian (Roman Catholic) father's paternal community and culture, and the defendant father was acquitted. See Maarit Jänterä-Jareborg in this volume, section 8.

31 Convention for the Protection of Human Rights and Dignity of the Human Being with Regard to the Application of Biology and Medicine: Convention on Human Rights and Biomedicine, Oviedo, 4 March 1997, *European Treaty Series*, no. 164. In fact, having regard to the precedent of the Finnish Supreme Court, *KKO 2008:93* (*ibid.*), from a legal point of view the case focuses on the question whether Finland's ratification of the said Convention called for another assessment of a basically similar case. Whereas in the opinion of the court of first instance (Helsinki City Court, judgment 30 December 2011) a religious circumcision of boys *is* contrary to the Convention, the Court of Appeal considered this not to be the case. The Court of Appeal pointed out that to its knowledge the Convention's ratification has not resulted in the prohibition of circumcision in any of the contracting states.

Finnish judges will be met favourably by everyone.[32] Instead, it appears that in Europe an ever louder voice is demanding that the pendulum should stop swinging between, on the one hand, support for "the dark side" of religion, tradition and identity and, on the other, the forceful plea for protection of the rights of children against violations of their physical integrity as provided for in human rights standards. Where physical integrity is involved, a balancing of the human rights at stake is in their view out of the question. In other words, advocates of this position will entertain no concessions: in their view the child's physical integrity should be the paramount consideration, so much so that no circumcision that is not strictly justified by medical reasons can be accepted any more. The conclusion drawn by Marlene Rupprecht at the public hearing of 28 January 2014 is very relevant in this regard: "It is the rights of the child that are foremost in our minds [...] I ask you to understand what motivates us". One may fear that the debate in Europe will find no easy resolution. For the same concern, namely the child's best interests, also preoccupies those who condemn the resolution, but for them, the interests of the child must be seen in a broader perspective, including all the *good* that religion and tradition can also give a child.

1.4. EUROPE IS NOT THE ONLY PLACE WHERE CIRCUMCISION IS CALLED INTO QUESTION: *PLONIT V. THE GREAT RABBINICAL COURT IN ISRAEL*

In Europe, as already indicated, some critics are of the opinion that over and above the concern for protection of the physical integrity of minors, there may be in the minds of some people a propensity to try to kill two birds with one stone, using the debate about children to stigmatise certain religious minorities in particular. If indeed it turned out that the rights of the child serve as a pretext in a debate where the real stakes lie elsewhere, this would thwart the situation and preclude a frank and open debate.

The latter interpretation is probably insufficiently nuanced, and should not be taken to mean that the practice of circumcision for religious reasons remains unchallenged in other parts of the world. As it happens, it is in fact in Israel, a country where the Jewish community constitutes the vast majority of the population, that the debate has been in full swing for some time, following a controversial decision handed down by a rabbinical court. True, the context is different, but the case reveals a growing sensitivity within the Jewish community as well to the interests of the child that is not dictated first and foremost by religious belonging. "The case shines a spotlight on a long-running debate over religious

32 The District Prosecutor in Helsinki immediately affirmed that she would seek leave to appeal to the Supreme Court, "since all the charges were rejected". Cf. *supra* note 29. The application for a review permit is pending (2015).

coercion in Israel, where generations of leaders have struggled to find a balance between the country's Jewish and democratic character", observed Daniel Estrin.[33] What was the case about?[34]

On 19 December 2013 Israel's High Court of Justice issued a temporary injunction freezing a rabbinical court's decree that had ordered a mother to circumcise her son against her wishes. On 29 October 2013 the Netanya Rabbinical Court had imposed a penalty of NIS 500 (USD 140) per day on the woman who refused to have her one-year-old son undergo circumcision. It did so after having required the mother to verify with a medical doctor working in an Israeli hospital and also a *mohel* that there was no medical impediment to having the circumcision performed. The boy had not been circumcised at eight days old, as is the rule in Jewish law, because the child was born prematurely. In such circumstances, Jewish law prescribes that circumcision be postponed. Shortly thereafter, the parents' marriage broke down,[35] and subsequently the woman decided she no longer wished to have her son circumcised. Later she claimed she had her husband's consent for taking that position. During the divorce proceedings, however, the husband asked the rabbinical court to compel his wife to allow circumcision to be performed upon the boy. According to the Attorney General's response to the Court, the wife sought to have the Family Court decide the question of the circumcision, as part of the claim brought for settling the marital property. However, the Family Court dismissed her application since it considered that this matter could not be adjudicated as a part of that claim. The Rabbinical Court not only granted the father's request, holding that the circumcision was for the child's welfare and thus ordering the mother to have the circumcision performed within seven days, but it also ruled that she would have to pay a daily penalty until she complied with the court order.[36] In the opinion of the judges, the mother refused to have the son circumcised as a way of forcing reconciliation with her husband. On appeal before the Supreme Rabbinical Court of Appeals, the judges, at the very end of their ruling, also mentioned their concern that allowing a Jewish Israeli woman to leave her son uncircumcised

---

33 D. Estrin, "Rabbinical court in Israel orders circumcision. Official role of religion under spotlight", *The Boston Globe*, 29 November 2013.

34 I would like here to thank Talia Einhorn sincerely for clarifying the legal situation in Israel to me, in particular regarding the jurisdiction of the rabbinical and secular courts, and the cases.

35 According to the Supreme Rabbinical Court's decision, the wife, in answer to a question put to her by the Rabbinical Court, told the Court that she did not want to be divorced but rather wanted conciliation. Thus the Supreme Rabbinical Court concluded that all the wife wanted in fact was to postpone the divorce until her husband agreed to resume their marital life.

36 The fine was initially imposed, as a sanction for contempt of court, because the mother refused to appear before the rabbinical court. The court could have chosen to order the police to bring her, but instead it sanctioned her with a daily financial penalty. It chose the latter solution because it considered that it would be improper to order the police to bring a mother who has to look after a baby to be heard by the court. When the mother appeared the sanction was frozen; however, it was re-imposed as a sanction for contempt of court, should the mother not carry out the circumcision.

would encourage the anti-ritual circumcision movement in Europe and the United States, thereby giving political weight to the reasoning of the judges involved in the case.[37]

The case has given rise to debate in Israel that can be followed through the media and social networks: it reveals disagreement between those who give clear priority to the autonomy and protection of the integrity of minors (with comments such as "this is a clear example of a court forcing a physical assault on a child" or "this rabbinical court ruling is dangerous for democracy") and those who, on the contrary, see circumcision as part of the integrity of Jewish minors, even perfecting their body, and claim respect for this view as being part of freedom of religion. The arguments invoked on both sides are very similar to those found within the debate in Europe. The positions are associated with uncompromising, not to say mutually incompatible values and priorities. Values associated with *pro*-circumcision arguments are: upholding religion and respect for tradition and thus accepting conventional practices in order to conform to group expectations; and to a lesser extent, stoicism and endurance. Values associated with *anti*-circumcision arguments are: individual rights and freedom of choice as of paramount importance; intolerance of avoidable pain/risk; surgery should be allowed for therapeutic purposes only; and, to a certain extent but difficult to measure, sexual pleasure at adult age.

The commotion that is perceptible behind the debate is probably linked to the fact that it is the first time a religious court in Israel has punished a parent for refusing to circumcise a child. The mother had argued, among other things, that the rabbinical court does not have jurisdiction over the matter but the court rejected that argument.

The Israeli Court for Family Affairs Act, §3, provides that family affairs, as defined by the Act, are adjudicated by the family court. However, §25 of the same Act provides that: (a) the Family Court Act will not derogate from the powers of the religious courts and the labour courts; and (b) if a matter is subject to concurrent jurisdiction of the family court and the religious court, the family court may assume jurisdiction, on the condition that the case was not brought before the religious court

37 A. Fogg, *supra* note 4. The court notes a growing global trend *against* acceptance of infant circumcision. After a discussion of the factual situation obtaining between the parents in this particular case and the Jewish Law (*halakhah*) in this matter, the rabbinical court concludes with the statement: "It is unthinkable that the matter of performing or failing to perform circumcision will be taken out of the hands of halakhic scholars (*hakhmei Yisrael*) and be subject to the discretion of a civil court, where each person has his own opinions and worldview – God forbid that this should happen in Israel [here meaning the People of Israel, not the land]". The court then adds the following two sentences: "Furthermore, we are witnessing, since a long time in many European states and in the US, public and legal campaigns against circumcision, whereas the public in Israel is united against such campaigns and considers them another aspect of anti-Semitism which should be fought against. We welcome any statement and act by the leaders of these countries that support our position. What will the world make of it, if here too circumcision will be left to each person's discretion according to his perceptions".

first. The competence of the rabbinical courts is set out in the Rabbinical Courts Jurisdiction Act (Marriage and Divorce), 5713–1953. With respect to maintenance, the wife has, in principle, the option of bringing a claim for alimony in either the rabbinical court *or* in the family court (§4, Rabbinical Courts Jurisdiction Act). If she chooses to bring the case before the Family Court, the latter may exercise jurisdiction provided that the husband had not first filed a case for divorce in the Rabbinical Court and included in his claim an application for the Rabbinical Court to decide the issue of maintenance as an ancillary matter, in which case the rabbinical court exercises exclusive jurisdiction (Rabbinical Courts Jurisdiction Act, §3).

"The 'race' for jurisdiction has always been, and still is, a thorny issue in Israeli family law", Talia Einhorn comments on this division of judiciary competences. "The law as it stands has thus provided an incentive for each spouse to rush to the court of his or her choice before the other spouse fixes jurisdiction with the less favourable court".[38] To prevent the husband from frustrating the option available to the wife (who, in many cases, prefers to litigate in the civil court), the civil courts developed the test of "sincerity", that is, the husband's inclusion of maintenance, or any other ancillary matter, in his claim for divorce has to be "sincere". In this case, the husband filed the case for divorce in the rabbinical court and included in his claim an application for the court to decide the matter of circumcision as an ancillary matter. As mentioned above, the court granted his request. The mother appealed the decision to the Supreme Rabbinical Court, but her appeal was dismissed with respect to both the order and the financial penalty. Hence she petitioned the Israeli Supreme Court, which, when sitting as the High Court of Justice, is competent to exercise judicial review of rabbinical courts' decisions. As indicated above, on 19 December 2013 the High Court issued a temporary injunction freezing the Rabbinical Court's decree ordering the mother against her wish to circumcise the couple's son. And, six months later, on 29 June 2014 it issued a ruling that was passed by an extended panel of seven justices and that voided the ruling by the Supreme Rabbinical Court. The focal point of the mother's petition to the High Court was whether a demand to circumcise could be attached to a divorce proceeding. In the opinion of the judges (six out of seven) there is nothing about circumcision that is materially linked to divorce proceedings; instead, the jurisdiction is with the Family Court, and hence a demand to circumcise will have to be decided by the Family Court on the basis of evidence, something with which the High Court does not deal. The father will have to initiate proceedings in the Family Court, which may later be appealed to the High Court.

From the discussions on social media in the period between the first and the second ruling of the High Court, three positions emerged: for some, it is high time for the question of whether or not to circumcise to be dealt with as a matter of principle by an expanded panel of High Court justices, and to state clearly that

[38] T. Einhorn, *Private International Law in Israel*, 2nd edition, Kluwer Law International 2012, para. 612.

circumcision is contrary to the best interests of a Jewish child; for a second group, the High Court ought to adopt precisely the opposite position, since in their view the decision not to circumcise a boy means uprooting the child from a vital aspect of his Jewish identity. Finally, the third position insists on the fact that it is not up to the judicial authorities to decide questions of religious upbringing, but that only a clear separation of synagogue and state can help ensure that inter- and intra-religious aspects of family disputes and issues of guardianship and parental authority in particular do not become a source of (religious) oppression.[39]

To the Court, as we now know, there is no justification for tying circumcision to a divorce proceeding and the rabbinical court had exceeded its authority with its decision. Earlier court decisions in Israel also concerned male circumcision in Israel. In 1998, a petition was submitted to the Supreme Court, sitting as the High Court of Justice (HCJ 578/98), by a charity, *The Society Against the Scission of Baby Genitals v. The Minister of Health*, appealing for a ban to be imposed on circumcision in Israel. The Supreme Court dismissed the petition, holding that circumcision was not a medical treatment and therefore the Ministry of Health was not authorised to issue such a ban, as requested by the aforementioned Society.[40] The Supreme Court's decision in this petition has not been reported in the Israeli case collections, but it has been referred to in later cases. And in 2010 the Family Court in Tel Aviv (secular, civil section; Case no 39553-09-10) ordered that a baby be circumcised at the request of the mother. The mother submitted a medical document stating that it would be in the child's best health interests to be circumcised, and that any delay may make the procedure more painful and more prone to infection. As a result, the burden of proof was shifted to the father, who did not provide any medical statement to the contrary. Furthermore, the judge tried to help the father by appointing a lawyer *ad litem*, on behalf of the court, who sought a neutral medical opinion. However, the father refused to see the expert, notifying the lawyer that he was going on vacation. The judge also mentioned the wife's statement that her husband, like all males in his family, is circumcised. In the end, the court, given the circumstances, accepted the evidence submitted by the wife. In its ruling it specified, moreover, that it had the impression that the quarrel among the spouses was not primarily about the best interests of the child but about other issues, the circumcision issue being only part of a wider disagreement between them. Ultimately, the court, having gone as far as it could in trying to obtain neutral expert information, in particular on the balance of evidence in the case, ordered the circumcision.[41] The case was decided on 7 November 2010, and

---

39 It may be useful, in particular for this third position, to note that the issue only gives rise to a case in situations where the parents disagree between each other. If neither parent wants the child to be circumcised, or if both agree to the circumcision, this will not raise a legal issue in Israel.

40 Reported in: *Nocirc Annual Report*, Spring 2000, vol. 14 (Lawsuits and Legislation), 3.

41 The judge-appointed guardian *ad litem* was to verify the correctness of the expert opinion, submitted by the mother, that there were medical reasons for carrying out the circumcision.

the father did not appeal the decision. No doubt, given the importance of ritual circumcision in Judaism, other court decisions will follow.

Clearly, infant boys' circumcision is a topic that increasingly divides opinions and communities in various places worldwide. Though I cannot be exhaustive here, there are many other ongoing debates that could be cited indicating that the discussion on infant and young boys' circumcision is occurring in many parts of the world.[42] Non-therapeutic circumcision for newborn males has been banned, for example, in Australian public hospitals, but the discussion is still ongoing.[43] For some, advocates of circumcision for religious reasons use the available medical literature selectively for their own purposes, making a mockery of the claim that the benefits of infant and young boys' circumcision would outweigh the risks. For reasons of lack of space I will stop the overview of ongoing discussions here, but what becomes clear from various recent documents that address and illustrate these debates is that, slowly but surely, genital integrity in the case of both young girls and boys is becoming a human rights issue in various countries, including outside Europe. This is true, among others, for Canada, Australia, New Zealand, and also most Central and South American countries. The plea for appropriate legal action to safeguard genital integrity of children has been sounding ever louder, also in recent years with a view to protecting infants and young boys.

2. DIFFERENT PERSPECTIVES ASSOCIATED WITH THE APPRAISAL OF CHILD CARE, IDENTITY AND PERSONHOOD

2.1. THE RESPECT DUE TO CHILDREN AND THEIR PHYSICAL INTEGRITY: THE SOCIAL NORM IS SHIFTING

It is a basic tenet of human rights protection that one right may well conflict with another. In practice, the right to religious freedom often clashes with other rights.[44] As regards the circumcision of young boys the recent debates discussed above show how complex, not least because of its extreme sensitivity, the question of what to

The father refused to pay the costs of the expert opinion, however, and refused to cooperate with the guardian (going on vacation was more important to him). The mother refused to pay for an additional expert opinion, and so the judge had to rule on the basis of the evidence that had been submitted, emphasising that this is not a principled decision.

42 See among others: N.C. Walker, "Rites v. Rights. Exemptions for Ritual Circumcision?", paper presented at the 2014 Annual Meeting of the Law and Society Association (panel on "Religion, Gender and Inequality", 30 May 2014).

43 See: *News about Circumcision from Australia and around the World*: 2012, www.circinfo.org.news_2012.htlm#guardian.

44 See, for illustrations: A. Scolnicov, *The Right to Religious Freedom in International Law. Between group rights and individual rights*, Routledge 2011.

prioritise is: the freedom of parents to bring up their children in their religion and therefore abide by the consequences of their faith, i.e. their freedom to introduce their children in a particular religious community, *or* the autonomy of the child and the requirement to safeguard his physical integrity by every possible means until he has reached the age of consent. Disputes about circumcision – to cut or not to cut – are likely to become more common in the context of contemporary society, where different groups and communities disagree among each other about answers to such basic questions as "how best to give bodily expression to one's identity, if at all".[45] Practices such as infant boys' circumcision are perceived by large portions of Jewish and Muslim communities, in particular, to be constitutive and to "build on deeply personal beliefs about the existential meaning with the human condition".[46] These are not convictions one is easily prepared to discuss, let alone to compromise on. But among majority society, public opinion over the last thirty years has become ever more responsive when it comes to the respect due to children and their integrity. The tide is turning, it seems, and the social norm is gradually changing, to the point that mainstream opinion in different countries – and this is certainly true for Europe – is increasingly vehement in opposing the physical subjection of young children to surgery that does not meet the definition of medical treatment but is practised for the sake of a group (*in casu* religious) norm. "The European reluctance to circumcise boys becomes even more apparent when requested for religious or cultural indications", Robert Wheeler and Pat Malone note.[47] The ruling in the Cologne case and Resolution 1952 (2013) adopted by PACE reflect this shifting of the social norm in Europe toward non-circumcision of young boys.

The Cologne case does not stand on its own. While circumcision lawsuits are not frequent in Europe, when disputes do arise with regard to the matter, this is usually in conflicts between parents, one of them requesting to circumcise their child and the other opposing the surgery. Understandably, the dispute most often arises between divorced spouses where the parent with custody wishes to circumcise an older child who was not circumcised at birth (for example, due to the opposition of the other parent). In a critical analysis of the case law in the United States, the lawyer David J. Llewellyn some years ago expressed concern that the courts too often follow the parent with custody and allow a physician to operate on a child with the consent of only one parent.[48] In his view, the obvious solution would be to require the consent of both parents or, even better, "to take the general approach that a parent is a good parent and a smart parent for not

45 R.A. Shweder, *supra* note 14, p. 358.

46 M. Kristiansen and A. Sheikh, "Legislation on male infant circumcision in Europe: a call to avoid paternalism and to promote evidence-based patient-centred care" (2013) 3(2) *Global Discourse: An Interdisciplinary Journal of Current Affairs and Applied Contemporary Thought* 342–347, 345.

47 R. Wheeler, "Male Circumcision. Risk versus Benefit" (2013) 98(5) *Archives of Disease in Childhood* 321–322.

48 D.J. Llewellyn, "Strategies for Litigation", in G.C. Denniston et al. (eds), *Bodily Integrity and the Politics of Circumcision. Culture, Controversy, and Change*, Springer 2009, pp. 219–232.

circumcising".[49] In Europe, the few court decisions we know of are moving the social norm even further, taking the view that the decision whether or not to be circumcised ultimately belongs to the child.[50] These court decisions therefore generally suggest waiting until the child has reached the age of consent, based on the assumption that each person alone has rights over his own body and what is done to it.

The view that the individual person should have the final say about what happens to his or her body is consistent with classic liberal legal thinking and can count on broad support today: the body has become a space of personal investment. "Body practices are increasingly positioned in various ways as expressing, reflecting, or revealing various aspects of the self, and in myriad ways bodies are seen to make the inner self visible, render it public, manage it, or establish or even affirm its authenticity", writes Victoria Pitts-Taylor.[51] In the 1970s and 1980s, bodily modifications, largely at the initiative of women wishing to align their physical appearance with the canons of female beauty, were virulently criticised by certain authors, primarily feminists. The latter saw such practices as an obstacle to the emancipation of women, since they condemn women to conform ever more completely to norms not of their own choosing, even at the expense of considerable suffering such as in sometimes extreme forms of plastic surgery. Authors such as Naomi Wolf have influenced the debate considerably, notably by showing how women, consciously or not, allow masculine norms of physical appearance to be imposed on them from outside. These norms often cause them terrible suffering, not to mention the commercial speculation on the part of those who seek to benefit from women's vulnerability in wishing to look ever more beautiful, while concealing the price they are prepared to pay for their appearance.[52] Cosmetic surgery is seen by some critics as a particularly pernicious form of self-destruction, to be equated with body dysmorphic disorder:[53] cosmetic surgery makes gullible women run the risk of becoming addicted to beauty and being prepared to invest their time and energy in a (neverending) quest to improve their body image. For similar reasons some suffer from eating disorders, albeit to varying degrees.

---

49 *Ibid.*, p. 229.

50 See for example: Tribunal de première instance [Court of First Instance] Liège, 28 June 1991, *Revue du Droit des Etrangers*, no. 64, May-August 1991, pp. 220225. The Swedish and Finnish courts have, however, taken a more nuanced and accommodating position. See Maarit Jänterä-Jareborg in this volume, section 8.

51 V. Pitts-Taylor, "Medicine, Governmentality and Biopower in Cosmetic Surgery", in S.W. Smith and R. Deazley (eds.), *The Legal, Medical and Cultural Regulation of the Body*, Ashgate 2009, pp. 159–170, 159.

52 N. Wolf, *The Beauty Myth: How images of beauty are used against women*, Chatto & Windus 1990. Other more recent works taking a similar and equally critical position include: V. Blum, *Flesh Wounds: The Culture of Cosmetic Surgery*, University of California Press 2003; S. Jeffrey, *Beauty and Misogyny: Harmful Beauty Practices in the West*, Psychology Press 2005.

53 The term was introduced by: P. Clough, "The Affective Turn: Political Economy, Biomedia, and Bodies" (2008) 1 *Theory, Culture and Society* 1–22.

For some time, however, less critical voices have been heard, suggesting that people who, out of a desire to improve their appearance, subject their bodies to various forms of physical modification or draconian personal discipline should not necessarily be seen as victims but, on the contrary, these women take their fate into their own hands, the result of which may be regarded as a new type of relationship between a person and her body. This is the position taken by Pitts-Taylor, among others, cited above: "cosmetic surgery foregrounds the relation between the body and the self and promotes the body as a site of self-management, self-care and wellness".[54] She refutes the thesis of the woman as victim, adopting instead an interpretation that restores a woman's mastery of her body. She does so in terms which present women who make use of the available surgical techniques not as submitting to dictates that come from outside themselves, but as acting out of self-esteem. Such a view takes a completely different perspective on the issue: "Far from being [...] a painful outcome of internalising patriarchy that obliterates an authentic sense of self [...] body image can be considered in the governmentality framework as a key part of the architecture of the modern self, built by certain vocabularies of self-awareness, that is neither inauthentic nor authentic, neither free of power – part of a 'true' self – nor only an expression of power working against a 'true' self".[55]

Cosmetic surgery is presented as a practice of self-care, along the lines of personal fitness and health improvement. Since new surgical and pharmacological applications are being marketed in the form of various medicalised practices, women in particular have started making use of them. In Pitts-Taylor's view, this should not be seen in the first instance as manipulation by the cosmetic surgery industry, but instead "as ways of relating to the self in the context of individual and collective enmeshment in various notions and measurement of bodily risk and value".[56] I have deliberately quoted at length a number of passages from Pitt-Taylor's article, as they give a clear formulation to what could be called the new relationship between the human being and the body, which leaves it exclusively to the individual to make decisions about his or her body. Like the French anthropologist Maurice Godelier, who published a revelatory work about what he so elegantly termed "metamorphoses of kinship"[57] in contemporary societies, we may speak here of a veritable metamorphosis of the relationship between human being-physical body in our societies: the body belongs in the fullest sense of the word to the person who inhabits it, and who is free to do with it as he or she wills.[58]

54 Cf. *supra* note 53, p. 160.
55 *Ibid.*, p. 162.
56 *Ibid.*, p. 166.
57 M. Godelier, *Metamorphoses of Kinship*, Verso 2011 (translated from French: *Métamorphoses de la parenté*).
58 A similar trend seems to be present with regard to treating reproductive rights as human rights: see among others D.S. Davis, *Genetic Dilemmas. Reproductive Technology, Parental Choices and Children's Futures*, Routledge 2001; K. Walker, "Should there be limits on who may access assisted reproductive services? A legal perspective" in J. Gunning and H. Szoke (eds.), *The Regulation of Assisted Reproductive Technology*, Ashgate 2003; J. Robertson, *Children of Choice:*

This perspective on the relationship between the person and his or her body, once it has been accepted, probably explains the great rise in cosmetic surgery today across Europe and more generally in consumer societies, where a growing prosperous class has the financial means to afford surgical modifications without these being necessary for medical reasons. Contrary to what one might think, recourse to surgery is not limited to those who are prepared to suffer to make their physical appearance match the classical "Western" ideals of beauty. In the United States, for example, the demand for "ethnically appropriate" cosmetic surgery at a person's own request is growing: "cosmetic surgeries are being planned to 'help' a person express her ethnic identity".[59] Pitts-Taylor looks ahead with optimism: "[t]he global cosmetic surgery industry is giving us a constant stream of new choices, new areas of the body to enhance, new reasons for cosmetic surgery and new technologies to explore. It is part of a new 'politics of vitality' in which the constant technological optimization of the body is presented, at the level of the individual, as a key aspect of one's relation to herself, and at another level, is creating population slices out of many millions of patients and potential patients while generating transnational trade in tourists and organic and inorganic body parts".[60] In this view, there may be various good reasons to undergo cosmetic surgery and modify the human body, including the genitals, aside from preventing, relieving or curing a disease; it may just mean "improving" the body in order to have a positive effect on a person's sense of wellbeing.

The subject deserves further discussion. One may indeed profoundly disagree with the author's perspective on the future, in which she sees a growing world market in cosmetic medicine. In her optimism, she passes over in silence the innumerable injustices and inequalities that also come with the rampant expansion of this new market, as well as the profound suffering that is often its corollary. But that is not the issue here. What is interesting is the message that comes through in her prognosis, for it reflects a new kind of anthropological vision of the relationship between a person and his or her body that regards the latter as entirely "available", as it were, to be moulded according to the wishes of the person who inhabits it. This applies to adults, of course, and the liberal credo is thereby upheld: persons who have reached the age of consent have the freedom to choose how they "care" for their body, even if that involves changes to it, as long as their choice does not intentionally inflict harm on others.[61]

In sum, the acceptance of this new conception of the relationship between human beings and their body simply reinforces the reasons invoked by those

---

Freedom and the New Reproductive Technologies, Princeton University Press 1996; S. Wilkinson, *Choosing Tomorrow's Children. The Ethics of Selective Reproduction*, Oxford University Press 2010.

59 *Ibid.*, p. 166.

60 *Ibid.*, pp. 166–167.

61 This is consonant with John Stuart Mill's often quoted concept of liberty: liberal rights and freedoms are subject to whether their exercise involves harming others or violating their rights. See: J.S. Mill, *On Liberty and Other Essays* (ed. with an introduction by John Gray), Oxford University Press 1998.

who, in the debate on circumcision of young boys, argue for maximum respect for the physical integrity of the child. Only the fullest possible respect for such integrity will make it possible to preserve the young man's autonomy until he has reached the age of consent.[62] In law, it is then up to him to make a decision about his own body, once he has reached the age at which, by law, he has autonomy to take decisions on his own and any act which might violate his bodily integrity but which is taken with his full consent, will concern no one but himself.

Yet the notion that physical integrity is a paramount value in legal terms and that it is in the child's interests for it to have priority over other human rights is not only fairly new in Western legal thinking, but it sharply contrasts with other views on social aspects of a person's identity and mechanisms of bodily identification that are still generally accepted among various groups and communities worldwide. These differences in perspective further complicate the debate on which views should prevail, rendering it difficult to proceed in a reasoned and constructive manner where the values at stake have to do with a person's belonging and identity, a subject that is highly sensitive and, as history demonstrates, can often prove inflammatory.[63]

In the final part of this contribution, I outline the three main responses that have to date been formulated, in particular in Europe, to the question of how to safeguard the bodily integrity of minors in the specific case where the group to which the family belongs has a conception of the interests of the child that is divergent from the prevailing view in the majority society, and in the name of – often ancient – cultural and/or religious precepts claims the right to make decisions that affect the child's body. In these traditions, body modifications – such as ritual scarifications, genital stretching, extensions or elongations, insertion of studs, tattoos or circumcision – are not only commonly permitted and serve as a means of perpetuating group membership, but are also in some cases a powerful way of expressing resistance to majoritarian suppression of cultural practices. Before succinctly outlining these three responses (section 2.3), therefore, it may be useful to take a brief interdisciplinary detour through social and cultural anthropology, which for decades has turned its attention to seeking to understand, among other things, the motives behind the various ways in which societies intentionally modify the bodies (and appearance) of their members and the extent to which these manifold practices serve to identify individuals and groups. Anthropologists have examined a whole range of body modification practices and discussed their significance for the preservation of groups. Their studies suggest that current discourses centred on individual autonomy as regards respect for

62 Which in law usually, but not necessarily, coincides with the age of majority.

63 See esp.: J.T. Levy, "Cruelty and Conflict in Multiethnic Politics" in J.T. Levy (ed.), *The Multiculturalism of Fear*, Oxford University Press 2004, pp. 40–65; S. Hall, "Political Belonging in a World of Multiple Identities" in G. Baumann and S. Vertovec (eds.), *Multiculturalism. Critical Concepts in Sociology. Volume IV. Crises and Transformations: Challenges and Futures*, Routledge 2011, pp. 151–157.

the physical integrity of children appear unusual when compared with other cultural views of the construction of identity and identification, and the use of the biological body for this purpose.

2.2. BODILY IDENTIFICATION: INSIGHTS GAINED FROM ANTHROPOLOGY

In the conclusion to their monograph on the significance of the biological body in determining identity and identification and vice versa, Rebecca Gowland and Tim Thompson write: "The construction of identity is complex, multidimensional, sometimes passive, sometimes active, relational and above all body-mediated, whether through individual agency or through the body's capacity to respond dynamically and absorb the by-products of the social fabric. Identity as a concept is difficult to pin down, and teasing out the individual facets of a person's identity (e.g. gender, ethnicity) is harder still, because in essence they are interwoven both biologically and socially".[64] The authors consistently argue and illustrate in the various chapters of the book that the treatment of the human body as an object of intense cultural investment across the globe and throughout history of mankind has given rise to a whole range of practices of intentional modification of the body, whether dermal or skeletal or via surgical implants. They also note that most types of modification of the human form involve pain "and in so doing the experience or process is firmly located in a corporeal plane".[65]

If one considers physical integrity from a global perspective, it turns out that an astonishing number of societies around the world use physical markings to symbolise identification with one's culture.[66] Ethnographic evidence shows that, worldwide, modifications of the human body often serve, within the given context, to mark a person's status and/or affiliation as a sign of inclusion in the community. These practices can also involve children: the scarification of a sister at the time of her brother's initiation, the practice of inserting lip plates,[67] or the custom of

64 R. Gowland and T. Thompson, *Human Identity and Identification*, Cambridge University Press 2013, p. 175.

65 *Ibid.*, p. 159.

66 See: E. Schildkrout, "Inscribing the Body" (2004) *Annual Review of Anthropology* 319–344; S. Gilman, *Making the Body Beautiful: A Cultural History of Aesthetic Surgery*, Princeton University Press 1999; M. Featherstone (ed.), *Body: Social Processes and Cultural Theory*, Sage 1991; G. Mackie, "Ending foot binding and infibulation: a convention account" (1996) *American Sociological Review* 999–1017; R. Ikehara-Quebral and M.T. Douglas, "Cultural alteration of human teeth in the Mariana Islands" (1997) *American Journal of Physical Anthropology* 381–391; P.L. Geller, "Altering identities: body modifications and the Pre-Columbian Maya" in R.L. Gowland and C.J. Knüsel (eds.), *The Social Archeology of Funerary Remains*, Oxbow 2006, pp. 168–178; D. Blom, "Embodying borders: human body modification and diversity in Tiwanaka society" (2005) *Journal of Anthropological Archaeology* 1–24; S.R. Cummings and K. Stone, "Consequences of foot binding among older women in Beijing, China" (1997) *American Journal of Physical Anthropology* 1677–1679.

67 This practice is underpinned by the logic according to which you start at a fairly young age, at menarche, to wear a lip plate in order to increase the chances of a good marriage. See among

the fattening room, where a young woman is prepared in order to make her more attractive. The binding of women's feet in ancient China started at a very early age and served an identical aim. It is known from testimonies how painful this procedure is. Some of these practices have now been abandoned,[68] sometimes through pressure from the outside but for the most part from within.[69] By scrutinising human behaviour ethnographically, i.e. using an in-depth, long-term, field-based approach, anthropologists have observed that intentional modification of the human form goes far back in history: cultures have used the body as a common medium through which identity is expressed using various types of modification. "Succinctly put, the modification of the body is the simplest means by which human beings are turned into social beings", notes Margo DeMello.[70] In a way, body modifications are part of the complex process of creating and re-creating personal and social identities. They regulate people's belonging and, by so doing, have a role to play in maintaining the social structures of groups and societies.

Alterations of the body can be permanent or temporary. Temporary adornments such as the use of body paints or elaborate headdresses are most typically used to mark transitional statuses or for specific social events,[71] whereas permanent (irreversible) modifications such as some forms of piercing, scarification, or the wearing of large lip plugs are more commonly meant to mark status, affiliation or even wealth.[72] Other body modification practices such as the fattening (beautifying) of girls prior to marriage serve to demonstrate marriageability. What these and a myriad other practices have in common is that they turn the human body into products of our own (cultural, religious, ethnic, etc.) making. The very act of modification of the human form is thus a centrally human act, and provides a crucial tool for identifying individuals, including children.[73]

---

others, S. LaTosky, "Reflections on the lip-plates of Mursi women as a source of stigma and self-esteem" in I. Strecker and J. Lydall (eds.), *The Perils of Face: Essays on Cultural Contact, Respect and Self-Esteem in Southern Ethiopia*, LIT-Verlag 2006, 371–385; S. LaTosky, *Predicaments of Mursi (Mun) Women in Ethiopia's Changing World*, Köppe 2013.

68 S.D. Gamble, "The disappearance of foot binding in Tinghsien" (1943) *The American Journal of Sociology* 181–183.

69 Today, according to Western legal thinking, it is perfectly justifiable, including from a human rights point of view, to remove part of the human body, as long as the surgery is practiced for medical/therapeutic reasons. By contrast, bodily modification on penal grounds has become more problematic regardless of the age of the person considered to be punishable. Some of these practices, such as cutting off the hand as a punitive measure, are considered repugnant and thus totally unacceptable. In reality, this happens rarely, but cutting off the hand is indeed a typical culturally grounded bodily mutilation for penal reasons.

70 M. DeMello, "Modification. Blurring the Divide: Human and Animal Body Modifications" in F.E. Mascia-Lees (ed.), *A Companion to the Anthropology of the Body and Embodiment*, Wiley-Blackwell 2011, p. 338.

71 *Ibid.*, p. 339.

72 DeMello notes that among cultures like the Makonde of Tanzania, lip plates often indicate status, as the size of the lip increases with the wealth of the woman. In other cases the type of tattoo worn represents status or rank.

73 There is no space here to discuss the many abuses that have also accompanied these practices throughout history, such as branding to mark human slaves and convicts, or practices like

Yet in anthropological literature one will not easily find the term "mutilation" used to designate cultural practices of bodily modification, since from an epistemological point of view this would be to devalue a practice in light of standards that come from outside the world of the people involved. In principle, the anthropologist is less concerned about taking a stand personally; his or her own opinion is indeed of lesser – not to say no – relevance; instead the aim is to strive for an ethnographically based/documented comprehension of human behaviour. Are anthropologists therefore cultural relativists? Not in the sense of an "anything goes" attitude. The main reason they do not wish to "judge" what they see on the ground is the desire accurately to apprehend and translate empirical ethnographic findings into nuanced and contextualised insights.[74] And that is probably precisely what lends such depth to many ethnographic findings: they do not cast an evaluative glance at the facts, but rather what matters is the insiders' view.[75] One of the concerns of the anthropologist is to identify the normative logic at play behind the practices observed, and he/she approaches this through questions such as whether a given practice is religiously inspired; to what extent people feel it to be (still) binding upon them; from where or from whom does the authority come to continue it; how much pressure is involved, from inside or outside; what are the sanctions, etc. One such sanction, ostracism, is a very harsh punishment, since to be ostracised might mean that in time one no longer belongs to the group.

---

genital mutilation aimed at controlling people who were considered deviant or unruly. But clearly these, too, are practices of modification of the human body; they have taken place since antiquity and were endured under colonisation. Body markings were seen as a sign of submission, deviance or degeneracy.

74 Some anthropologists do take a stand and forcefully protest where they see a need. But for methodological and epistemological reasons, most anthropologists prefer to refrain from taking an explicit normative stance. For a more thorough examination of the anthropological literature on which relativists usually base their claims and of the critiques of moral relativism, see esp.: J.W. Cook, *Morality and Cultural Differences*, Oxford University Press 1999; M.M. Moody-Adams, *Fieldwork in Familiar Places. Morality, Culture and Philosophy*, Harvard University Press 2002; Cl. Geertz, *Available Light: anthropological reflections on philosophical topics*, Princeton University Press 2000 (esp. Chapter II: "Ethical Dimensions of Anthropological Fieldwork in the New States" and Chapter III: "Anti Anti-Relativism"); M.E. Spiro, "Cultural relativism and the future of anthropology" in G.E. Marcus (ed.), *Rereading Cultural Anthropology*, Duke University Press 2000, pp. 124–151; M.O. Hinz, "Human rights between universalism and cultural relativism? The need for anthropological jurisprudence in the globalizing world" in A. Bösl and J. Diescho (eds.), *Human Rights in Africa: legal perspectives on their protection and promotion*, MacMillan Education 2009, pp. 3–32; W. Rudolf, *Der kulturelle Relativismus: kritische Analyse einer Grundsatzfragen -Diskussion in der amerikanischen Ethnologie*, Duncker & Humblot 1968.

75 A concept such as "false consciousness" – the notion that people are often not sufficiently conscious of various types of constraints or even oppressive mechanisms weighing upon them, and hence that one ought to raise their consciousness – is not of primary relevance within the framework of an anthropological investigation unless the anthropologist decides to take a critical position (as did ethnographers working in the vein of the school of "cultural materialism"). False consciousness is usually more the concern of political scientists or feminists, but for the anthropologist what matters above all is to identify the reasons why people feel bound by the mechanism that regulates their social identity.

For the anthropologist, appraisal and motivations of child care – as of any standards or values – are therefore relative in the sense that they relate to the culture in which they apply. In assessing motivations and various forms of child care in human societies, anthropologists have come across all sorts of practices that regulate identities, yet they make sure to locate these practices *within the subjects' own context.* For the anthropologist, there is no other valid, empirically based way to understand these practices. One may certainly feel some discomfort with ethnographic writings, insofar as they generally offer "mere" description. Yet an anthropologist will in the first place scrutinise the normative logic at play according to which one practice is deemed to meet the standards of acceptability by the group who continues to observe it, while others are not. Why, in the perception of the outside world, are some practices considered banal and unproblematic, while others are deemed *un*acceptable, even though the "damage" done to the body may be very similar? These are questions addressed by anthropologists.

Moreover, empirical observations from fieldwork also show that perceptions of what ought or ought not to be done with a person's body – whether a minor or an adult – not only vary with the cultural context but also change over time, and can do so to a considerable extent. In Western mainstream opinion, as things stand it appears that the *age of consent*[76] has now become the decisive line of demarcation between body marking practices – traditional or newer forms – that are regarded with approval and practices that are rejected as equivalent to "mutilation". As a consequence, in the case of consenting adults, even if a practice might lead to disfigurement or fatally injure the human body, it will be considered, as Pitts-Taylor phrases it, "to create [...] delicate affiliations between subjective hopes and dissatisfactions, and the capacities of technology",[77] and thus tolerated. Illustrations include genital piercing at the request of the person, some forms of extreme surgery for aesthetic reasons (the example of the "cat woman" some years ago) or tattoos covering large parts of the body. Anthropological research shows that these are recent developments, however; worldwide, societies that commit themselves to modern liberalism by leaving much scope for the personal autonomy and freedom of competent adults offer just one model of how to conceive of identity and social cohesion.

The view that a legislator – or any other public authority – should not interfere with the conduct of a competent adult citizen unless and until that conduct harms or seriously threatens to harm third parties clearly clashes with other views that disapprove of the focus on individual freedom and are instead more preoccupied with the perpetuation of particular patterns of behaviour (grounded in tradition, religion or culture) and therefore require specific restraints to be imposed on the conduct of individual persons. Is it disquieting

76 Cf. *supra* note 64.

77 V. Pitts-Taylor, *supra* note 51, p. 167.

to think that particular groups and communities in contemporary European societies would therefore continue *resisting* the liberal stand with its emphasis on individual choice? It would be tempting to think that this resistance is all the more understandable since in majority societies, particularly in Europe today, "various other practices involving the bodies of youngsters – such as elongating ear lobes, lips, and head shapes, and ear lobe piercing, insertion of studs, and tattooing that have no associated health benefits are yet commonly permitted".[78] Why would similar surgeries, when performed for religious reasons, be referred to as mutilations? The resistance on the part of communities that perform ritual (infant boys') circumcision is all the more vehement since in their view not only is there no consistent reason to claim that the above-mentioned practices are more acceptable than young boys' circumcision, but in the case of the latter practice, it is nothing less than the perpetuation of religious communities in multicultural societies that is at stake.

How, then, on a practical level, to overcome these divergences in views? For the moment it would be difficult to say that listening to the many ways in which human societies around the world treat the body – whether of minors or adults – and show concern (or not) for its unity is the majority view taken in Europe. Yet it would be far too easy to claim that it would suffice to listen to the contribution of anthropology to learn how to find common ground among the different cultural perspectives on the human body.[79]

Clearly it will not be easy to find a solution, for the hope of changing the perspectives of either side would require nothing less than introducing a cultural change, and this is not something that happens overnight. To what extent can law assist in finding the right balance between an approach that demonises religious practices and "rushes to dark judgments about [...] others" as Richard Shweder puts it,[80] and a hands-off policy that would let minority groups and communities continue their practices unhindered? In the next section, which is the last part of this analysis, I look briefly at the question of whether over the short term a compromise that would satisfy everyone might come from within the law. As things stand, the answer is a nuanced one.

---

78 G.B. Levey, *supra* note 14, 328.

79 The challenge of how to transpose, adequately, ethnographic knowledge into legal reasoning is an issue in legal anthropological circles today: can (anthropologists) be there at the point when a decision-maker (courts, legislator or any other corporate or non-governmental organisation) could benefit from ethnographic expertise, and how would it impact on the decisions to be taken? See among others: P.J. Stewart and A. Strathern (eds.), *Anthropology and Consultancy. Issues and Debates*, Berghahn 2005; B. Morris and R. Bastin (eds.), *Expert Knowledge, First World Peoples, Consultancy and Anthropology*, 2004; R.J. Currie, "The Bounds of the Permissible: Using 'Cultural Evidence' in Civil Jury Cases" (2005) 20(1) *Canadian Journal of Law and Society* 75–86; E. Oring, "Folklore and Advocacy" (2004) 41(2) *Journal of Folklore Research* 259–267; V. Sanford and A. Angel-Ajani (eds.), *Engaged Observer. Anthropology, Advocacy and Activism*, Rutgers University Press 2008.

80 R.A. Shweder, *supra* note 14, p. 364.

2.3. NON-MEDICAL MODIFICATIONS OF CHILDREN'S BODIES: THREE APPROACHES

With regard to the physical integrity of minors and its protection under state law today, three different approaches have, generally speaking, been explored: (a) turning to the courts, either because the law is unclear or because the parties do not agree on its interpretation, or sometimes simply because there is no legislative response that is immediately applicable; (b) the views of experts, whose position is put forward in one or more reports; and finally (c) the legislative approach, which can take the form of a general criminal law forbidding any attack on the bodily integrity of a minor not dictated by medical necessity, or a special law targeting a particular practice; alternatively, a non-punitive law may be passed that emphasises certain conditions that must be fulfilled whenever parents, for reasons other than therapeutic ones, decide to have their child circumcised.

In what follows I sum up the three approaches and the responses they offer in particular to the difficult question of the circumcision of infant or young boys.

2.3.1. The Case Law or Case-by-Case Approach

Put very briefly, two normative positions can be distinguished in addressing the circumcision of boys on religious grounds: the first prioritises religious liberty and thus tends to take a lenient attitude to the practice, while the second position is that decisions about what ought or ought not to be permitted should not be dependent upon collective/group conceptions of the "good" – such as those prescribed by a religion – and is inclined to take a more prohibitive attitude. As long as no formal policy is put in place, in practice it is up to the judiciary to take the role of deciding whether or not to outlaw ritual circumcision of young boys. To date, there is scant case law in this area in Europe.

In many countries there is more case law on the equally contentious issue of female excision. France, for example, has gone through a remarkable development in this regard. At first, judges faced with cases of the excision of girls showed understanding, arguing that recent migrants belonging to cultural and ethnic minorities should not be "punished" for being ignorant of French laws and that withdrawing a young daughter from the guardianship of her parents would amount to disproportionately harsh treatment, all the more so since it would not necessarily prove an effective way of eliminating the practice. On the contrary, it would put them even further on the margins of French society. In this approach, the best interests of the child should preferably be protected by cautiously accompanying the parents, familiarising them with the French approach to children's rights and the way to safeguard these. This position comes close to a pedagogical approach.[81] The French case law has, however, taken a real U-turn. The period of understanding and accommodation was followed by a much harsher position on the part of the judiciary: since the late 1990s French judges have not hesitated to penalise the parents in such cases. And this leads to the paradox that the courts punish a mother and father who have the best interests of their child at heart, albeit from their own perspective. These are dramatic responses, but the (French) judges' aim is to give a signal, so that the parents understand and accept that in France these practices are not tolerated. This is now very much the French approach.[82]

In many European countries, courts have ruled that in the absence of a clearly discernible regulation or competent regulatory body, ritual circumcision should be placed *beyond* the reach of parental authority and, in the best interests of the child, be performed only after the child has reached the (legal) age of consent. According to this reasoning, parents or legal guardians should not have the right to authorise, on behalf of (their) minor children, surgical procedures for non-medical reasons; instead the child should decide for himself. This was implicitly also the position of the Cologne court and it fits well with the liberal view that it is the individual involved who is best placed to decide what use he or she effectively makes of his rights and freedoms. A similar conclusion had already been reached by a Belgian civil court in the 1980s with regard to a case of two boys, aged fifteen and twelve.[83] As the father – on the grounds that he is a Muslim – was in the process of divorcing their mother, he requested that the boys be circumcised. Yet the court noted that with the approval of both parents, the boys had attended a Catholic school and had no acquaintance with the Islamic religion. The court considered that in the best interests of the boys the education so far provided was to be continued and that, consequently, it was up to the boys to decide, when they reach the age of majority, whether or not to be circumcised. By so ruling, the court kept religion out of the way, at least provisionally. For the court, in this case the best interests of the children were to *continue* being educated in the same manner as initially determined by the parents.

To delay circumcision, i.e. to allow the boys to participate in the decision in an age-appropriate manner, is an option supported – directly or indirectly – by courts in various countries, even if, as some critics observe, this will place the (adult) individual at higher risk, since complications are more likely to occur and the protective effects against various infections and diseases is lower if the procedure is performed in adulthood. Not only do the (alleged) health benefits decrease the later in life the procedure is performed, but one should also take into account that,

81 M.-C. Foblets, "Les délits culturels: de la répercussion des conflits de culture sur la conduite délinquante. Réflexions sur l'apport de l'anthropologie du droit à un débat contemporain" (1998) 1 *Droit et Cultures* 195–122.

82 For a very fine analysis of this development in the French case law, see: L. Bellucci, *Consuetudine, diritte e immigrazione: la pratica tradizionale dell'escissione nell'esperienza francese*, Giuffrè 2012.

83 Cf. *supra* note 52.

with aging, the pain, discomfort and anxiety of the operation increase.[84] But these appear to be ancillary concerns, given the shift of priorities.

Without waiting for legislative solutions to be found, the courts have thus sought to offer a few options, but the scarce decisions available do not make it possible to draw unambiguous conclusions, at least not in Europe. Moreover, it is well known that case law often only represents the tip of the iceberg and does not reflect daily reality. In all likelihood, the vast majority of cases remain invisible, though precise figures are not available.[85] Anecdotal evidence will have to suffice for now. For instance, there was the testimony given about three years ago by a female surgeon at a conference in Brussels on the practice of excision of young girls. The case presented by the surgeon involved a mother who had given birth and then requested to be re-infibulated. The surgeon asked herself what an acceptable alternative would be. If she refused to perform the procedure, the husband would send his wife back to their country of origin, and who knows under what circumstances she would be re-infibulated. And so the surgeon, after consulting the midwife, decided to accede to the woman's request, despite it being against the (Belgian) law. In her view the law did not offer, in this particular case, an appropriate answer. I discuss below (section 2.3.3) the third option, which is regulation by law. But it may be useful at this stage to make a preliminary observation: what is true for the case law is also true for regulation by law: so far neither covers the full picture, that is, neither tackles the reality on the ground. Despite all the efforts of courts and legislators, in practice myriad cases remain *outside* the scope of state-organised control and therefore "escape" legal reasoning.

2.3.2. *Expert Committees*

An approach that does not exclude the possibility that circumcision of boys may be decided by judicial means or regulated by law is the recourse to committees or working groups. As regards circumcision of young boys, the reports available are mainly the fruit of reflection by medical associations that have deemed it necessary to take a position on the question.

The views of medical professionals are quite divergent. On the whole, there are three positions: the first can be found in reports that categorically reject circumcision in every case not justified on strictly medical/therapeutic grounds; by contrast, other reports emphasise the benefits of circumcision at (very) young age. Between the two extremes are the reports that propose a middle way, namely laying down certain conditions to ensure that the operation is performed with all due care, but once those have been met, see no reason to oppose the parents' decision.

---

84 G.B. Levey, *supra* note 14, 328.

85 For a comparison with the practice of genital modification(s) performed on young girls: M. Exterkate, *Female Genital Mutilation in the Netherlands. Prevalence, incidence and determinants*, Pharos 2013.

The British Medical Association (BMA), for example, opted in 2006 for the third position. It produced a guide to the law and ethics of the circumcision of boys in which it recognises its legality, provided it is performed competently, is in the child's best interests, and there is valid consent.[86] In the BMA's view "circumcision of boys has been considered to be either medically or socially beneficial or, at least, neutral", and "the responsibility to demonstrate that non-therapeutic circumcision is in a particular child's best interests falls to his parents". Interestingly, in a checklist the BMA identifies the following as relevant to an assessment of the child's best interests: the patient's own ascertainable wishes, feelings and values; the patient's ability to understand what is proposed and weigh up the alternatives; the patient's potential to participate in the decision, if provided with additional support or explanations; the patient's physical and emotional needs; the risk of harm or suffering; the views of the parents and family; the implications for the family of performing or not performing the procedure; religious or cultural background; and the prioritising of options which maximise the patient's future opportunities and choices.[87]

The BMA Guide points out that, like with any medical procedure, action can be taken against the doctor if a circumcision was carried out negligently, but that "action cannot be taken against a doctor simply because a man is unhappy about having been circumcised at all" (e.g. in infancy).[88] In sum, the BMA Guide gives clear professional and legal directives: it does not prohibit doctors in the UK from performing non-therapeutic circumcision, but it also states that the General Medical Council reserves the right to take action if a doctor performed such an operation incompetently.[89] In practice, however, some concrete questions and how to address them appear to remain. Thus, for example, what should be done if parents disagree between themselves, or in the case where only one parent consents? In commenting on a study done among paediatric surgeons throughout England and Wales, Richard Robinson, Erica Makin and Robert Wheeler are of the opinion that both professional organisations and the courts could perform much better in giving due regard to the request that every effort be made to ensure that both parents consent (dual parental consent).[90] But all in all, even if there is still room for improvement in their application, the directions contained in the BMA Guide appear to provide sufficient guidance, making regulation by specific legislation not (yet) necessary. Thus, in England and Wales, young boys' circumcision – including non-therapeutic circumcision – remains legal.

86 British Medical Academy, *The Law and Ethics of Male Circumcision. Guidance for Doctors*, 2006.

87 *Ibid.*, pp. 3–4.

88 "A valid consent from a person authorized to give it on the patient's behalf (such as the parents) is legally sufficient in such cases" (*ibid.*, p. 4).

89 The authors of the Guide explicitly advise that doctors must "have the necessary skills and experience to perform the operation and use appropriate measures, including anesthesia, to minimise pain and discomfort".

90 R. Robinson, E. Makin and R. Wheeler, "Consent for Non-Therapeutic Male Circumcision on Religious Grounds" (2009) 91(2) *Annals of the Royal College of Surgeons of England* 152–154.

Yet as regards the benefits of neonatal circumcision, as mentioned above, the opinions of physicians and in particular of paediatricians worldwide diverge; not all of them see the benefits associated with male circumcision performed at a (very) young age as equally important. The German Academy for Paediatric and Adolescent Medicine (*Deutsche Akademie für Kinder- und Jugendmedizin e.V.*, DAKJ),[91] the German Association for Paediatric Surgery (*Deutsche Gesellschaft für Kinderchirurgie*, DGKCH)[92] and the Professional Association of Paediatric and Adolescent Physicians (*Berufsverband der Kinder- und Jugendärzte*),[93] for example, took a firm stand *against* non-medical routine infant circumcision. So did the Royal Dutch Medical Association.[94] The Swedish Paediatric Society likewise urged, in 2012, that the circumcision of young boys for religious and non-medical reasons be banned.[95]

At the opposite extreme, there is the position of the American Academy of Pediatrics (AAP), published in August 2012, supporting non-therapeutic circumcision of boys.[96] Their policy statement concludes that, based on the scrutiny of a large number of complex scientific articles, current evidence indicates that the health benefits of newborn male circumcision outweigh the risks of the procedure, which is well tolerated when performed by trained professionals under sterile conditions with appropriate pain management. In the United States, non-therapeutic circumcision of male children has long been assumed to be lawful provided that one parent grants informed consent on the child's behalf, and thus the report can be said to reflect US mainstream opinion on the issue, which is to *not* problematise the matter.

It is precisely this lack of critical distance with regard to a sociological reality, so characteristic of an American society that is still profoundly religious, that evoked a critical reaction to the AAP report on the part of medical colleagues abroad: seen from the outside, the cultural bias reflected in the treatment of non-therapeutic circumcision in the United States as normal seems obvious, and the report's conclusions differ from those reached by physicians in other parts of the Western world, including Europe, Canada, and Australia.[97] In a 2013 article signed by 38 doctors – all non-Americans – the validity of the AAP report was called into question as culturally biased.

Their comment demands further reflection: clearly there remains controversy about the medical indication for the circumcision of infant boys and young boys, but the observation that, particularly in Europe, the matter meets with such

---

91 http://dakj.de/pages/posts/stellungnahme-zur-beschneidung-von-minderjaehrigen-jungen-123.php; http://dakj.de/media/stellungnahmen/ethische-fragen/2012.

92 Cf. *supra* note 22.

93 www.kinderaertze-im-netz.de.

94 Cf. *supra* note 21.

95 "Swedish Official Call for Circumcision Ban", *The Denver Post*, 28 September 2013.

96 "American Academy of Pediatrics Task Force on Circumcision. Circumcision policy statement" (2012) 130(3) *Pediatrics*, available at: www.pediatrics.org/cgi/content/full/130/3/e756.

97 M. Frisch et al., "Cultural Bias in the AAP's 2012 Technical Report and Policy Statement on Male Circumcision" (2013) 4 *Pediatrics* 796–800.

critical positions is probably the sign of a deeper – ever more apparent – reluctance regarding the practice. Can the manifest differences of opinion among medical associations, all of which are made up of professional experts, be explained solely as the result of a lack of incontrovertible medical evidence, or should one conclude that, absent such proof, the ideological convictions of the individual experts ultimately prevail? The ideological gulf that was evident in the public debate, as we saw recently within PACE with regard to Resolution 1952 (2013),[98] also seems to divide professionals within the field of paediatric surgery. In the English-speaking world, until recently, male circumcision was widely recognised as beneficial for the health of the boy; this view has now become less popular, for various reasons, of which we have identified some in the course of this chapter. It is probably no coincidence that for the past few years it has been mainly the medical associations of countries where secularisation has been gaining ground that have been speaking out with a view to limiting, if not halting, the practice of circumcision of minors. This would also explain the diametrically opposite position expressed in the AAP report.

On the question of whether the law should permit the circumcision of young boys, there is not only case law, which appears to vary widely, but also medical experts, who to date are equally divided. In the face of these profound disagreements, what kind of response may one expect from the legislative branches, themselves likely torn between the different positions? Should the law intervene?

2.3.3. Legislative Responses

In Europe to date, non-medically justified modifications of children's bodies have been the subject of two types of specific legislation. In some countries, criminal law prohibits any act affecting the physical integrity of a minor not dictated by medical necessity; such body modifications are punishable either as "assault" or "child abuse", or are prohibited under a specific provision. In other countries, there are non-criminal laws that emphasise certain conditions that must be fulfilled in any case where parents, for reasons independent of therapeutic necessity, decide to have their child circumcised.

The criminal option has been adopted by several countries in Europe over the past twenty years, notably in response to practices of female genital mutilation, thereby banning specific practices by criminalising them. In criminal law the principle of *nulla poene sine lege* applies: unless a law provides for it, a behaviour cannot be penalised. Some states have passed specific provisions qualifying the practice of female genital mutilation as a punishable offence. This is the case in Sweden, Austria, Belgium and the United Kingdom.[99] In other states, female genital mutilation is considered punishable as a specific variant of

98 Cf. *supra* note 19.

99 R. Kool, "Female Genital Mutilation: a matter for criminal justice?" in I. Westendorp and R. Wolleswinkel (eds.), *Violence in the domestic sphere*, Intersentia 2005, pp. 99–123.

child abuse, as gross maltreatment justifying increased sentences, but without a *lex specialis* (specific provision) being passed. This is the case, for example, in the Netherlands.[100] In practice however, whether the violations approach is grounded in a particular law or in other general (but relevant) criminal law provisions, an approach that is exclusively punitive may well turn out to be not only excessively limiting but above all inefficient. A basic premise in penal law is that criminalisation can only be the last resort. Whenever possible, and provided other – more nuanced – means would allow for equally efficient action against practices that are considered clearly abusive and therefore unacceptable, public authorities should resort to these other means, *in casu* laying down conditions that can serve as an important tool for bringing about a change in the parents' view of what is in the best interests of their children.

Education and institutions such as faith-based organisations, trade unions, sport and recreation programmes, to name but a few, could prove more efficient in this regard than punitive laws could possibly be.[101] Another approach may be to ensure the availability of symbolic scarification, as was proposed in the case of female genital mutilation.[102] Ultimately, the aim is to find solutions that maintain a balance between the parents' wishes and the good health of their child. A supportive approach is to be preferred – by far – over a punitive approach that considers the matter only in terms of violations; practice shows that the latter approach rarely proves useful as a proactive instrument against contentious practices. Specific legal provisions thus turn out to be primarily symbolic, having hardly any real impact. In Belgium, the excision of young girls is still an ongoing practice.[103] Yet there is evidence that an exclusively punitive approach that singles

100 *Ibid.*, pp. 99–123.

101 For an argument in the same vein: D. Peacock et al., "Men, HIV/AIDS, and Human Rights", *Journal of Acquired Immune Deficiency Syndrome*, 1 July 2009, 51 (Suppl 3), 119–125 at 122.

102 As was the case in the Netherlands: K. Bartels and I. Haaijer, *'s Lands wijs, 's lands eer? Vrouwenbesnijdenis en Somalische vrouwen in Nederland* [A Country's way, a country's honour? Female excision and Somali women in the Netherlands], Pharos 1992; and in Italy by Omar Abdulcadir, a Somali gynaecologist who graduated in Florence and now heads the centre for the prevention and therapy of female genital mutilation at the Careggi Hospital, Florence. In 2003 he submitted a proposal to the Ethics Committee in Florence to perform a symbolic *sunna*. The proposal consisted in a pricking on the clitoris with the use of anaesthetic cream, under medical supervision, in order to have only a symbolic "drop of blood". The principle was rather simple: a symbolic rite, without physical harm, as an alternative to FGM. The proposal was adopted unanimously first by the Florence Ethics Committee in December 2003 and then by the Regional Bioethics Committee in 2004. The proposal elicited a massive reaction in the media and gave rise to much debate. However, the proposal was opposed by the Regional Council of Tuscany in 2004 and by several feminist organisations in Italy. See: M. La Barbera, *Multicentered Feminism: Revisiting the 'Female Genital Mutilation' discourse*, Compostampa 2009, pp. 184–187; E. Bottini, "Is juridicization of female genital mutilation an effective way of eliminating it? Western Democracies facing the violation of female integrity and dignity: illegal FGM as an integration problem", *Jura Gentium* (Review of International Philosophy and Global Politics), 2009, available at www.juragentium.org/forum/mg/sunna/en/bottini.htm.

103 M. Dieleman, *Excision et migration en Belgique francophone* (Rapport de recherche de l'Observatoire du sida et des sexualités pour le GAMS, Belgique), Brussels, GAMS, 2012.

out particular practices and imposes serious constraints upon specific minority groups and communities adds to the stigmatisation of those who continue to abide by their practices and traditions; in effect, criminalisation comes down to "victim blaming".[104]

In the case of the circumcision of young boys, the situation is different, insofar as it is more difficult to speak in that case of bodily mutilation. Clearly this is an irreversible body modification, and in many cases non-therapeutic in nature, but the comparison ends there, as the term "invasive" does not apply to the same extent to both procedures: the extreme nature of some forms of female genital mutilation, such as clitoridectomy and infibulation, does not have an analogue in male circumcision. This difference also explains the fact that to date no government has invoked criminal law to take action against the circumcision of young boys on grounds of grievous bodily harm. While anti-circumcision groups have occasionally proposed legislation aiming at banning young boys' circumcision, so far it has not been supported by any legislature: "there is no jurisdiction globally, that rules out religious circumcision", observes B. Fateh-Moghadam.[105] And it is not likely that, in the short term, this situation will change, not least due to the strong interest of religious groups in this matter and its controversial nature.

Faced with an unregulated practice such as young boys' circumcision, the legislature may have recourse to other, alternative statutory regulations. One such alternative is to clarify the conditions under which parents may validly consent to their child's circumcision. Such regulations could be part of family law. Another option would be a more elaborate statute that regulates the practice in greater detail as regards both (single or dual) parental consent and the qualification of the persons entitled to perform the surgery, as well as time limits, and that also requires all boys to enjoy the same standard of care in circumcision, irrespective of whether the procedure is carried out for therapeutic or religious reasons. The law would make sure that parents or legal guardians have the right to authorise surgical procedures in the best interests of their children.

The latter approach was adopted in Germany after the Cologne judgment had left parents, legal practitioners and surgeons in legal uncertainty: on 12 December 2012, following a series of hearings and consultations, the Bundestag adopted the proposed law explicitly permitting non-therapeutic circumcision to be performed under certain conditions.[106] The pros and cons of the legal framework provided for male circumcision in German domestic law deserves to be further assessed, not

---

104 The latter effect may explain why there is some hesitation on the part of prosecutors to take action against practices such as FGM, which would likely drive the practices underground. In Europe, with the exception of France (see *supra* note 84), very few cases have so far been brought before the courts.

105 B. Fateh-Moghadam, "Criminalizing male circumcision? Case note: Landgericht Cologne, Judgment of 7 May 2012 – No. 151 Ns 169/11" (2012) 13(9) *German Law Journal* 1131–1145.

106 Cf. *supra* note 13.

least since the response on the part of the legislators is not a repressive one but one that has been negotiated with the main stakeholders and in a process of democratic deliberation. Boys' circumcision has thus in a sense been accommodated.[107]

3. SOME PERSONAL REFLECTIONS BY WAY OF A CONCLUSION

There are of course many more views in favour of or against the circumcision of boys than I have identified and dealt with here. In the discussion on whether or not to accommodate minority practices, in Europe it appears that young boys' circumcision is taking over the role previously played by other contentious practices such as ritual slaughtering of animals, arranged marriages or unilateral divorce (also known as repudiation): in various countries, non-therapeutic circumcision of boys increasingly generates a debate about whether or not to regard it as a harmful custom and, if so, how to help end it.

While historically male circumcision has been much less controversial than modifications of the body performed on girls, it now appears that cultural acceptance on the part of mainstream opinion is gradually decreasing, to the benefit, ever more forcefully, of the right to bodily integrity of a young child who is unable to consent to an invasive and irreparable medical procedure. The question to be addressed is thus whether state authorities are obliged to protect what is understood to be the best interests of children even against the religious rights of their own parents and their right to educate their child as they see fit.

The discussion is vital in countries – Europe offers a clear example – where minorities continue to perform religiously motivated circumcisions. The suggestion that this practice is equivalent to causing grievous bodily harm to minors not only indicates that the circumcision of boys is seen in a new light, but also amounts to passing a moral judgment on what is regarded by millions of parents worldwide as an important rite in Islam and Judaism. Unless one were prepared to admit that the consent of an adult and the reversibility of some forms

[107] Not everybody agrees with this conclusion. In B. Fateh-Moghadam's view, for example, it would be wrong to conclude that the German legislative response to the circumcision of young boys is an example of accommodation, since for him "[p]arents who circumcise their sons following Jewish or Muslim tradition do not claim a legal privilege or 'reasonable accommodation'; rather, they utilize the parental right to the care and custody of the child and freedom of religion as guaranteed by the general law (in Germany)" (B. Fateh-Moghadam, *supra* note 105, p. 1143). The fact remains that simply invoking general principles has not been sufficient, in this case, to resolve the debate that broke out in Germany after the highly controversial court ruling, and a detailed solution was necessary for the medical profession to be able to determine under what precise conditions the surgical procedure remains indisputably legal. An accommodation enshrined in legislative was necessary. As B. Fateh-Moghadam noted, one may deplore the fact that reiterating a set of principles did not suffice, in and of itself, to put to rest the anxieties aroused by the court decision in question.

of body modifications have become standards in their own right of what is to be considered "good" and thus to be prioritised at all costs, even over freedom of religion, this stance is highly questionable. The wish to ban the practice comes from a clear notion of superiority and causes outrage among the religious minorities who feel targeted by this position.

Seen from a minority position, one would be tempted to conclude that the disapproval of neonatal circumcision of boys, notwithstanding the absence of medical consensus that it endangers the boy's health, comes close to provocation, not to say arrogance: to criticise a practice performed by minority religions since time immemorial, without considering that various interventions on the body that are widely accepted in Europe today may be potentially much more damaging and unnecessarily painful, lacks consistency. Neither the fact that the latter modifications may be performed on a consenting adult person nor the reversibility of some of these practices can justify this stance.

Should the legislators intervene? Critics of the Cologne judgment see the court's position as "an attempt to legally enforce a single comprehensive doctrine of good education, tacitly accepting the exclusion of Jewish and Muslim families for the sake of the intactness of the body".[108] "Yet there is one worry", as Sherry Colb warns against attempts to ban the circumcision of young boys, "and it is significant. The worry is perhaps that, out of the many painful things that people do to their children the law could be singling this one out for prohibition at least in part because the practitioners are religiously motivated, and the religions in question are minority religions".[109]

This is clearly a forceful accusation, but there are two reasons why it deserves particular attention. First, Muslims have performed the circumcision of young boys for hundreds of years and Jews for thousands, and both groups believe it to be a religiously required practice. Moreover, the rite serves as an affirmation of their religious and cultural belonging and is experienced by many as an essential component of their religious and cultural identity. Second, the circumcision of boys has long been welcomed – in "Western" countries as well – as a procedure that could be beneficial to health; only recently have professionals started opposing the practice.

Unless, in the years to come, medical professionals provide decisive evidence that young boys' circumcision should be banned *for evident health reasons*, there is probably more to gain from a position of prudence than from categorically banning a practice regarded by many as a religious mandate. There is not much to gain from passing excessively burdensome legislation that makes (certain targeted) minorities pay the price of an inconsistent policy. To do so would be to wreak havoc with the future of a multicultural society.

108 B. Fateh-Moghadam, *supra* note 105, p. 1142.

109 S. Colb, "A proposed bill to ban male circumcision", *FindLaw*, 8 April 2005, available at http://edition.cnn.com/2005/LAW/04/08/colb.circumcision/index.html.

MALTA PROCESS AND CROSS-CULTURAL ASPECTS IN FAMILY DISPUTES

Louise Ellen TEITZ*

1. INTRODUCTION: THE CHALLENGES OF CROSS-BORDER FAMILY RELATIONSHIPS

Globalisation in the 21st century has expanded international trade in goods and services and led to increased movement by families and children across frontiers. As people cross borders, often for work, they meet others, fall in love, and have children – though not necessarily in that order – and as a result, there have been marked increases in the number of marriages and family relationships that touch

* The author gratefully acknowledges the assistance of Ha-kyung Jung, Judge on Secondment and Judge, Chuncheon District Court, Republic of Korea; Ariel Xue, Intern; and Kerstin Bartsch, Senior Legal Officer. The presentation on which this chapter is based was given while serving as First Secretary of the Hague Conference on Private International Law. Any comments are those of the author and not of the Hague Conference. The author also thanks Roger Williams University School of Law, Bristol, RI, USA; Boston University School of Law; Brendan Sullivan, RWU School of Law Class of 2016; and Brian Goodrich, Boston University School of Law Class of 2014 for assistance.

on more than one culture, nationality or religion. When these relationships break down, children in particular are caught in the turmoil: they can be the focus of disputes on custody, visitation, and terms of upbringing. Often they are the victims of child abduction, and as a result are denied access to one of their parents. The resolution of these issues is complicated by disparate legal systems, diverse cultural and religious customs and rules, and opposing ideas of how these differences should influence the outcome of a dispute.

The Hague Conference on Private International Law (HCCH) is well known for its seminal work in the area of cross-border family law, especially in creating structures for international legal cooperation in addressing international child abduction and child protection. These frameworks are exemplified by the 1980 Hague Convention on the Civil Aspects of International Child Abduction[1] and the 1996 Hague Convention on Jurisdiction, Applicable Law, Recognition, Enforcement and Co-operation in Respect of Parental Responsibility and Measures for the Protection of Children,[2] which both create binding international legal instruments for the contracting states. While 93 countries are contracting states to the 1980 Convention,[3] and 41 are contracting states to the 1996 Convention,[4] many countries, referred to herein as non-contracting states, still remain outside of the Conventions' framework. Where no such binding structure exists, non-binding legal mechanisms are increasingly important tools in protecting the rights of the child in a multi-faith and multi-cultural society.

Currently, the majority of the world's Muslim countries are not contracting states to the 1980 Convention;[5] however, these countries have not been immune to

1 Oct. 25, 1980, 1343 U.N.T.S. 49 (1980 Convention).

2 Oct. 19, 1996, 35 I.L.M., 1391 (1996 Convention).

3 For a full list of contracting states, see *Status Table 28: Convention of 25 October 1980 on the Civil Aspects of International Child Abduction*, Hague Conference on Private International Law [HCCH] (10 April 2014), www.hcch.net/index_en.php?act=conventions.status&cid=24 (1980 Convention Status Table).

4 *Status Table 34: Convention of 19 October 1996 on Jurisdiction, Applicable Law, Recognition, Enforcement and Co-operation in Respect of Parental Responsibility and Measures for the Protection of Children*, HCCH (18 August 2015), www.hcch.net/index_en.php?act=conventions.status&cid=70 (1996 Convention Status Table).

5 Many countries have legal systems which have been influenced by, or based on, some form of Sharia law, reflecting the different schools of Islamic legal thought. Similarly, the extent of the inclusion of Sharia into the applicable family law rules varies as well, as does legislation on personal status. See generally J. Nasir, *The Islamic Law of Personal Status*, 2nd edition, 1990. Examples of these countries not all of which are primarily Muslim include: Afghanistan, Algeria, Bangladesh, Brunei, Comoros, Djibouti, Egypt, Eritrea, Ethiopia, The Gambia, Ghana, India, Indonesia, Iran, Iraq, Israel, Jordan, Kenya, Kuwait, Lebanon, Libya, Malaysia, the Maldives, Mauritania, Morocco, Nigeria, Oman, Pakistan, the Philippines, Qatar, Saudi Arabia, Singapore, Somalia, Sri Lanka, Sudan, Tajikistan, Tanzania, Thailand, Uganda, the UAE and Yemen. Of these countries, six (Egypt, Israel, Malaysia, Morocco, the Philippines and Sri Lanka) are currently members of the Hague Conference. Israel is a signatory to the 1980 Convention, and Morocco, Sri Lanka, and Iraq have acceded to the Convention; Egypt, Malaysia, and the Philippines are non-contracting states. See *1980 Convention Status Table*, *supra* note 3. Thailand and Singapore, which are not members of the Hague Conference, are signatories to the 1980 Convention. *Ibid.*

cross-border child abductions.[6] The means and extent of implementation of Sharia among countries of Islamic tradition varies by country,[7] and family law pertaining to the role of women within the family structure, divorce, and child custody differs from that in the Western legal tradition.[8] The 1980 Convention relies upon the concept of "habitual residence" in providing a mechanism for the prompt return of a child wrongfully removed or retained in breach of custody rights. Whether a return is ordered in cases involving abductions from non-contracting states has in some contracting states been determined by reference to the "best interests of the child".[9] Often in those cases, the outcome of the "best interests of the child" inquiry is dependent upon the deciding court's conclusions about the specific Sharia-influenced law and how it would apply in a particular case, which leaves a judge

> "compelled to act as a multistate decision maker in a way that will affect relationships among family members who, by definition, are not confined to the judge's culture.

Morocco is also a signatory of the 1996 Convention. See *1996 Convention Status Table*, *supra* note 4.

6 In 2008, statistics from reunite International Child Abduction Centre showed that the highest numbers of abductions to non-contracting states occurred in India (11 cases), Pakistan (9 cases), Nigeria (8 cases), and Dubai (6 cases). See M. Freeman, "When the 1980 Hague Child Abduction Convention Does Not Apply: The UK-Pakistan Protocol" (2009) 3 *Int'l Fam. L.* 181–85.

7 The BBC World Service's website provides the following short summary of the implementation of Sharia law among the world's predominately Muslim societies in its case study of Sharia law: "[In some countries, Islam is viewed as a] political ideology as well as a personal faith, and a strict interpretation of the Sharia serves as the supreme law of the land. In the majority of Muslim countries, however, the Sharia is applied selectively. Some countries adopt only a few aspects of Sharia law; others apply the entire code, and still others have only parts of the country which adhere to aspects of Sharia law." *Case Study: Sharia Law*, BBC World Service, www.bbc.co.uk/worldservice/people/features/ihavearightto/four_b/casestudy_art07.shtml. It should also be noted that normative religious concepts may permeate legal systems in Muslim-majority countries, even those that may not outwardly profess to adhere strictly to Sharia law. See E. Schnitzer-Reese, "International Child Abduction to non-Hague Convention Countries: the Need for an International Family Court" (2004) 2 *Nw. U. J. Int'l Hum. Rts.* 1, 7.

8 See C. Gosselain, *Child Abduction and Transfrontier Access: Bilateral Conventions and Islamic States – A Research Paper*, HCCH, Prel. Doc. No. 7 for the attention of the Special Commission of Sept./Oct. 2002 (Aug. 2002), available at www.hcch.net/upload/abd2002_pd7e.pdf. For example, "[i]n the Muslim world, children continue to belong to the father and his family, the mother's rights being subordinate and restricted, during and after marriage." M. Jänterä-Jareborg, *The Hague Conference Report on Family Law: Contact Rights/visitation*, Int'l Law Assoc. Int'l Family Law Comm., p. 7 (2010). In contrast, the Western model of custody is increasingly turning toward a baseline of equal parental responsibility and custody. See *ibid.*

9 See, e.g., *B v. El-B* [2003] EWHC (Fam), [2003] 1 FLR 811 (Eng.) (ordering return of child in a dispute between mother residing in England and father residing in Lebanon after assessing the best interests of the child, taking into account the child's religious, ethnic and cultural background). Some countries, such as the UK, have bilateral agreements for return of children and may return children to other non-contracting states even when not under the agreement or occasionally in cases where two contracting states are not "partners" under Article 38 of the 1980 Convention. See *infra* note 11.

Cross-cultural family conflicts require the judge to consult unfamiliar foreign law which, he or she may find, is as unsatisfactory as [domestic] law."[10]

In the absence of a Convention framework, mediation and soft law tools may serve as effective means of bridging the gap between different legal and cultural traditions in cases involving abductions to or from states with Sharia-based or influenced legal systems, in the same way that certain bilateral agreements also foster similar aims of enabling contact between a child and parent living in different countries.[11] This chapter focuses on the recent work of the Hague Conference that attempts to span the gap between contracting states to the 1980 and 1996 Conventions and non-contracting states with legal systems influenced by, or based on, Sharia through the use of non-binding soft law principles and mechanisms, such as mediation and amicable resolution and specifically, the Malta Process and the Working Party on Mediation.[12]

Section 2.1 provides an overview of the 1980 and 1996 Conventions. Sections 2.2 and 2.3 then discuss the Hague Conference's work of a non-binding nature, establishing a context and principles to accommodate religious and cultural diversity with respect to: (a) the Malta Process and its focus on legal systems that have been influenced by, or are based on, Sharia/Islamic concepts; and (b)

10 M. Foblets, 'Family Disputes Involving Muslim Women in Contemporary Europe', in D. Westerlund and I. Svanberg (eds.), *Islam in the West*, 2011, pp. 409–411; see also *Re J.* [2004] EWCA (Civ) 417, [2004] 2 FLR 85 (Eng.) (ordering return of child in a non-Convention dispute between mother residing in England and father residing in Saudi Arabia and discussing legitimacy of alternative legal systems despite their lack of equal treatment of men and women).

11 Though outside of the scope of this chapter, a number of countries have adopted bilateral agreements to address cross-border child abductions involving non-contracting states with Sharia-influenced legal systems. For examples of these, see *Non-Hague Convention Child Abductions – Bilateral Agreements*, HCCH, www.hcch.net/index_en.php?act=publications.details&pid=5215&dtid=28 (listing bilateral agreements between: Australia–Egypt (2000); Belgium–Morocco (1981); Belgium–Tunisia (1982); Canada–Egypt (1997); Canada–Lebanon (2000); France–Algeria (1988); France–Egypt (1982); France–Lebanon (2000); France–Morocco (1983); France–Tunisia (1982); Sweden–Egypt (1996); Sweden–Tunisia (1994); Switzerland–Lebanon (2005); and USA–Egypt (2003)). See C. Gosselain, *supra* note 8, pp. 13–27 (analysing the operation and effectiveness of bilateral conventions on cross-border child abduction and access); see also M. Freeman, *supra* note 6 (discussing challenges to implementation of the bilateral UK–Pakistan protocol due to lack of necessary support and enforcement measures).

12 The "Malta Process" was launched in 2004 as a dialogue between contracting states to the 1980 Convention and non-contracting states with Sharia-based or influenced legal systems. In March 2009, the participants at the third Malta Conference acknowledged the need to give individuals involved in cases to which no international legal framework applies some assistance, in the interim, by encouraging the development of mediation structures. They recommended the establishment of a Working Party to draw up a plan for the development of mediation services to assist in the resolution of cross-frontier disputes concerning custody of and contact with children. This suggestion was approved by the Council on General Affairs and Policy of the Hague Conference. See Conclusions and Recommendations of the Council (31 March–2 April 2009), p. 2 (available at www.hcch.net under "Work in Progress" then "General Affairs"). Information on the Malta Process and the Working Party on Mediation is available at www.hcch.net under the "Child Abduction Section". See *infra* section 2.3.

the use of mediation as a means for cooperative protection of the child. Section 2.4 will discuss next steps with respect to these initiatives. Finally, section 3 will conclude with a discussion of future work toward the ultimate goal of accession to the 1980 and 1996 Conventions by a broader group of countries, especially those with Sharia-based or influenced legal systems, as well as more "non-Western" cultures.[13]

2. DISCUSSION

2.1. OVERVIEW OF THE 1980 AND 1996 CONVENTIONS IN A CROSS-CULTURAL, CROSS-RELIGIOUS CONTEXT

Children crossing borders and caught in cross-border conflict are the focus of much of the Hague Conference's work. This work, developing binding international law in the form of multilateral treaties, accords with and helps countries to implement parts of the 1989 United Nations Convention on the Rights of the Child (CRC).[14] Article 10(2) of the CRC provides that when a child's parents reside in different states, the child shall have a right to maintain direct contacts with both parents on a regular basis.[15] Article 21 of the 1980 Hague Convention[16] helps ensure this access of a parent to a child, but the 1980 Convention more generally provides for protection from abduction, which is the concern of Article 11 of the CRC.[17] The 1996 Hague Convention, which focuses on cross-border child protection in general, from the point of view of parental responsibilities, also helps ensure the right to contact with both parents by providing recognition and enforcement for access orders and also covers protection of vulnerable children, such as children who are runaways or exiles.[18]

The 1980 Convention focuses on the prompt return of a child wrongfully removed or retained in breach of custody rights. The 1980 Convention provides

13 The contracting states to the 1980 Convention have recently added two non-Islamic "non-Western" countries – the Republic of Korea and Japan. Interest has also been generated in mainland China.

14 UN Convention on the Rights of the Child, 20 November 1989, 1577 U.N.T.S. 3 (CRC).

15 *Ibid.* at Art. 10(2).

16 Article 21 allows applications to be made to a Central Authority "to make arrangements for organising or securing the effective exercise of rights of access." *Ibid.* at Art. 21. Under Article 7, Central Authorities must "promote the peaceful enjoyment of access rights and the fulfilment of any conditions to which the exercise of those rights may be subject" and "shall take steps to remove, as far as possible, all obstacles to the exercise of such rights." Further, Central Authorities may initiate or assist in the institution of proceedings aimed at securing these rights.

17 Article 11 of the CRC states that "1. States Parties shall take measures to combat the illicit transfer and non-return of children abroad. 2. To this end, States Parties shall promote the conclusion of bilateral or multilateral agreements or accession to existing agreements."

18 See, e.g., 1996 Convention, Art. 6 (providing for jurisdiction over children whose habitual residence cannot be established and displaced and refugee children).

a mechanism that ensures the prompt return of a child up to the age of 16 to his or her country of "habitual residence" in the belief that *that country* is in the best position to make determinations of custody and is able to determine what is in the best interests of *that* child.[19] The 1980 Convention is often referred to as a "venue" convention as it does not change the underlying substantive custody law. The 1996 Child Protection Convention is focused on providing clear and uniform rules concerning jurisdiction, applicable law, and recognition and enforcement in connection with "measures of protection" for children up to the age of 18.[20] The 1996 Convention also covers a broad range of areas within "measures of protection" for children and is particularly useful in cases concerning access between a child and a parent who live in different states, cross-border placements of children, and cross-border relocation of families with children.

In discussing how these Conventions fare in cross-cultural, cross-religious marriages and relationships, one must first stress that both Conventions, especially the 1996 Convention, are neutral toward legal and cultural systems – that is, they establish a framework for legal cooperation but do not strive to change the underlying substantive law. Thus, the Conventions may determine which country has jurisdiction to make determinations on custody, but they do not intrude into the way in which those custody decisions are made. For example, if religion is a factor in custody determinations, the Conventions do not change that. Nor do they ignore this aspect where the underlying law incorporates it.

The 1996 Convention more openly embraces cultural and religious differences than the 1980 Convention. The most obvious example of this is the inclusion of *kafala* as a measure of protection in Article 33 on cooperation in cross-border placements.[21] The institution of *kafala*, which was included in the Convention at the urging of Morocco,[22] varies from adoption in that it does not change parental rights directly.[23] Another example is Article 10 of the 1996 Convention, which concerns a contracting state's jurisdiction to include claims on parental

19 1980 Convention; see also T. Heine, 'Home State, Cross-Border Custody, and Habitual Residence' (2011) 17 *Ann. Surv. Int'l & Comp. L.* 9 (describing the operation of the 1980 Convention).

20 1996 Convention, Art. 1, 2.

21 1996 Convention, Art. 33.

22 Morocco signed the 1996 Convention at the conclusion of the Eighteenth Session of the Hague Conference on Private International Law and ratified the 1996 Convention in 2002, eight years before it acceded to the 1980 Convention in 2010. 1996 Convention Status Table, *supra* note 4.

23 The Secrétariat à l'adoption internationale Québec explains the difference between adoption and *kafala* as the following: "Adoption is prohibited in most countries whose judicial system is based fully or partly in Islamic law. Those countries have other measures for protecting children, the best known being *kafala*. *Kafala* is generally defined as a voluntary commitment to take charge of the needs, upbringing and protection of a minor child. In certain cases, *kafala* is combined with tutorship. As *kafala* does not create a legal parent-child relationship between the child who is taken in charge and the person holding the right, it cannot be considered adoption." *Kafala and Adoption*, Secrétariat à l'adoption internationale Québec, www.adoption.gouv.qc.ca/en_adoption_kafala.phtml; see also *Harroudj v. France*, App. No. 43631/09 (ECtHR 2012).

responsibility in connection with divorce proceedings. Article 10 is drafted so that countries with religious courts for divorce may simply exclude its application.

Second, both Conventions give no role to nationality or religion, instead placing an emphasis on the habitual residence of the child, though this term is not defined.[24] In theory, the Conventions' jurisdictional bases should make it easier for countries to become contracting states. However, the habitual residence basis has created difficulties for some countries where family law is part of religious personal law and where there are separate religious courts. Thus far, Morocco, which has religious courts, is the only country in the Islamic world that is signatory to both the 1980 and the 1996 Conventions.[25] Israel, which also has religious courts as a part of its faith-based personal law system, joined the 1980 Convention in 1991 and is in the process of preparing to join the 1996 Convention.[26]

Third, both Conventions provide for efficient international legal cooperation to resolve the complex legal issues that arise with respect to cross-frontier family relationships. This collaboration is not limited to judicial channels, such as through direct judicial cooperation, but also involves administrative cooperation, and thus the Central Authority model.[27]

In terms of direct judicial cooperation, the principles and means to encourage direct judicial communication, especially in connection with the 1980 Convention, are very important and serve to bridge cultural and religious differences. One of the soft law mechanisms developed to allow better operation and to reach out to both contracting and non-contracting states, especially when a child has been abducted to a non-contracting state, is the International Hague Network of Judges (IHNJ).[28] This network includes over 90 judges, from 60 states, some of which are non-contracting states – such as Pakistan – and relies on non-binding instruments[29] to provide better protection for children. Direct judicial cooperation is particularly helpful in cases where there is concern of a "grave risk of harm" or concern with safe return.[30]

Both the 1980 and 1996 Conventions also encourage finding amicable solutions outside the court systems through mediation, conciliation or other means, which

---

24 See 1980 Convention, Art. 3; 1996 Convention, Art. 5, 7.

25 See 1980 Convention Status Table, *supra* note 3; 1996 Convention Status Table, *supra* note 4.

26 See 1980 Convention Status Table, *supra* note 3.

27 See 1980 Convention, Art. 7; 1996 Convention, Chapter V.

28 For members of the IHNJ as of May 2014, see *International Network of Judges*, HCCH (December 2013), www.hcch.net/upload/haguenetwork.pdf.

29 Such non-binding instruments include, for example, the principles for Direct Judicial Cooperation. See *Emerging Guidance Regarding the Development of the International Hague Network of Judges and General Principles for Judicial Communications, Including Commonly Accepted Safeguards for Direct Judicial Communication in Specific Cases Within the Context of the International Hague Network of Judges*, HCCH, Prel. Doc. 3A-Revised for the attention of the Special Commission of June 2011 on the practical operation of the 1980 Hague Child Abduction Convention and the 1996 Hague Child Protection Convention (July 2012), available at www.hcch.net/upload/wop/abduct2011pd03ae.pdf (Principles for Direct Judicial Cooperation).

30 The section of the 1980 Convention that addresses grave risk of harm is Article 13(1)b.

as discussed below in more detail, has been particularly valuable in connection with the cases of abduction or access when one of the countries has a legal system based on or influenced by Sharia. The 1980 Convention requires Central Authorities of contracting states to take all appropriate measures to secure the voluntary return of the child or to bring about an amicable resolution of the issues.[31] The 1996 Convention requires the Central Authorities that have been designated under the Convention in each contracting state to facilitate, by mediation, conciliation or other means, agreed solutions for the protection of the person or property of the child.[32] In fact, the Hague Conference is currently considering further work on the recognition and enforcement of mediated and other voluntary agreements in international child disputes,[33] as discussed later.[34]

Mediation may transcend cultural and religious barriers more easily than legal concepts and offers the possibility of working even in the absence of agreed notions of jurisdiction or common family law rules or laws. Additionally, from a child-centred perspective, an amicable resolution is always more desirable than a court-imposed resolution, and will facilitate better long-term relationships among family members.

As part of its work in the area of nonbinding soft law, the Hague Conference has produced multiple Guides to Good Practice (GGP) under the 1980 Convention, including a guide for trans-frontier access,[35] which was drafted to encompass shared values transcending the 1980 Convention. The newest Guide to Good Practice on Mediation,[36] which was issued in July 2012, created in the context of the 1980 Convention, may also be read to reach the 1996 Convention and topics outside of a convention framework, such as mediation with non-contracting states and as part of the Malta Process. The European Commission translated the Guide to Good Practice on Mediation not only into all of the official EU languages, but also into Arabic, reflecting the understanding of its use and relevance in the European Union and in processes with non-contracting states.[37]

While mediation may cross cultural and religious divides, bi-cultural and religious mediation is difficult to execute. It requires skill and sensitivity on the

---

31 See 1980 Convention, Art. 7.

32 1996 Convention, Art. 31.

33 The 2007 Hague Maintenance Convention also encourages mediation and provides for enforcement of agreements. Hague Convention on the International Recovery of Child Support and Other Forms of Family Maintenance, Art. 6, 34. 23 November 2007, 47 I.L.M. 257.

34 See *infra* text accompanying notes 38 and 39.

35 *Transfrontier Contact Concerning Children: General Principles and a Guide to Good Practice*, HCCH (2008), available at www.hcch.net/upload/guidecontact_e.pdf.

36 *Guide to Good Practice under the Hague Convention of 25 October 1980 on the Civil Aspects of International Child Abduction*, HCCH (2012), available at www.hcch.net/upload/guide28mediation_en.pdf.

37 The European Union has an extensive multi-phase project, Euromed, a portion of which focused on family law and mediation on the model of the Hague Conference work. See The Judges' Newsletter on International Child Protection – Vol. XX / Summer-Autumn 2013, available at www.hcch.net/index_en.php?act=publications.details&pid=6090.

part of the mediators, often involves multiple languages, and mandates knowledge of and familiarity with multiple legal systems, especially where the agreed solution must be rendered enforceable cross-border. On the question of enforceability, in April 2012, the Council on General Affairs and Policy of the Hague Conference mandated that there be an

> "Experts' Group to carry out further exploratory research on cross-border recognition and enforcement of agreements 'reached in the course of international child disputes,' including those reached through mediation, taking into account the implementation and use of the 1996 Convention. Such work shall comprise the identification of the nature and extent of the legal and practical problems, including jurisdictional issues, and evaluation of the benefit of a new instrument, whether binding or non-binding, in this area."[38]

The Experts' Group met in December 2013 and discussed both the legal and practical challenges that parties face when seeking recognition and enforcement of voluntary agreements using existing instruments, both those of the Hague Conference and of regional organisations. The Experts' Group recognised the possible need for non-binding principles or guidelines, to assist parents, lawyers, mediators, and judges with securing cross-border recognition and enforcement using the existing legal framework for "package agreements" that may include a range of issues, from custody to maintenance to access to education. The Experts' Group noted the desirability and feasibility of new instruments and recommended "that the Council authorise the continuation of the Experts' Group to explore further the nature and content of such instruments in greater detail, which would enhance the existing Hague Conventions", and it will meet again in late 2015 or early 2016.[39] The next step would be to go to the Council on General Affairs and Policy for a mandate to undertake further work.

---

38 This mandate was made on the basis of the recommendations and conclusions of the Special Commission of January 2012. See *Conclusions and Recommendations of Part I and Part II of the Special Commission on the Practical Operation of the 1980 Child Abduction Convention and the 1996 Child Protection Convention and a Report of Part II of the Meeting*, HCCH 10 (2012), available at www.hcch.net/upload/wop/concl28–34sc6_en.pdf (Conclusions and Recommendations of the 2012 Special Commission).

39 The Conclusions and Recommendations of the Experts' Group include: "10. The Experts' Group noted that further instruments are likely to encourage and foster voluntary agreements in international child disputes. 11. The Experts' Group recognised the need for those concerned, including parents, mediators, lawyers and judges, to be provided with a 'navigation tool', *e.g.*, non-binding principles or guidelines, to assist them in securing cross-border recognition and enforcement of 'package agreements' in the existing legal framework. 12. The Experts' Group noted the additional benefit of a binding instrument that could provide a 'one-stop shop' to accommodate the 'package' that parents in particular conclude…" See *Annex A Conclusions and Recommendations of Experts' Group on Recognition and Enforcement of Voluntary Cross-Border Agreements 12–14 December*, included in *Prel. Doc. No 5 of March 2014 – Report on the Experts' Group Meeting on Cross-border Recognition and Enforcement of Agreements in International*

2.2. THE MALTA PROCESS: A BRIDGE BETWEEN CONTRACTING AND NON-CONTRACTING STATES

Having provided a general discussion of mechanisms that may work in cross-cultural and multi-faith cross-border situations, we turn next to the Hague Conference's work specifically focused on finding a means for contracting states to the 1980 Convention (and 1996 Convention) to work with non-contracting states that have legal systems influenced by or based on Sharia – in particular, on child abduction, access, and visitation issues – all of which has become known as the "Malta Process".[40] The Malta Process, now more than a decade old, is based on shared concerns for the best interests of the child and encouraging mutual respect for different legal systems. The focus of the Malta Process is on the protection of children. It particularly seeks to support the child's right to have continuing contact with parents living in different countries, and to combat international child abduction that may occur following arrangements for one parent to relocate or return home with the child.

The Malta Process seeks to find solutions to cross-border family law disputes in situations where the relevant international legal structure is not applicable, by encouraging dialogue and improving cooperation between contracting states to the 1980 and 1996 Conventions, and states with legal systems that are influenced by or based upon Sharia and which have not joined these Conventions. The basic approach has been to agree on certain common core understandings and shared positions: (a) equal respect for the different legal traditions and systems; (b) a willingness to explore and consider new solutions; and (c) the search for approaches arrived at through a process of consensus.[41] At the heart of the Malta Process are the three Malta Conferences, held in St. Julian, Malta in 2004, 2006 and 2009, which laid the groundwork for a gradually increasing dialogue and engagement between Western and Islamic jurisdictions over issues of child abduction and access.

The three conferences were composed of high-level experts, many from the judiciary, from contracting and non-contracting states. One of the most significant and successful parts of all three conferences was the use of hypothetical cases – where the participants, working through similar case studies, learned and shared their approaches – which led to the understanding of the importance of both common principles and agreed solutions. All three conferences focused on trying to identify common legal principles, such as

Child Disputes (from 12 to 14 December 2013) and recommendation for further work, available at www.hcch.net/upload/wop/gap2014pd05_en.pdf (*Conclusions and Recommendations of the Experts' Group on Voluntary Agreements of the Meeting*).

40 *See Press Release*, HCCH (26 March 2009), available at www.hcch.net/upload/maltapress2009.pdf.

41 *Ibid.*

concepts of jurisdiction, and shared values, such as the child having contact with both parents and the best interests of the child, which could lead to basic tools for better cooperation and for the development of a "rule of law" between the states concerned.

For example, at the first Malta Conference in 2004, the experts attending the conference were confronted with practical and rather typical case scenarios, such as when a Muslim mother, living in a contracting state with her Muslim husband and their five-year-old child, allows the father to take the child to visit grandparents living in a non-contracting state. The father and child do not return and the mother has been unable to have access to her child for many years. They considered how these cases would be handled under existing rules and procedures, and what common approaches might be possible in developing improved systems. The outcome of these deliberations was that although the Islamic countries would apply their own national laws and private international law rules rather than the 1980 Child Abduction Convention, they nonetheless came up with similar answers, which those attending considered an encouraging result. At the conclusion of the meeting, those present agreed upon the first "Malta Declaration".[42] Although this Declaration is non-binding and not intended to replace possible bilateral or multilateral binding agreements among states, it contains principles that may be seen as much more than purely aspirational, but rather as laying the foundation for next steps.[43]

For example, among the first Malta Declarations was the recognition of the need to develop common jurisdictional standards and to give mutual respect to decisions made on those bases.[44] It was also significant that all the countries present at the conference proclaimed the importance of specialist judges and the limitation of the number of courts exercising jurisdiction in international child cases.[45] Furthermore, it was agreed that speed is of the essence in cases

42 See *Declaration of 17 March 2004*, HCCH (2004), available at www.hcch.net/upload/maltadecl_e.pdf (*Malta I Declaration*).

43 See *ibid.*

44 Declaration #5 states: "The importance is recognised of having common rules which specify which country's courts or authorities are competent to make decisions concerning custody and contact." *Ibid.* The need to develop common jurisdictional standards continued to be recognised in the second Malta Conference, as evidenced by Declaration #5 of the second Malta Declaration: "It is in the interests of children that courts in different States should apply common rules of jurisdiction and that custody and contact orders made on the basis of those rules should as a general principle be recognised in other States. Competing jurisdictions add to family conflict, discourage parental agreement, and can encourage the unlawful removal or retention of children." *Declaration of 22 March 2006*, HCCH (2006), available at www.hcch.net/upload/maltadecl2_e.pdf (*Malta II Declaration*).

45 See, e.g., Declaration #8 of the first Malta Declaration: "The cases under consideration need to be handled by experienced judges. Judicial training, as well as concentration of jurisdiction among a limited number of courts, contribute to the development of the necessary expertise." *Malta I Declaration*, *supra* note 42.

where parent and child have been separated.[46] Another principle, on inter-state cooperation, may have set the tone for the continuation of the Malta Process and highlighted the overarching need for developing mutual trust:

> "Successful inter-State cooperation in child protection depends on the development of mutual trust and confidence between judicial, administrative and other competent authorities in the different States. The regular exchange of information, as well as meetings between judges (and other officials) at a bilateral or a multilateral level, are a necessary part of building this trust and confidence."[47]

A second Malta Conference took place in March 2006, followed by a third Judicial Conference in Malta in March 2009. At these conferences, the dialogue continued to proceed on the basis of a shared set of values and objectives, equal respect for the different legal systems, and a willingness to explore and consider new solutions. The Malta Process expanded its participation: in 2004, 14 states were represented; in 2006, 19 states were represented; and the third Malta Conference in 2009 had even more participants (24). As part of the process, the attempt was made to have an equal number of contracting and non-contracting states at each Malta Conference.[48]

---

46 Declaration #7 of the first Malta Declaration states: "Speed in both administrative and judicial processes is of the essence because delays which prolong the separation of a child from a parent may have devastating consequences for the parent-child relationship." *Ibid.* at #7.

47 *Ibid.* at #10.

48 Sweden was a participant in all three Malta Conferences. The participants in the First Malta Conference (2004) were judges and experts from: Algeria, Belgium, Egypt, France, Germany, Italy, Lebanon, Malta, Morocco, the Netherlands, Spain, Sweden, Tunisia, the United Kingdom, the European Commission, the Council of the European Union, the International Social Service and Reunite, and the Hague Conference on Private International Law. The participants in the Second Malta Conference in 2006 (19–22 March 2006) were judges and experts from: Algeria, Australia, Belgium, Canada, Egypt, France, Germany, Indonesia, Lebanon, Libya, Malaysia, Malta, Morocco, the Netherlands, Sweden, Tunisia, Turkey, the United Kingdom, and the United States of America. The international, regional and non-governmental organisations/bodies included the European Commission, the European Parliament, the Council of the European Union, the International Social Service, the International Centre for Missing and Exploited Children and Reunite, as well as the Hague Conference on Private International Law. The participants in the Third Malta Conference in 2009 were judges and experts from: Australia, Bangladesh, Belgium, Canada, Egypt, France, Germany, India, Israel, Jordan, Malaysia, Malta, Morocco, the Netherlands, Oman, Pakistan, Qatar, Spain, Sweden, Switzerland, Tunisia, Turkey, the United Kingdom, the United States of America, the European Commission, the European Parliament, the Council of the European Union, the United Nations Committee on the Rights of the Child, the League of the Arab States, International Social Service, the International Centre for Missing and Exploited Children, and Reunite, as well as the Hague Conference on Private International Law.

2.3. THE THIRD MALTA CONFERENCE AND THE WORKING PARTY ON MEDIATION

Following the third Malta Conference in 2009, many of the participants wanted to move forward with more than broad Declarations in an effort to secure better protection for cross-frontier rights of contact for parents and their children and the problems posed by international abduction between the States concerned. Participants at the third Malta Conference had acknowledged the urgent need to provide assistance to individuals involved in cases where no international legal framework applied, in the interim, and suggested encouraging the development of mediation structures.[49] They therefore recommended the establishment of a Working Party on Mediation to draw up a plan of action for a manageable project – the development of mediation structures and services to assist in the resolution of cross-frontier disputes on custody and contact with children.[50]

Mediation allows common values and trust to transcend legal boundaries to bridge the gap where no underlying legal structure is shared by the parties to a conflict. Further, the role of mediation in Islamic culture is well established in some countries, such as Jordan, Lebanon and Egypt.[51] Based on demographic factors and legal traditions, a small group of states was convened to form the Working Party. These states consisted of an equal number of contracting states (Australia, Canada, France, Germany, the United Kingdom, and the United States) to the 1980 Convention and non-contracting states (Egypt, India, Jordan, Malaysia, Morocco[52] and Pakistan).

In 2010, the Working Party completed a draft of the Principles for the Establishment of Mediation Structures in the Context of the Malta Process[53] and

---

49 *Declaration of 26 March 2009*, HCCH, Info. Doc. 8 (January 2012) (*Malta III Declaration*) #7.

50 *Ibid.*

51 See, e.g., J. Wagner, 'Islamic Mediators and Germany's "Two Legal Systems"', *Der Spiegel*, 18 June 2012 (discussing prevalence of mediation among Muslims living in Germany); *B v. El-B* [2003] 1 FLR 811, 814–817 (Eng.) (stating understanding that family mediation involving the parents and their family members is customary in Muslim countries and summarising English precedents involving non-contracting states with legal systems influenced by or based on Sharia law).

52 At that time, Morocco was considered a non-contracting state. In 2010, Morocco ratified the 1980 Child Abduction Convention which created an "imbalance" between the number of contracting and non-contracting states in the Working Party. As a result, the current Working Party members agreed to expand the Working Party and invited several new countries to join (Qatar, Indonesia, Bangladesh, Senegal, South Africa), but with a commitment to ensure sufficient and equal participation by non-contracting states with Sharia-influenced or -based legal systems. Senegal and South Africa officially joined the Working Party. The current co-chairs of the Working Party are Chief Justice Jillani of Pakistan and Mr William R. Crosbie of Canada.

53 HCCH (Nov. 2010), available at www.hcch.net/upload/wop/mediationprinc_e.pdf (*Mediation Principles*).

of the related Explanatory Memorandum,[54] which were welcomed by the Sixth Special Commission in June 2011.[55]

The Mediation Principles call for the establishment of a "Central Contact Point" for international family mediation in each state.[56] The Central Contact Point is intended to facilitate the provision of information on available mediation services in the respective jurisdictions, access to mediation, and information regarding other important related issues, such as relevant legal information and obtaining help to locate a child.

> "A. CENTRAL CONTACT POINT
> States should establish / designate a Central Contact Point for international family mediation which should undertake, either directly or through an intermediary, the following tasks,
>
> - Serve as contact point for individuals and at the same time as network point for mediators working in cross-border family disputes.
> - Provide information about family mediation services available in that country, such as:
>   - List of family mediators, including contact details and information about their training, language skills and experiences;
>   - List of organisations providing mediation services in international family disputes;
>   - Information on costs of mediation;
>   - Information on the mediation models used / available; and
>   - Information on how mediation is conducted and what topics may be covered in mediation.
> - Provide information to assist with locating the other parent/ the child within the country concerned.
> - Provide information on where to obtain advice on family law and legal procedures.
> - Provide information on how to give the mediated agreement binding effect.
> - Provide information on the enforcement of the mediated agreement.
> - Provide information about any support available to ensure the long-term viability of the mediated agreement.
> - Promote cooperation between various experts by promoting networking, training programmes and the exchange of best practices.
> - Subject to the principle of confidentiality, gather and make publicly available on a periodic basis information on the number and nature of cases dealt with by central contact points, actions taken and outcomes including results of mediation where known."[57]

---

54 *Explanatory Memorandum on the Principles for the Establishment of Mediation Structures in the Context of the Malta Process*, HCCH (Nov. 2010), available at www.hcch.net/upload/wop/mediationmemo_e.pdf (*Explanatory Memorandum*).

55 *Special Commission on the Practical Operation of the 1980 and 1996 Hague Conventions (1–10 June 2011), Conclusions and Recommendations adopted by the Special Commission*, HCCH, available at www.hcch.net/upload/concl28sc6_e.pdf.

56 See *Mediation Principles*, *supra* note 55, §A.

57 *Ibid.*

The Mediation Principles further refer to certain standards for identifying international mediation services, as well as for the mediation process and the mediated agreement itself.[58] The Mediation Principles also emphasise the importance of rendering a mediated agreement binding or enforceable in all the legal systems concerned before the time for implementation.[59]

Some participating states have already taken measures to implement the Mediation Principles and have designated Central Contact Points. Australia, Germany, France, Pakistan and the United States have already established Central Contact Points for international family mediation.[60] Thus far, it has been mostly the contracting states that have established Central Contact Points to handle incoming cases with non-contracting states that have Sharia- or Islamic-influenced legal systems. The Slovak Republic, the Netherlands, Hungary and the Russian Federation, all contracting states that are not members of the Working Party, have also designated Central Contact Points which are designed to provide assistance to parents seeking returns when a child has been abducted from a non-contracting state. Of the non-contracting states, only Pakistan has set up a Central Contact Point, and it has been difficult to obtain empirical information on cases.[61] Egypt established a "Good Office Committee" to facilitate the solution of cross-border family conflicts by using alternative dispute resolution mechanisms, and it has been actively considering establishing a Central Contact Point. Jordan has recently opened a Mediation Center for international family conflicts as well, reflecting the importance of mediation in resolving these disputes in Sharia countries. The shared belief in the importance of mediation as a means of dispute resolution in family conflicts may pave the way for further exploration of cooperative solutions in access, custody, and abduction cases.

2.4. THE FUTURE OF THE MALTA PROCESS AND THE WORKING PARTY ON MEDIATION

Although some have suggested that the Hague Conference should organise another large-scale Malta Conference, at this point, the Member States through the Permanent Bureau have been focused on creating more concrete and substantive "deliverables", as some Member States have called them, based on the Declarations already generated. A stronger and broader foundation needs to be established before the Hague Conference can undertake a new foray. More concrete assistance is necessary to address the problems faced by contracting states and

58 *Ibid.*, §B.

59 *Ibid.*, §C.

60 *Central Contact Points for International Family Mediation*, HCCH, available at www.hcch.net/index_en.php?act=publications.details&pid=5360&dtid=52.

61 *Ibid.* Most CCPs have not yet provided comprehensive data for their countries.

non-contracting states to the Conventions, including cooperation in arranging for communications and more understanding of the underlying legal systems.

Dialogue, confidence building and exchange of information are essential components of the Malta Process. There is still a need to learn from each other, and the importance of the process of understanding why things are done in different ways in the various legal systems should not be underestimated. The Malta Process will therefore continue to be a learning experience leading to an increased understanding of other legal systems. However, the consensus achieved among judges and other experts at the Malta Conferences still must be translated into a broader and more efficient state of cooperation with practical working arrangements involving more administrative and governmental authorities.

In the future, the Malta Process might apply a wider methodology with the view to achieving tangible, practical results, and these efforts would require full commitment not only on the part of the judiciary but also on the part of other governmental entities. Rather than a large conference, the thought is therefore to have smaller sub-regional meetings. This approach lends itself to further work by the Working Party, not limited to building mediation structures, but also building cooperation in family disputes and access cases while in addition encouraging non-contracting states to consider acceding to the 1980 and 1996 Conventions.

Such an approach was initiated at a recent conference in October 2013, organised by the Hague Conference and the *Deutsche Stiftung für Internationale Rechtliche Zusammenarbeit* (IRZ) in Tunisia, where the Hague family law conventions received significant attention and the Working Party on Mediation held a separate, pre-conference one-day meeting.[62] More than 65 experts from throughout the Middle East and North Africa (MENA) region, including representatives from Tunisia, Algeria, Egypt, Jordan, Lebanon, Mauritania, Morocco, Qatar and Saudi Arabia, as well as Germany and Canada, attended this two-day conference at which they unanimously adopted several Conclusions and Recommendations, including:

"1980 Child Abduction Convention and 1996 Child Protection Convention

7. The 1980 Child Abduction Convention provides a structure to support family relationships, by providing a civil, non-criminal procedure to return a child when taken by a parent or a custodian.
8. The 1996 Child Protection Convention is a valuable tool in providing protection for children in cross-border contexts and in supplementing and supporting the 1980 Convention.

---

62 See www.hcch.net/index_en.php?act=events.details&year=2013&varevent=332. See also *Cross Border Co-operation in Civil and Commercial Matters through The Hague Conventions, Tunis, Tunisia 28–30 October 2013, Conclusions and Recommendations*, available at www.hcch.net/upload/tunis2013concl_en.pdf.

9. Mechanisms should be developed to promote agreement between parties in Convention cases (e.g., mediation structures). However, States must ensure that efforts to promote agreement between parties in Convention cases do not unduly delay the decision as to whether to return the child.
10. Non-Contracting States to the 1980 and 1996 Hague Conventions are encouraged to make available mechanisms leading to agreed solutions in cross-border family disputes involving children and to ensure that these agreements are respected and if necessary, legally enforceable in the countries concerned.
11. Non-Contracting States to the 1980 and 1996 Hague Conventions where the legal systems are based on, or influenced by, Sharia law are encouraged to consider joining the Working Party on Mediation and to implement the Principles for the Establishment of Mediation Structures in the context of the Malta Process, including establishing a Central Contact Point on International Family Mediation."[63]

Currently, more concrete work is being done by the Working Party on Mediation as part of the Malta Process. The Working Party, led by co-chairs William R. Crosbie from Canada and Chief Justice Jillani of Pakistan, have held yearly meetings for the last three years on the margin of the annual meeting of the Hague Conference's Council on General Affairs and Policy. The one in April 2014, hosted by the Dutch government, offered a day programme that provided insight into concepts of Islamic law and Islamic legal perspectives on cross-border family disputes. These meetings have been undertaken to provide the opportunity for exchange between experts in Islamic family law and Working Party members.

The implementation of the Mediation Principles by several states represents a concrete outcome laying the groundwork for practical solutions. In particular, the establishment of Central Contact Points for international family mediation as entry points for information, assistance, and cooperation has the potential to assist parents and protect children effectively in cross-border disputes. For that reason, a primary focus of the Working Party is to further promote the implementation of the Mediation Principles, encourage all members to establish Central Contact Points, and to expand the concept of the Central Contact Point beyond providing information on mediation structures and services.[64] One can see the Central Contact Points in non-contracting states as an early stage of a Central Authority, as a mechanism for cooperation, judicial and administrative, with contracting states. In other words, Central Contact Points may help lay the foundation for ongoing collaboration and trust that would, in the future, make accession to the 1980 and 1996 Conventions possible. In the interim, the Central Contact Point can play a role in providing a structure for cooperation and building trust that will benefit children and parents in these non-contracting states.

---

63 *Ibid.* at 7–11.

64 See *Conclusions and Recommendations of the 2012 Special Commission*, HCCH, *supra* note 38, at Part 1.

3. CONCLUSION

3.1. FUTURE WORK TOWARD GAINING ACCESSIONS

From the point of view of many members of the Hague Conference, the Working Party and the Malta Process more generally, while the promotion of mediation and other means to find amicable solutions in cases of cross-border, cross-cultural family disputes is a priority, they are ultimately focused on promoting accession to the Hague Conventions. Mediation may offer solutions in some – perhaps many – cases, especially those with cross-cultural and multi-faith aspects, but it is not a panacea for all cases. Mediation may not resolve all issues and it may not offer a total or lasting solution. The absence of binding certainty as a "stick" may also hinder full cooperation between parents. The 1980 and 1996 Conventions offer a legal framework for cooperation and communication as well as legal certainty for parents and children, especially as they cross borders.

The accession of Morocco in 2010 as the first Muslim contracting state to the 1980 Convention and the more recent accession by Iraq in 2014 are milestones demonstrating the possibility of applying the multilateral convention framework to both countries with legal systems influenced by Sharia and those adhering to purely Western principles of family law. Already-existing bilateral agreements also illustrate the potential for using a Convention framework for abduction cases involving Islamic countries, while simultaneously revealing the need for a more comprehensive multilateral solution.[65]

Before wider accession to the Hague Conventions is possible, however, further work must be done to identify and address possible obstacles to states with Sharia-influenced or -based legal systems joining the 1980 and 1996 Conventions.[66] Such work may focus on developing shared values and principles on jurisdiction, and on the roles of religion, habitual residence, and nationality. For example, as mentioned earlier, habitual residence under the 1980 Convention is a concept that is neutral with respect to nationality, religion, and the sex of the child.[67] Under a Sharia-influenced system, however, these can be determinative factors in analysing the best interests of the child, which might create a conflict between what is mandated by some Sharia law and the automatic return mechanism in certain cases.[68]

---

65 See *supra* text accompanying note 11.

66 For research already conducted by the Permanent Bureau identifying some of the special issues arising in relation to cross-border abduction cases involving an Islamic country, see C. Gosselain, *supra* note 8. See also *infra* text accompanying note 73.

67 See 1980 Convention, Art. 3.

68 See, e.g., Z. Kamaruddin, Int'l Islamic Univ. Malay., Keynote Presentation at the HCCH Int'l Seminar: *Islamic Legal Perspectives on Cross-Border Family Disputes Involving Children*, pp. 12–13 (7 April 2014) (discussing different rules that apply to various circumstances depending on the habitual residence or religion of the parties involved in cross-border family disputes relating to custody of child).

Furthermore, under traditional Sharia law, a child is considered Muslim if the father is Muslim, and it is considered in the best interests of the child to be raised as a Muslim within an Islamic culture. "[P]arental care in traditional Islamic jurisprudence is divided into custody and guardianship with the mother (and other female relatives of the child) having a stronger claim to the former and the father (and other male relatives of the child) being primarily entitled to the latter."[69] Child custody and guardianship under Sharia law have been traditionally determined by the age and sex of the child, and men and women are allocated specific, complementary parental responsibilities.[70] "The relationship between *hadanah* [custody] and guardianship (*wilayah*) can be seen as a complex structure of rights and duties distributed between the entitled person(s). The main distinction between the two concepts is that *hadanah* is more related to the emotional taking care of and nursing of the infant, whereas *wilayah* is more concerned with decisions that in some way or another affect the child's present and future welfare."[71] Generally speaking, guardianship is a male-oriented function and *hadanah* is a more female-oriented function. "The father as the natural guardian of the child has the duty and responsibility to determine major decisions relating to the child's life, such as discipline, education, religious upbringing, medical consent, consent to marriage and future career."[72] This allocation of ultimate guardianship to the father, combined with Sharia law's preference for the Muslim parent, means that the best interests of the child under Sharia law might be viewed as inconsistent with the return of a child to a non-Muslim mother bringing a case under the 1980 Convention against a Muslim father.[73] Despite potential roadblocks posed by cultural and religious differences such as these, it must be emphasised that multilateral treaties are a framework for legal cooperation, not changing underlying legal systems or their substantive laws.

One recent example of the way forward can be seen in the First Gulf Judicial Seminar on Cross-Frontier Legal Co-operation in Civil and Commercial Matters,

---

69 See L.-M. Möller, "Improving Women's Rights Through Children's Rights: The Reform of Custody Laws in Contemporary Muslim Jurisdictions", in M. Jänterä-Jareborg and H. Tigroudja, *Women's Human Rights and the Elimination of Discrimination*, The Hague Acad. of Int'l L., Martinus Nijhoff Publishers 2016 (forthcoming) (draft of article shared by author). See generally J. Nasir, *The Islamic Law of Personal Status*, 2nd edition, 1990; M. Zahraa and N. Malek, "The Concept of Custody in Islamic Law" (1998) 13 *Arab. L.Q.* 155; E. Schnitzer-Reese, *supra* note 7.

70 See L.-M. Möller, *supra* note 69. "[T]he overall theme can be summarized as the father and mother being endowed with different abilities and qualification which enable them to take care of children of a specific gender and age. Whereas the mother was seen as better suited to care for young children with a preference for girls, the father was to intercede and oversee the upbringing of children, boys in particular, at a later stage in life. Such division of parenting functions along gender lines was seen as the logical consequence of different 'natural' qualifications of women and men, i.e. mothers and fathers, for fulfilling the child's needs."

71 M. Zahraa and N. Malek, *supra* note 69, p. 157.

72 *Ibid.*, p. 158.

73 See S. Ayar, "International Child Abductions Involving Non-Hague Convention States: The Need for a Uniform Approach" (2007) 21 *Emory Int'l L. Rev.* 277, 283.

held in Doha, Qatar, in June 2011, when approximately eighty participants from Member States of the Gulf Cooperation Council (GCC) – Kuwait, Qatar, Saudi Arabia, the United Arab Emirates and Oman (Bahrain was excused) – including ministry officials, academics, professionals and members of the Permanent Bureau of the Hague Conference, met to discuss the relevance and possible implementation of some of the Conventions within the GCC Region in the area of child protection, along with Hague Conventions on legal cooperation and litigation. The Conclusions and Recommendations from the meeting illustrate the possibilities for cooperation when there are shared values, such as the "best interests of the child", and mutual trust in protecting children. Specifically, they acknowledged:

> "that the 1980, the 1996 and the 2007 Conventions implement the principles set out or implicit in the United Nations Convention on the Rights of the Child of 1989, such as:
> i. the best interests of the child as a primary consideration in all actions concerning children;
> ii. the right of a child whose parents reside in different States to maintain on a regular basis, save in exceptional circumstances, personal relations and direct contacts with both parents; and
> iii. the opportunity for a child to learn, to know and respect the culture and traditions of both parents;
> all of which are underlying principles of *sharia* law."[74]

3.2. THE ROAD AHEAD

Mediation has much to offer parents when faced with the realities of conflicting cultures and values in child-rearing. Mediation may be able to create a bridge where the underlying legal framework is not shared. One critical element necessary to encourage and nourish mediation and other forms of amicable resolution for cross-border disputes involving children is the ability to recognise and enforce agreed solutions across borders – to make the voluntary agreements "portable" from contracting to non-contracting states and back. Indeed, the Conclusions and Recommendations of the Experts' Group on Voluntary Agreements, which met in The Hague in December 2013, emphasised the need for and use of additional tools

[74] See *First Gulf Judicial Seminar on Cross-Frontier Legal Co-operation in Civil and Commercial Matters Qatar, Doha – 20 to 22 June 2011 Conclusions & Recommendation*, available at www.hcch.net/upload/2011_doha_conc_en.pdf. They also acknowledged that: "A. the use of the 1980 Child Abduction Convention in providing a structure to support family relationships, by providing a civil, non-criminal procedure to return a child to his or her habitual residence when taken by a parent or a custodian; B. the value of the 1996 Protection of Children Convention in providing protection for vulnerable children in cross-border contexts and in supplementing and supporting the 1980 Convention; C. the potential merits of establishing focal points in each GCC State to co-operate with each other and with Central Authorities established under the 1980 and 1996 Conventions."

to help make these agreements achieved through amicable resolution enforceable not only in contracting states but in non-contracting states.[75] Although the cross-border recognition of voluntary agreements has broader implications than just for abduction and access cases involving Islamic countries, and is relevant for relocation cases generally, enforceability will help encourage the use of agreed solutions in cases involving children from contracting and non-contracting states, including those with Islamic traditions, by providing certainty and confidence for parents as their children come and go across borders.

Future efforts at increasing legal cooperation and understanding should also concentrate on issues such as the nature of abduction cases as civil as opposed to criminal cases; the role of state and non-state courts in handling abduction cases; issues of immigration and visas for visitation or access; challenges related to the implementation of Central Contact Points and structures for mediation, such as the costs, funding, governmental support in the form of legislation and establishment of legal structures; and the difficulty of adherence to binding Hague instruments in countries where there are multiple legal systems governing family relations.[76] Recognising that achieving the requisite understanding surrounding these issues and, ultimately, accession may take a great deal of time, mechanisms for international cooperation, starting with mediation and the Malta Process more generally, are the best way to start building the necessary bridges between states and creating practical legal tools to help multi-religious, multi-cultural families handle cross-border challenges.

75 See *supra* section 2.1 and notes 38 and 39.

76 See, e.g., Z. Kamaruddin et al., "Assessing the Working Draft of the Hague Convention on the International Recovery of Child Support and Other Forms of Family Maintenance: Malaysian Shari'ah Perspective" (2010) 2 *Malay. J. of Syariah and L.* 95, 116 (addressing the problems Malaysia confronts in complying with the Hague Conventions given the country's history and cultural heritage, particularly its concepts of the family from the Sharia perspective).

THE CHILD AS THE "SACRIFICIAL LAMB" TO SOCIETY, FAMILY, RELIGION AND CULTURE

A Comment

Esin Örücü

This is a brief comment reflecting concern and scepticism related to the rights of the child and the concept of "in the best interests of the child". We are talking of a child who until a certain age does not have a voice at all and, after learning to use his or her voice, is either not heard or is disregarded or overridden by the voices of others such as law makers, parents, NGOs, social workers, teachers and doctors. The child is furthermore surrounded by the values of belief systems, religion, tradition and customs which she or he has not played any part in creating. Where is the child in this? When seemingly deciding in the child's best interests, are the above-mentioned persons and systems not in fact all sacrificing the child?

In issues such as settling custody disputes, child marriages, circumcision of boys and genital mutilation of girls, placement of children in foster homes, the child's right to receive essential education in segregation from the "different", domestic violence, and even in small matters like dress codes, the child does not have an effective right to develop his or her identity but rather is suffocated, used and abused. If we cast our eyes worldwide, there are other more menacing issues, such as child soldiers, kidnapped children raised for terrorist armies, children sold for gain by their parents, girls sold into forced marriages, child labour, child prostitution, child pornography, and even ritual slaughtering of children. The list appears endless.

It is the authorities that decide on who can foster and be fostered, and who can adopt and be adopted. Even in this context, it is the authorities and not the child who exercise rights. In addition it appears to be the parents' rights rather than the child's that have priority, as it is the values and beliefs of the parents that determine whether the child is circumcised, which school she or he attends, what she or he may or may not eat. So, should we then call the child's rights the "parents' rights"? The child becomes the "sacrificial lamb", sacrificed to the values, religious or otherwise, of society and the parents; has little or no say; is not believed when reporting abuse and is ignored most of the time. How can the child be truly nurtured and protected? Is neutrality achievable in the process?

The answer is in fact yes; things have improved. Children are not regarded, at least in law, as possessions of their fathers, which was the case in ancient Roman law. They are not seen usually as helpers in family chores, and they have to be sent to school. However, we cannot be smug just because we have international instruments which regard the child as a person and bestow rights on him or her. Hidden behind the concept of "the best interests of the child", the authorities, and their physical manifestation, the courts, ultimately make decisions for children, place them, move them, separate them from family and friends, or force them back into their families, which may prove detrimental to their future development. Children on the whole have no say in these life choices, especially if they are toddlers. A toddler has no religion, no specific identity as yet, no culture, and is a body being shaped into someone else's religion, culture and customs.

The rights of the child are a strange kind of right where others decide what is in the best interests of the holder of the right, where the holder of the right cannot determine the scope of his or her rights, or exercise them or make claims arising from their violation, but depends on others to do so, which will happen only if those others so choose. Could one assume a presumed delegation of this fragmented right? This right should then not be called a right but something else!

In the intersection between family, society, religion and culture, *the child* is squeezed and sacrificed to these outside values without being consulted and without his or her consent or choice. Even the pluralistic mixed-faith and multicultural society is trying to mirror itself onto children born into it. We know that, for instance, Article 9 of the European Convention for the Protection of Rights and Fundamental Freedoms (ECHR) and the Convention's Additional Protocol No. 1 (Article 2) do not include a right to force a child to share in the religious beliefs and practices of the parents. This applies equally to the Convention on the Rights of the Child (Article 14). And yet, parents want and have the power to instil in the child their own values and beliefs. At times, I would argue, the body and soul of the child need to be saved from parents, family, society, religion and culture and even the state. Who can do that?

The questions then are: Who should have the right to determine the becoming of a person? Who can truly protect this nucleus of a person from society, family, religion and culture? Are the present laws, instruments and implementation capable of delivering? How will this child fare in adulthood, especially in an increasingly globalising world? Who is he or she to blame for his or her misfortunes?

ANNEX

Summary of the Report of the Swedish Law Commission: *Strengthened Protection against Forced Marriages and Child Marriages* (Statens Offentliga Utredningar 2012:35)

THE PROBLEM AND THE PROPOSALS

How extensive is the problem of forced marriages and child marriages? It would be good to have some figures. How many people are married off against their will, how many are afraid that this will be the case, how many child marriages are there?

However, it is the stories of individuals that really convince us regarding the need for enhanced protection against forced marriages and child marriages. The story of the 15-year-old girl who was sent to Iraq, married off to a considerably older cousin and ever since has been informing the world around by means of a hidden computer of the abuse she is subjected to. The story of the young woman who wanted to get an education in Sweden but became part of a barter transaction between two families, protested but was threatened, assaulted and finally married off. Or the story of the girl who escaped from a forced marriage and had a child with the man she loved, a child whom the family subsequently killed.

As the inquiry neared completion, a nineteen-year-old woman was stabbed to death. Her sixteen-year-old brother is a suspect and is at present in police custody. As a child the victim had been taken to another country and there been married off against her will at the age of fourteen. After a while she succeeded in fleeing back to Sweden. As we write, a police inquiry has just been initiated and a discussion is ongoing concerning why the young woman was not given the protection she needed to survive.

There are many of these stories, each one more gripping than the other. They bear witness to a widespread lack of freedom and young people who are not aware that they themselves have the right to decide over their lives.

It is difficult to give exact figures but, based on the information available to us; we estimate that in 2011 at least 250–300 people experienced an acute or fairly acute risk of being married against their own will. Previous investigations indicate that some 70,000 young people have restrictions in relation to marriage or have conditions laid down by the family for choice of partner. About 8,500 young people were estimated to be anxious that they will not be allowed to choose for themselves whom they marry.

It clearly emerges in our investigation that forced marriage and child marriage are often connected with honour-related violence and oppression. This knowledge is of importance for how we tackle the problems. But it is more important - quite apart from culture, religion, traditions and values - to start from the human rights due to every individual, rights laid down in several international conventions and recommendations - such as the UN Convention on the Rights of the Child, the UN Convention on the Elimination of All Forms of Discrimination Against Women and the Council of Europe's Convention for the Protection of Human Rights and Fundamental Freedoms.

We have carried on this work since June 2010. According to our terms of reference, among other things we were to:

- increase knowledge about forced marriage and child marriage,
- consider whether such marriages should be made criminal offences, and
- consider whether the possibility of exemption for child marriage should be removed.

In addition we were instructed to think of measures that could be taken apart from legislation, inter alia in order that the authorities' work to counter forced marriage and child marriage should become safer and better.

Legislating against forced marriage and child marriage is a complicated matter. From a legal point of view there are almost insurmountable obstacles regarding child marriage. In addition there are fears that legislation of this type would have a stigmatising effect on society's view of minority groups and their traditions. It is therefore tempting to abstain from legislation. But then you must remember the stories and be aware that there are people, particularly girls and women, who are in very great need of the help and protection of legislators and authorities. Some measures should therefore be taken in spite of our instinctive reaction not to.

We propose, among other things, the following:

(1) Forced marriage be made a criminal offence through a special penalty stipulation. This would also include certain alliances similar to marriage, but which are not valid marriages. We call these informal marriages.
(2) Child marriage be made a criminal offence. Here too the informal marriages are included.
(3) The possibility of exemption to enter into child marriage be removed.
(4) A national so-called competence team be established to lead, coordinate and support efforts to counter forced marriage and child marriage and also honour-related violence and oppression.

Along with these proposals we submit a further four that are less conspicuous but from a practical point of view probably equally important:

(5) The National Board of Health and Welfare should be commissioned to carry out a supervision project concerning forced marriage and child marriage at municipalities' social services departments.
(6) For religious communities and wedding officiators to be granted permission to perform marriages, it should be required that they do not carry out any religious "forced marriages" or "child marriages", which do not result in legal marriages but lead to alliances with the same effect in practice.
(7) In its ordinary operations, the Committee for state support to religious communities shall carry on a dialogue with the communities and marriage officiators about child marriage and marriage against a person's wishes.
(8) A recommended method be formulated for family work in acute situations. It should be based on, among other things, an evaluation of the methods used in some parts of the country today.

On some matters we abstain from presenting proposals which would in themselves strengthen protection against forced marriage and child marriage. For example, we do not propose any limitations to the possibility of recognising in Sweden what is known as a proxy marriage entered into abroad nor the criminalisation of such marriages even when they take place against the wishes of one of the couple. Nor do we propose any further restrictions to the possibility of recognising child marriages that have been entered into abroad. In these cases we consider that the arguments against legislation override. This also applies to an otherwise conceivable possibility of withholding in some very distressing cases the true grounds for a decision to refuse a residence permit.

Below we summarise the experience, knowledge and insight we have gained concerning forced marriage and child marriage, and also the considerations that are the basis for our proposals and other conclusions. When we use the word child marriage we mean all marriages where one of the parties is under the age of 18. By forced marriage we primarily mean marriage that has been entered into as a result of punishable force. When we also include marriages that have been entered into following other forms of pressure we say married against a person's will. That term also includes cases where there has been no pressure as such, but where the person is not able to decline a marriage that others wish him or her to enter into, or where he or she can decline only with great difficulty.

THE EXTENT AND NATURE OF THE PROBLEM

We mentioned above some figures that apply to the extent in Sweden of the problem of marriage against a person's will. We estimate that in 2011 at least 250–300 people experienced an acute or fairly acute risk of being married against their own will. Previous inquiries indicate that about 70,000 young people have restrictions in relation to marriage or from conditions laid down by the family for choice of partner. The Swedish National Board for Youth Affairs has estimated that some 8,500 young people are worried that they will not be allowed to choose whom they marry.

From the inquiries carried out in, or in connection with, our work the following, inter alia, further emerged:

- At least 16 people in 2011 were kept abroad to be married off against their will.
- In December 2011 there were thirteen children in Sweden aged 15–17 who were registered as married.
- The number of children living in relationships that are not legally valid as marriage but which in practice are similar may be assumed to be several times greater than the figure just mentioned.
- The Swedish Migration Board in one year handled 11 cases of child marriage and 8 cases of suspected forced marriage in matters concerning residence permits.
- In one year the Swedish Tax Agency handled a total of 70 cases regarding national registration of a child marriage contracted abroad where at least one of the couple was either a Swedish national or a resident of Sweden at the time when the marriage was contracted.

It should be clear from these figures that the problem of forced marriage and child marriage is considerable in Sweden even in purely quantitative terms. There is no doubt that it is a major and concrete problem for many of the individuals concerned.

Our investigation indicates that a majority of the people who are married or engaged to be married against their will, or who are worried about being married off against their will have a foreign background. Furthermore, there is a clear connection between forced marriage and child marriage on the one hand and, on the other, honour-related violence and oppression. However, as mentioned previously these circumstances should not influence our attitude towards forced marriage and child marriage. Instead, in the first instance it is a matter of securing the human rights of those exposed.

SOME OTHER POINTS OF DEPARTURE

Attempts to deal with child marriage have been ongoing for many years in the international arena. There is an almost forty-year-old UN Convention on, inter alia, a minimum age for marriage. The discussion in this country on forced marriage and child marriage began in the early 1970s and has intensified over the past 10–15 years. It is clear that in many cases there is a connection between forced marriage and child marriage on the one hand and, on the other, honour-related violence and oppression.

In 2004 some amendments to laws were implemented in Sweden for the purpose of strengthening protection against forced marriage and child marriage. The amendments meant, among other things, that no one may enter into marriage before a Swedish authority before the age of 18 without special permission (marriage exemption). Furthermore, the conditions for marriage exemption were tightened. The rules for recognition of foreign marriages were also tightened in order to strengthen the possibility of refusing recognition in the case of forced and child marriages. The possibility of divorce without a preceding time for consideration was extended to include cases where marriage was entered into in Sweden under compulsion or in contravention of the age requirement.

Since 2003 the Government has taken initiatives for far-reaching efforts to counter honour-related violence and oppression. In May 2010, a special action plan was adopted to prevent young people being married against their will. It comprises a total of fifteen measures in four areas, namely strengthened preventive work, reinforced support and protection, enhanced collaboration between authorities and increased knowledge. One of the measures was to set up this inquiry.

However, some other countries in Europe appear to have made more progress than we in this country in work to counter forced marriage and child marriage. This applies in particular to the United Kingdom and Norway where partly different paths were chosen. We have studied their work and experience and tried to learn from them.

The discussion in the report is based on some fundamental building blocks. One of these is the view of marriage as an important legal and social institution which may, however, involve very negative consequences for the individual who does not want to, or is not ready to marry. Another building block is that both marriage against one of the party's wishes and child marriage are in violation of human rights. This approach is confirmed by several international agreements.

The UN has defined among other things forced marriage, early marriage and dowry as harmful practices that constitute a form of violence against women and a violation of women's human rights. The UN General Assembly and other UN organs have urged governments to develop and fully implement laws and other measures to eradicate harmful practices and traditions including early marriage, forced marriage and honour-related crime.

In 2011 the Council of Europe adopted a Convention on preventing and combating violence against women and domestic violence. It establishes that forced marriage is to be regarded as a form of violence against women and states are enjoined to make forcing a person to marry a punishable offence.

To be forced to marry and live with someone against one's will is clearly in itself a major encroachment. Expectations that the marriage should lead to sexual cohabitation and children imply in these cases a major risk of sexual assault.

Experience shows that many of the girls and women who are married against their will are exploited and badly treated in their marriages. Difficulties in obtaining a divorce accepted by their own group and the stigmatisation of divorced women in this group can further exacerbate the situation.

Other disadvantages include the fact that early marriage may lead to discontinued schooling. Lack of education can result in long-term alienation and major difficulties in getting into the labour market and earning a living.

In discussions about forced marriage, child marriage and honour-related violence and oppression, fears are often expressed that an "us and them attitude" will emerge and racist and xenophobic ideologies gain support when particular groups are pointed out because they are considered to represent negative behaviour and opinions. In view of this risk, and of the danger that people will be subjected to prejudice, it is important to emphasise that legislation against forced marriage and child marriage is intended to protect vulnerable people, not to attack or point out particular groups. Protection of those exposed safeguards equal human rights for all and is not dependent on the group to which the individual belongs.

A fear of xenophobia or stigmatisation cannot be allowed to result in a lack of attention on the part of society to the individual's exposure. We have seen examples of the existence of this type of danger in our work. There are many descriptions of how society does not intervene when very young girls are married off and become parents. It cannot be accepted that children from minorities are refused the protection considered self-evident for children belonging to the majority in Swedish society.

At the same time it must be underscored that people, groups and cultures deserve basic respect even to the extent their traditions and approach include values that are unfamiliar to the majority in the country. To be sure, basic respect of this nature can never be allowed to mean any departure from fundamental rights and freedoms. But it should mean that amendments to laws that may be perceived to be directed against a group or tradition be implemented in a tone of voice and with an approach in general that does not create unnecessary confrontation and which does not play into the hands of xenophobic forces. It must be admitted that in this instance the legislator is in an area that is unusually difficult to master.

NO POSSIBILITY OF EXEMPTION FOR CHILD MARRIAGE

Persons under 18 may not marry in this country unless the county administrative board grants permission, known as marriage exemption.

The provisions were tightened in 2004. Nowadays exemption is only granted if there are special reasons.

We mapped out cases of exemption for the years 2008–2010. The survey shows that the number of young people applying for marriage exemption has more than halved since the year 2000. During the three years we studied, a total of 68 children applied to be permitted to marry. Six were granted permission, that is to say nine per cent. 58 of the applicants were girls, 10 boys. The majority of applicants had a foreign background. Of the six who were granted exemption, three were girls and three boys, all of them 17 years old.

Although there may be reasons that appear in individual cases to be very deserving, we propose that the county administrative boards' possibility of granting marriage exemption for children be abolished. An essential reason for this is that the exemption rule does not only give a minor the right to enter into matrimony but also excludes that person from the protection the age limit provides. In our view it may be seriously questioned whether under any circumstances it should be accepted that children in Sweden take decisions with such far-reaching consequences as those involved in entry into marriage. By giving the opportunity for marriage exemption, society is in a way giving it its support.

In favour of the exemption possibility it is usually asserted that in certain groups great difficulties arise for both the mother and the child if a child is born out of wedlock. However, it must be called into question whether traditions in a group should outweigh the rights of the pregnant child. Swedish law makes no difference in a child's rights based on birth of the child in or outside of wedlock. The legislator should not contribute to preserving old-fashioned and discriminatory norms in another direction. If the possibility of marriage exemption is retained in order to protect girls who become pregnant against reprisals or displeasure in their own group, it would mean a neglect of society's obligation to treat all equally and a kind of support for norms implying that extramarital sexuality and pregnancy are shameful and prohibited. This is an approach Swedish society should reasonably repudiate.

The fact that the possibility of exemption exists may further mean pressure on children to marry. An advantage of its abolition is that young people who do not want to marry, and also parents who want to withstand pressure from others to marry off a child, are given better opportunities to gain a hearing for their wishes.

In practice the exemption possibility means that legislation does not provide the same protection for children from different religious, cultural or ethnic minority groups as for children of the majority of the population. An important point of departure must be that all children be given the same protection under the law.

It may be that families are so anxious that their under-age daughters marry a person selected by the family that the girls are pressured into becoming pregnant, which is assumed will increase their chances of marriage exemption. Forced parenthood must naturally be counteracted. Early parenthood increases the risk of negative consequences for the young person, such as lost educational opportunities and alienation.

CRIMINALISATION

Swedish law does not contain any penalty specially aimed at forced marriage. On the other hand, there are other provisions in the Penal Code that may be applicable in certain cases, in particular that of unlawful coercion.

Child marriage is not a criminal offence. In a report dated 2008, the inquiry into human trafficking proposed a penalty for guardians who allow children under 16 to enter into marriage but the proposal did not result in legislation.

We are of the opinion that the reasons for a criminalisation clearly outweigh those against and that this applies both to forced marriage and child marriage. Regarding forced marriage it is a matter on the one hand of creating a special penalty in order to underscore society's reaction more clearly and in a more focused way and, on the other, of widening the punishable area somewhat compared with what applies today.

Regarding child marriage there is a complication in that such marriages cannot in principle be entered into lawfully in Sweden and would not be possible at all under the regulations should the exemption possibility be removed. However, one problem is that children who are to be protected by the Swedish legal system but who have their background in another country may often run the risk of being married off on the initiative of their parents or other relatives in that other country. Another problem is that children enter into alliances similar to marriage in this country in a religious or traditional order. These are certainly alliances that do not become legally valid here but in practice the people involved are still considered married in their own environment and cannot always freely leave the relationship.

One of the most difficult issues for the inquiry was whether such "informal" marriages should also be criminalised. In spite of the delimitation difficulties that exist, we consider this should be the case. The decisive reason is that there are children and young people in great need of such protection from the legal system.

Thus, we propose that a special penalty provision be introduced into the Penal Code concerning forced marriage and an equivalent provision concerning child marriage. The offences should be designated marriage coercion and child marriage offence.

Marriage coercion is committed if, by unlawful coercion or through exploitation of a person's exposed situation, someone forces that person to marry. The sentence is imprisonment for at most four years. A child marriage offence is committed if someone induces a child to enter into matrimony or takes an initiative for or arranges a child marriage, providing the marriage comes about. The sanction is a fine or imprisonment for at most two years.

It is proposed that both marriage coercion and child marriage offences should also include what are known as informal marriages. They are described as alliances that can be equated with marriage in the sense that they are "binding under an established system of norms that includes special requirements for dissolution of the alliance and are entered into in accordance with that system of norms."

In accordance with a provision in the above-mentioned 2011 Council of Europe convention, we further propose punishment for any person who by deception induces a person to travel to another country for the purpose of forcing that person to enter into matrimony there. The scale of punishment shall be imprisonment for at most two years.

Regarding child marriage offences we propose that he/she who is him/herself a child shall not be punished if he or she contributed to a child marriage offence by marrying the child. Nor shall his/her partner be punished when the age difference is small and, in view of this and the circumstances in general, he/she should not be held liable.

We do not propose any provision that criminalises what are known as proxy marriages, not even if it is a case of someone entering into matrimony on behalf of another person against that person's will.

The limitation period for child marriage offences and for marriage coercion offences committed against a child shall be calculated from the day the injured party reaches the age of eighteen.

A NATIONAL COMPETENCE TEAM

The action of authorities is of fundamental importance for protection against forced marriage and child marriage. Knowledge, coordination and access to qualified advice are needed.

We therefore propose a National Competence Team be established with the task of promoting in different ways work to counter marriage against a person's will, child marriage and honour-related violence and oppression. The Team should be made up of people with special expertise in the problem areas and in different relevant fields.

The Competence Team should be instructed, among other things, to develop collaboration and make it more effective, promote good working methods, support authorities and other activities, produce educational and informational material, and create meeting places for practitioners and researchers.

Principle for the Competence Team should initially be the county administrative board in Östergötland, which has considerable experience and knowledge in the area. Work should be evaluated after a few years and in this connection it should be considered whether the task should be transferred to another actor.

Apart from the specified overall tasks, the Competence Team should be requested together with the Swedish National Agency for Education to develop and spread material concerning methods for work in schools which should aim to prevent forced marriage, child marriage and honour-related violence and oppression.

The Competence Team should also lead efforts to produce methods material for work on the question of marriage against a person's own will and child marriage in different activities pertaining to parental support and in the introduction to society for newly arrived immigrants. In addition, the Competence Team should offer training courses for relevant authorities and organizations, including operations that provide emergency telephone services. The Competence Team should also produce a check list that can be used in conversations about marriage against a person's own will. Furthermore, the Competence Team should consider how it can create in accordance with a Norwegian model the preconditions for special follow-up agreements with people who travel abroad in spite of a fear of being married off against their will.

SOCIAL SERVICES

Among the authorities that come into contact with child marriage and marriage against a person's will, the social welfare services play a main role. There have been clear deficiencies in the work of social services. We therefore propose that the National Board of Health and Welfare be instructed to carry out special supervisory efforts in the area in question. Apart from this, the Competence Team should play an important role in support of the development of work at social services departments.

An essential issue is whether social services should initiate efforts addressed to families where there is a threat of forced marriage, child marriage or honour-related violence and oppression. Obviously knowledge of such family work and of the complications and risks associated with it must be very good. A recommended method should be drawn up for these efforts. The formulation of the methods should include an evaluation of the methods used today in, for example, Västra Götaland, Uppsala and Stockholm. The Competence Team should lead the methods development work.

In order to ensure that there are no financial incentives to forgoing placement in sheltered accommodation for people who need it, the introduction of a state subsidy for the cost of this care should be considered.

RECOGNITION OF FOREIGN MARRIAGES, ETC.

The main rule is that a valid foreign marriage is recognised here in Sweden. It was easy up to 2004, even for a person with strong ties with Sweden, to evade the Swedish impediments to marriage by marrying abroad.

To prevent circumvention, a provision was introduced in 2004 to the effect that foreign marriages are not recognised in Sweden if at the time of the marriage there was an impediment to the marriage under Swedish law, for example a person under age, and at least one of the couple was a Swedish resident or a Swedish national. If it is probable that the marriage was entered into under duress, it is not recognised. But the marriage shall be recognised even so if there are special reasons. We do not propose any amendments to these provisions. We have given particular attention to the exemption for special reasons but are of the view that it should be retained.

There are no special restrictions under Swedish law regarding possibilities of recognising what are known as proxy marriages. We considered the matter and found no restriction should be introduced.

The rules on recognition of foreign marriages are of importance inter alia for people's chances of obtaining a residence permit in Sweden. There is a major difficulty when one of the parties in a valid or planned marriage says or intimates that pressure has been applied but does not dare maintain the claim. It has therefore been questioned whether the real motive for the rejection of an application for a residence permit in a case of this nature should be excluded from the decision of the Swedish Migration Board.

However, we assess that the preconditions do not exist to make special exemptions from the obligation to motivate decisions in matters concerning residence permits or to restrict parties' right to insight into the process.

Furthermore, an increased requirement of orality in connection with the processing of cases concerning family ties should not be introduced. However, in cases where duress is suspected, the Swedish Migration Board should introduce a routine of calling a meeting and giving detailed information about the action alternatives and possibilities of getting help that are available for persons who are married against their will or exposed to the risk of becoming so.

RELIGIOUS COMMUNITIES AND MARRIAGES

In some religious communities marriage ceremonies and similar rituals are performed that are not legally valid but from the practical point of view are binding for the parties. Thus, forced marriage or child marriage may in practice occur in this country. It was previously mentioned that we propose such "informal marriages" be criminalised if the alliance is "binding under an established system of norms that includes special requirements for dissolution of the alliance and are entered into in accordance with that system of norms". It is also essential, however, to try to prevent the occurrence of these informal marriages in other ways too.

We therefore propose that to obtain a permit to perform marriages, no rituals resulting in informal child marriage or forced marriage be performed in the religious community. A corresponding requirement shall also apply to persons ordained as marriage officiators.

We further propose that a dialogue be initiated between Swedish authorities and the religious communities concerning child marriage and marriage against a person's will. In its ordinary work the Committee for state support to religious communities should carry on a dialogue focusing on marriages of this type. Together with the Legal, Financial and Administrative Services Agency, the Committee should also be instructed to arrange study programmes on Swedish legislation concerning marriage for clergymen and other officials in the religious community working in Sweden but who have not had their education in this country.

THE PERSON TO BE MARRIED IS TAKEN ABROAD

A serious problem is that forced marriages and child marriages take place in a country to which the person under duress or the child has been taken. The person is often in a very difficult position in the other country. Girls and women in particular sometimes contact the Swedish foreign service requesting help. This type of help is in practice often difficult to provide.

To counteract these situations it is most important to make efforts to ensure that persons who run the risk of being married off abroad do not leave Sweden. The focus must be on discovering the problem here and seeing to it that these people receive information about their rights and possibilities of seeking help. Regarding children the matter of coercive measures must be brought to the fore in time. The role of schools and the social services are essential in this context.

As mentioned previously we propose a provision be introduced that inflicts a penalty on anyone who by deception induces someone to travel to another country for the purpose of forcing that person to enter into matrimony there.

In addition, the Ministry for Foreign Affairs, the National Board of Health and Welfare, the National Police Board and the Swedish Prosecution Authority should improve their collaboration regarding cross-border matters where there are problems connected with honour, marriage against a person's own will or child marriage.

It is also essential that in a suitable context the Government set up an inquiry into whether, regarding young people taken into care under the Care of Young Persons (Special Provisions) Act (1990:52), an express possibility should be introduced for the social services committee to decide on or take the initiative for the revocation or taking charge of passports and whether the social services committee should be able to prevent a passport from being issued.

OTHER MATTERS

It may be questioned whether forced marriage and child marriage entered into in this country should be invalid. We found that a special effect of this nature should not be introduced. Certainly, we consider the arguments in favour of invalidity carry great weight. But a provision to the effect that some marriages are invalid requires considerations of a kind that lie far beyond the issues that this inquiry is to discuss in accordance with its terms of reference. Therefore, if forced marriage and child marriage are to be rendered invalid this should take place following an inquiry with a broader base in marriage law.

The possibilities of receiving damages for infringement of rights for a person subjected to a forced marriage or a child marriage will increase slightly if the inquiry's proposal of criminalisation is implemented. Damages may be claimed from the person guilty of the offence. There are also some chances of claiming damages from the state or a municipality for infringement of rights, namely if an official has committed an error and thereby caused someone to be subjected to a forced marriage or a child marriage.

INDEX*

* References are given by author name and section number.

V

W

European Family Law Series

1. *Legal Recognition of Same-Sex Couples in Europe*, K. Boele-Woelki and A. Fuchs (eds.)
2. *European Family Law in Action Volume I: Grounds for divorce*, K. Boele-Woelki, B. Braat and I. Sumner (eds.)
3. *European Family Law in Action Volume II : Maintenance Between Former Spouses*, K. Boele-Woelki, B. Braat and I. Sumner (eds.)
4. *Perspectives for the Unification and Harmonisation of Family Law in Europe*, K. Boele-Woelki (ed.)
5. *Family Law Legislation of the Netherlands*, I. Sumner and H. Warendorf
6. *Indépendance et interdépendance patrimoniales des époux dans le régime matrimonial légal des droits néerlandais, français et suisse*, B. Braat
7. *Principles of European Family Law Regarding Divorce and Maintenance Between Former Spouses*, K. Boele-Woelki, F. Ferrand, C. González Beilfuss, M. Jänterä-Jareborg, N. Lowe, D. Martiny and W. Pintens
8. Inheritance Law Legislation of the Netherlands, I. Sumner and H. Warendorf
9. *European Family Law in Action Volume III : Parental Responsibilities*, K. Boele-Woelki, B. Braat and I. Curry-Sumner (eds.)
10. Common Core and Better Law in European Family Law, K. Boele-Woelki (ed.)
11. *All's well that ends registered?*, I. Curry-Sumner
12. *Model Family Code – From a global perspective*, I. Schwenzer and M. Dimsey
13. *Harmonisation of Family Law in Europe. A Historical Perspective*, M. Antokolskaia
14. *Brussels II bis: Its Impact and Application in the Member States*, K. Boele-Woelki and C. González Beilfuss (eds.)
15. *Tensions between Legal, Biological and Social Conceptions of Parentage*, I. Schwenzer (ed.)
16. *Principles of European Family Law Regarding Parental Responsibilities*, K. Boele-Woelki, F. Ferrand, C. González Beilfuss, M. Jänterä-Jareborg, N. Lowe, D. Martiny and W. Pintens
17. *Juxtaposing Legal Systems and the Principles of European Family Law on Divorce and Maintenance*, E. Örücü and J. Mair (eds.)
18. Convergence and Divergence of Family Law in Europe, M. Antokolskaia (ed.)
19. *European Challenges in Contemporary Family Law*, K. Boele-Woelki and T. Sverdrup (eds.)
20. *Children and their parents*, M. Vonk
21. *La capacité de l'enfant dans les droits français, anglais et écossais*, L. Francoz-Terminal
22. *Joint Parental Authority*, C.G. Jeppesen de Boer
23. *Debates in Family Law around the Globe at the Dawn of the 21st Century*, K. Boele-Woelki (ed.)

24. *European Family Law in Action Volume IV: Property Relations between Spouses*, K. Boele-Woelki, B. Braat and I. Curry-Sumner (eds.)
25. *Foundational Facts, Relative Truths. A Comparative Law Study on Children's Right to Know Their Genetic Origins*, R. Blauwhoff
26. *Imperative Inheritance Law in a Late-Modern Society. Five Perspectives*, Christoph Castelein, René Foqué and Alain Verbeke (eds.)
27. *Juxtaposing Legal Systems and the Principles of European Family Law on Parental Responsibilities*, Esin Örücü and Jane Mair (eds.)
28. *La justice des mineurs en Europe*, Yann Favier and Frédérique Ferrand (eds.)
29. *The Future of Family Property in Europe*, Katharina Boele-Woelki, Jo Miles and Jens M. Scherpe (eds.)
30. *The Place of Religion in Family Law: A Comparative Search*, Jane Mair and Esin Örücü (eds.)
31. *Reconstructing Marriage. The Legal Status of Relationships in a Changing Society*, Caroline Sörgjerd
32. *Legal Recognition of Same-Sex Relationships in Europe*, Katharina Boele-Woelki and Angelika Fuchs (eds.)
33. *Principles of European Family Law Regarding Property Relations Between Spouses*, Katharina Boele-Woelki, Frédérique Ferrand, Cristina González Beilfuss, Maarit Jänterä-Jareborg, Nigel Lowe, Dieter Martiny and Walter Pintens
34. *Der nacheheliche Unterhalt: Grundlagen und Ausgestaltung im deutschen Unterhaltsrecht und in den Prinzipien der Commission on European Family Law*, Philipp Beuermann
35. *Family Law and Culture in Europe: Developments, Challenges and Opportunities*, Katharina Boele-Woelki, Nina Dethloff and Werner Gephart
36. *Children's Rights in Intercountry Adoption. A European Perspective*, Claire Fenton-Glynn
37. *Nordic Cohabitation Law*, John Asland, Margareta Brattström, Göran Lind, Ingrid Lund-Andersen, Anna Singer and Tone Sverdrup
38. *European Family Law in Action Volume V: Informal Relationships*, Katharina Boele-Woelki, Charlotte Mol and Emma van Gelder (eds.)
39. *Divided Parents, Shared Children. Legal Aspects of Residential Co-Parenting in England, the Netherlands and Belgium*, Natalie Nikolina
40. *Family Forms and Parenthood. Theory and Practice of Article 8 ECHR in Europe*, Andrea Büchler and Helen Keller (eds.)

www.ingramcontent.com/pod-product-compliance
Ingram Content Group UK Ltd.
Pitfield, Milton Keynes, MK11 3LW, UK
UKHW051927100926
8556IPUK00022B/1415

9 781780 68